D1374223

Faculty Power:

Collective Bargaining
on Campus

Faculty Power:

Collective Bargaining
on Campus

Editor

Terrence N. Tice

Consulting Editor

Grace W. Holmes

The Institute of Continuing Legal Education

Hutchins Hall   •   Ann Arbor, Michigan

Copyright © 1972
by
The Institute of Continuing Legal Education

Library of Congress
Catalog Card Number
72-75641

Printed in the United States of America

THE INSTITUTE OF CONTINUING LEGAL EDUCATION

The University of Michigan
Law School

Wayne State University
Law School

State Bar of Michigan

Executive Committee

Frederick G. Buesser, Jr., President, State Bar of Michigan

Benjamin Carlin, Professor of Law, Wayne State University Law School

Robert E. Childs, Professor of Law, Wayne State University Law School

Carl S. Hawkins, Professor of Law, The University of Michigan Law School

R. David Henson, Professor of Law, Wayne State University Law School

Charles W. Joiner, Dean, Wayne State University Law School

Douglas A. Kahn, Professor of Law, The University of Michigan Law School

James A. Park, Fraser Trebilcock Davis & Foster, Lansing

William J. Pierce, Professor of Law and Director, Legislative Research Center,
The University of Michigan Law School

A. DeVere Ruegsegger, Dyer, Meek, Ruegsegger & Bullard, Detroit

Theodore J. St. Antoine, Dean, The University of Michigan Law School

Norman O. Stockmeyer, Jr., Commissioner, Michigan Court of Appeals

John W. Reed
Director

Foreword

Particularly in recent years the campus scene has tended to be a preview of coming events in the larger community. Movements and fads have begun on campus and then moved out into "the real world," there to flourish or die as the case may be. SDS, anti-war sentiment, rock music, the drug scene, communal living, ecological concern—these and other developments began or were given impetus and visibility on the campus.

But in at least one important matter the colleges and universities are followers rather than leaders. Collective bargaining has been a familiar part of the industrial and business scene for a long time, but only in the last year or two has it become noticeable on campus.

In response to this recent development, The Institute of Continuing Legal Education held a national conference in late 1971 to consider the legal, economic, and institutional implications of faculty collective bargaining. This volume, an outgrowth of that conference, sets forth the views of lawyers and educators who have considered and, in most cases, already dealt with this phenomenon in its new, ivied environment. As it did with its earlier volume on *Student Protest and the Law* (1969) and *Law and Discipline on Campus* (1971), the Institute here presents to the professionals of law and education a useful, pioneering treatment of problems where their concerns intersect.

John W. Reed
Director

Preface

Collective bargaining is rapidly becoming a fact of life in the public sector of higher education and in many private institutions. This book provides a detailed and systematic perspective over the numerous interdependent developments in this area since 1965 and an informed discussion of their implications. It supplies precise information for faculties and administrations considering or entering collective bargaining, evaluating their experiences, or seeking viable alternatives. It will be useful to those working to formulate or amend state legislation and to attorneys, officials, and other professionals.

Since this study is the only one of its kind in the field, it has been designed as a lasting foundation for any works that follow. Thus, a comprehensive bibliography is included. The appendixes contain surveys of state laws, contracts, and bargainable issues, two model statutes, and other basic documents. The five hundred pages of the Institute of Continuing Legal Education (ICLE) *Course Materials* which I compiled for the September, 1971, Ann Arbor conference on this subject are still available. They remain a valuable supplement to this publication, since there is little overlapping material.

Every contribution has been thoroughly edited to obtain an accurate, concise, comprehensive presentation of the issues. I have undertaken additional responsibility for the bibliography, the index, and the appendixes. Grace Holmes, ICLE publications director, has been a superbly exacting but gracious coworker throughout. Although I accept final responsibility for the text, her experienced hand has touched virtually every paragraph, as we have moved from a very loose transcript of spoken words to a more rigorous manuscript—sometimes through several drafts. Special credit also goes to John Reed, who conceived the idea, and Virginia Nordin, who planned with me, then skillfully organized, the conference out of which this book has emerged. The efficient, perceptive work of

Virginia Metz, who made editorial suggestions and coordinated the whole operation, has helped make the editing a pleasure. Warm appreciation is also due to Wanda Brown, who gathered some of the data on state laws, and to Harriet Kass, who was responsible for quality control and accurate legal documentation of the manuscript. I am indebted above all to the eighteen experts who have joined with us in this project.

Terrence N. Tice
March 30, 1972

Contributors

Robert T. Blackburn—Professor of Higher Education, Center for the Study of Higher Education, The University of Michigan, Ann Arbor.

R. Theodore Clark, Jr.—Seyfarth, Shaw, Fairweather & Geraldson, Chicago, Illinois.

Harry T. Edwards—Associate Professor, The University of Michigan Law School, Ann Arbor.

Tracy H. Ferguson—Bond, Schoeneck & King, Syracuse, New York.

Robert G. Howlett—Chairman, Michigan Employment Relations Commission.

Karl J. Jacobs—President, Rock Valley College, Rockford, Illinois.

J. David Kerr—University Attorney, Central Michigan University, Mt. Pleasant.

William P. Lemmer—University Attorney, The University of Michigan, Ann Arbor.

William F. McHugh—Associate Professor of Law, American University Law School, Washington, D.C.

Charles M. Rehmus—Professor of Political Science, The University of Michigan, Ann Arbor, and Co-director, Institute of Labor and Industrial Relations, The University of Michigan-Wayne State University.

Theodore Sachs—Rothe, Marston, Mazey, Sachs, O'Connell, Nunn & Fried, P.C., Detroit, Michigan.

Malcolm G. Scully—Formerly Assistant Editor, *The Chronicle of Higher Education,* Washington, D.C.

Allan F. Smith—Vice President for Academic Affairs, The University of Michigan, Ann Arbor.

Russell A. Smith—Professor of Law, The University of Michigan, Ann Arbor.

Kenneth M. Smythe—Office of the General Counsel, Wayne State University, Detroit.

Theodore J. St. Antoine—Dean, The University of Michigan Law School, Ann Arbor.

Alfred D. Sumberg—Associate Secretary, American Association of University Professors.

Terrence N. Tice—Assistant Professor of Philosophy, School of Education, The University of Michigan, Ann Arbor.

Belle Zeller—Professor of Political Science and Chairman of the Legislative Conference, City University of New York.

Table of Contents

PART II

INSTITUTIONAL DIFFERENCES

PART III

ALTERNATIVES TO
COLLECTIVE BARGAINING

PART IV

FACULTY ORGANIZATION

PART V

THE BARGAINING PROCESS:
PROBLEMS AND PROCEDURES

Introductory Remarks

Theodore J. St. Antoine*

The growth of public employee unionism represents the most significant development in the entire field of labor law during the past decade. This development has taken place primarily at the high school and elementary school levels, but it now seems clear that a substantial number of persons in higher education will be organized in one form or another during the next few years. A recent article in *Harper's Magazine*[1] suggests that one million persons in higher education could be organized by the 1980s. If this should occur, higher education personnel would comprise a substantial portion of the organized American labor force of twenty million.

I intend to make only a few general observations about the subject matter of this volume. An array of specialists is present to provide insights from the field of labor relations as it is in industry and as it has extended into the world of education over the last few years. One of the things we will have to recognize, of course, is that lessons gained from the one field cannot necessarily be transferred intact to the other.

I am reminded of the well-intentioned employer who decided to try to improve the esprit de corps within his establishment. He called a meeting of all his employees and told them: "I want to have a cheerful and efficient work force here. Therefore, I'm going to set up a suggestion box to solicit your views. I want you to tell me how I can be sure that when I walk down our main aisle, I'll find everybody hard at work." He installed the box and the next day found only a single slip in it. Confident that it must be a very profound observation, he plucked it from the box and read this

---

* Dean, The University of Michigan Law School, Ann Arbor.
1. Myron Lieberman, "Professors, Unite!", *Harper's Magazine*, Oct. 1971, pp. 61-70.

1

terse communication: "Take the rubber heels off your shoes!"

How does one relate that kind of insight to a field in which the most profitable portion of a person's working day may occur when he is looking pensively out the window? The marked difference between the two contexts hints at the difficulties we face in seizing upon the industrial experience and trying to apply it to the field of higher education. Quite candidly, I cannot assess the value of unionization in colleges and universities. I am firmly convinced that unionization has been of great value in our industrial society, but I simply do not know what it is going to mean for higher education or whether it is going to be worth the bother.

Comparisons to Industry

One point I think I can be confident about: things are not going to turn out as expected or as feared.

First of all, if the experience of industrial unionization is any indicator, such organization will not bring about the substantial economic change that many faculty members undoubtedly hope for. Labor economists are convinced that unionization has not substantially changed the proportion of corporate income going to wage earners. That conclusion is verified by experience in many different industries throughout the past seventy years. Let me repeat, because for many persons it is an astounding revelation. Overall experience shows that industrial unionization in the United States has not brought about any significant change in the percentage of corporate income going to the wage-earning group. In other words, the working force is getting approximately the same proportion it would have received in the absence of unionization, i.e., approximately 65 to 70 percent.

Certainly unions have not been without economic effect. The most noticeable change they have produced has been an average increase of 10 to 15 percent in rates of pay—a change employers have promptly offset by reducing the number of employees through more efficient production techniques. Productivity improvements, not unionization, are directly responsible for the overall increase in the real wages of working people.

Is this experience pertinent to higher education? How do you go about increasing the productivity of educators? Many persons say it simply cannot be done. I am not so sure. For example, I do not think it irrelevant that among the various schools and colleges, law schools have one of the highest ratios of students to faculty.

Whether the students are handled as well as they should be is, of course, another issue. In any event, it is customary for law school lecture classes, which are the chief means of instruction, to have 100 or more students. I know of no school that produces more semester credit hours per faculty member than the law school. The salary structures reflect that arrangement. A principal factor supporting requests for higher salary levels for law teachers is the large number of students being handled. It would seem likely that if salary levels are to be increased substantially throughout the university, one response administrations will make is to increase productivity. This will be done by putting far more emphasis upon large lecture courses and by trying to reduce the number of seminars, individual research projects, and the like.

In industry one of the particular benefits of unionization is not economic but humanitarian or psychological. That is, the individual working man is given a voice in the governance of the work place. He no longer fears becoming the helpless victim of an arbitrary management. How does that fit into the university setting? There undoubtedly are some faculties whose members feel imposed upon by administrators either at the school or university level. For them, obviously, unionization promises advantages akin to those it has provided industrial employees. But in many institutions the individual faculty member already has a considerable voice in the affairs of his particular school or college. In those institutions, especially those of higher quality where the faculties have traditionally controlled such critical matters as curriculum content and personnel selection, unionization would not play the vital role in advancing humane values that it has in the industrial setting.

Finally, political power is another significant benefit that unionization has brought to the working person. If unionization comes about in higher education, increased political power could well be a principal result. Whatever can be said about the direct economic gains working men may have achieved through collective bargaining, there can be little doubt that unions have secured a substantial body of legislation through their lobbying efforts and political activities. I suspect that in some respects this would be even more true of faculty organization. Faculty members have a good deal of flexibility in setting aside time to devote to political activities. They are likely to be unusually knowledgeable and articulate, and thus they should be capable of effective political activity in their communities. Therefore, my hunch would be that if there is extensive unionization on the part of faculties, political power will be one of the most significant means of achieving their objectives. Obviously, this is particularly true of public institutions, where organizations of faculties could bring their influence to bear directly upon the state legislators.

Special Circumstances

I have mentioned a number of ways in which faculty unions may not turn out as some persons have expected. It is also important to realize that the varied circumstances of different institutions will be controlling factors both as to the law and as to the practice of organization in those institutions. You cannot expect anyone to hand you a set of precise guidelines either as to what the law will be as applied to your own particular institution or as to what will be the best or most likely course of action for your particular institution. For example, two of the most important legal issues that must surely be resolved are the scope of the bargaining unit and the range of the subjects over which bargaining is mandatory. The National Labor Relations Board will deal with private institutions on these issues. The various state agencies, or the state courts, will deal with public institutions, which are excluded from the coverage of the National Labor Relations Act. These issues will be developed extensively by other writers, so I will not get into them now. Nonetheless, it should be recognized at the very outset that specific resolutions of all these questions will depend on the nature of the given institution.

How large should the unit be? Should it include department chairmen? Should there be a single unit for the entire university, or should particular "craft" groups such as doctors and lawyers be carved out and permitted to bargain separately? The handling of these issues may largely turn upon the facts of the particular situation. In a given school, departmental chairmen may exercise responsibilities of such significance that they ought to be treated as part of management. In other institutions they may have merely ministerial functions to perform, in which case they might appropriately be included in the faculty bargaining unit.

An Evolutionary Process

The last broad proposition I shall submit is that whatever form bargaining may take initially, the entire process is very likely to be evolutionary. I do not think anybody ought to worry too much about making some dreadful mistake at the outset because of the specific form devised for a union or guild in a particular institution. Time will make the need for accommodations apparent, and they will occur.

Indeed, I think there will be an interesting interrelationship between the development of unionization in higher education and that in other areas. From the general perspective of labor relations, this interrelating development will surely be among the most significant results of any widespread unionization in higher education. Unions, for example, have so far found it almost impossible to break the white collar barrier in American industry. Clerical and technical employees have insisted that by and large they are above the blue collar class, that they are really allied with management, however ill-paid they may be. I would expect unionization of high school teachers, and especially of professorial staffs, to have a marked sociological impact upon that kind of genteel thinking. It could bring about a substantial change of attitude and a correspondingly substantial increase in the scope of unionization across the country.

Finally, I would simply encourage you to enjoy this whole process. Many humorous stories are told about professors. Now an entirely new lot of tales is on the horizon—the legend and lore of the work place. Many of us in academia's worsening job market, for example, might consider it quite apropos to muse on the situation of one young fellow. This lad was trying to get a job at a plant, and he was told by the personnel office: "No chance, no chance at all. We are overstaffed; we simply have no need for more work." The young man wasn't at all discouraged. He replied: "But you don't know me. The little bit of work I would do wouldn't even be noticed!"

Part I

Principles and Practices
of Collective Bargaining

CHAPTER 1

Legal Principles of
Public Sector Bargaining

*Russell A. Smith**

In the absence of specific legislation, the applicable law concerning rights of organization and collective bargaining is derived from three sources: the common law (as expounded in judicial decisions), municipal law (basic legislation, including home rule provisions defining the powers of local government), and constitutional law. The public sector presents a different mix of elements from that prevalent in the private sector, as we shall see. Those who deal with the public sector must have a correspondingly different expertise.

The traditional view has been that public employees have no legal right to protection against the employer's interference in attempts at unionization. A countertrend may be forming, however. A few recent court decisions (so far none by the Supreme Court of the United States) have taken the view that the First Amendment guarantees the right to form or join or belong to an organization concerned with working conditions.

Suppose, then, that a body of public employees, such as a college faculty, organizes for bargaining purposes. Unless applicable legislation specifically requires public employers to bargain collectively, these people will have no legally protected right to bargain. At best they will have a de facto right, where the employer agrees to bargain either voluntarily or in response to pressure tactics. The traditional view of strikes is the same. Moreover, where legislation does not specifically provide it, public employees have no legal mechanism for handling representation issues (who has

---

* Professor of Law, The University of Michigan, Ann Arbor.

9

the right to represent particular groups of employees), for resolving impasses, or for dealing with other kinds of disputes. In such situations, attempts to organize are hampered by the lack of legal protection.

Recent Developments

A highly significant development over the past decade has been the enactment of legislation dealing with public sector unionism. Wisconsin enacted the first comprehensive legislation in 1959. Now over thirty states have done so. Comprehensive legislation covers entire categories of public employees, sometimes all categories. As a general rule, such legislation grants and protects the right of self-organization; establishes the principle that the majority determines the representative of an "appropriate" employee group; places upon the employer the legal obligation to "bargain collectively" or to "meet and confer" with an organization having representation rights; and provides for help in resolving disputes (usually mediation plus factfinding), but prohibits strike action. A few states even provide for compulsory arbitration in certain types of disputes, principally those involving police and firefighters.

Some important changes have also occurred at the federal level. In 1962, President Kennedy issued Executive Order 10988, applying broadly to federal employees and conferring on them limited rights of unionization and collective bargaining. President Nixon has continued the same general policy, with some modifications, in Executive Order 11491,[1] issued in 1969 and recently amended. Another interesting development is the grant of rights of unionization to postal employees under the Postal Reorganization Act of 1970[2]— rights comparable to those operative in the private sector.

Cornell University

In 1970, departing from tradition, the National Labor Relations Board (NLRB) elected to enter the field of higher education in the private sector. In the *Cornell University*[3] case it decided to assert jurisdiction over the University in its relationships with nonacademic employees. The NLRB has since ruled that it will assume

---

1. See Appendix C for text.
2. Aug. 12, 1970, P.L. 91-375, 84 Stat. 719.
3. 183 NLRB 41, see Appendix D for text.

jurisdiction over private educational institutions which have at least a million dollars of annual revenue for operating purposes.[4]

The question of whether the NLRB would extend its jurisdiction to academic employees in private institutions was soon answered. In April, 1971, the board asserted jurisdiction over two branches of Long Island University—the C.W. Post Center and the Brooklyn Center—in a representation proceeding initiated by the United Federation of College Teachers, an affiliate of the American Federation of Teachers. In one branch there was an intervening petition by the local chapter of the American Association of University Professors (AAUP).[5] The University did not contest the assumption of NLRB jurisdiction although representation of academic employees was being sought. The issues litigated concerned the scope of the bargaining units.

Fordham University

In the *Fordham University*[6] case in 1971, again an AAUP chapter petitioned the NLRB for certification as the bargaining representative of the entire faculty. (This is also true in the Manhattan College case, currently pending.) Fordham University hoped to persuade the board to refuse jurisdiction over faculty, if not to obtain the exclusion of large segments of the faculty from the collective bargaining unit. The board decided to assume jurisdiction. The briefs present an interesting analysis of the structure of the academic community at Fordham. Much of it is comparable to the structure of The University of Michigan.

State Legislation

The federal government has not as yet extended NLRB jurisdiction to public employees. Thus, developments at the state level are far more important in the public sector than in the private sector.[7] This could change. Meanwhile, the considerable development that has occurred at the state level is beneficial. The states are free to do some experimenting, a valuable approach if we are to identify our problems and find ways to meet them. Experimenta-

---

4. 186 NLRB 153, see Appendix F for text.
5. C.W. Post Center, 189 NLRB 109.
6. 193 NLRB 23, see Appendix F for text.
7. See appendix A—Public Employee State Laws.

tion is possible where a monolithic legislative structure is not imposed, as would be true if the NLRB were to assume jurisdiction over public employees as well.

In a recent seminar at The University of Michigan Law School, Chairman Robert Helsby of the New York Public Employment Relations Board usefully characterized the states in three categories: (1) The "do nothing" states have not yet faced up to the problem and are restricted to applying the principles first mentioned—the common law, municipal law, and constitutional law. Public sector employees in these states have little or no legal protection in their efforts at organization and collective bargaining. Changes can be expected soon in some of these states, notably Illinois and Ohio. (2) The "squeaky wheel" states have crisis legislation, enacted piecemeal to meet problems with teachers, police, firefighters, or municipal employees. Comprehensive legislation is lacking. Many of these statutes, in Mr. Helsby's view, grant less than full rights and fail to deal effectively with the problems that are bound to emerge. (3) The "real confrontation" states have faced up to the problems of public sector unionism and have taken a broad view, trying to decide the proper approach as a matter of overall policy. These states have more comprehensive legislation, often drawing upon the recommendations of study commissions. At least sixteen states have enacted legislation applicable to the academic community.[8]

Informed observers generally believe that unless Congress elects to step in with superseding legislation, the trend toward enactment of state legislation will continue. The probability is that within five or six years forty or more states will have enacted legislation granting rights of self-organization and collective bargaining to some or all categories of public employees. This may stimulate an already strong trend toward unionization, as was true in the private sector following enactment of the National Labor Relations Act (NLRA) in 1935.[9]

Remarkably, organization among public white collar and professional groups far exceeds the organization of such groups in the private sector. Obviously something is happening which appeals more strongly to public employees than to private employees.

---

8. Connecticut, Delaware, Hawaii, Maine, Massachusetts, Michigan, Minnesota, New Jersey, New York, Oregon, Pennsylvania, Rhode Island, South Dakota, Vermont, Washington, and Wisconsin.

9. National Labor Relations Act of July 5, 1935, 29 U.S.C. §151 et seq.

Two Agencies?

An administrative problem arises in those states which have a little Wagner Act or a little Taft-Hartley Act covering the private sector. Should the same agency administer the legislation for both sectors? New York separates the two. Michigan entrusts administration to a single agency.

Proponents of separate agencies wish to avoid the use of too many private sector concepts in the implementation of public sector legislation. They believe that public sector legislation presents unique problems calling for the undivided attention of an agency created for its specific administration—an agency not overly attuned to or influenced by decisions already made in the private sector. Proponents of a single agency claim economy of operation and assert that problems peculiar to the public sector can be identified and adequately treated.

I see benefit in the variety of approaches, state and federal, now developing. We cannot yet say exactly what we need or what we want on the statute books. We are not ready to specify the most effective kind of administration or the general principles which should govern. This is particularly true with regard to the extension of unionism to college and university faculties. We can now examine a potpourri of state legislation and experiences under that legislation. Hopefully the experimentation will enable us to identify and learn to deal with the problems peculiar to the public sector.

The Bargaining Unit

Among the important problems to be considered in enacting and administering legislation is the determination of appropriate units for collective bargaining purposes. In this country we accept the principle of majority determination within a defined group of employees and therefore deny bargaining rights to minority groups. This concept is uniquely American. We first accepted it in 1934— in an amendment to the federal Railway Labor Act of 1926 and in the administration of the National Industrial Recovery Act. The principle was incorporated in the NLRA of 1935 and continued in the Taft-Hartley Act of 1947. All state legislation has followed the same principle.

A necessary corollary of this principle is that the boundary lines of the voting group must be determined. A ruling must specify which employees may vote to decide whether they want to be represented by a particular labor organization or by one among competing labor organizations or by none. This is a key issue and the implications are obvious. For a time, at least, the decision spells life or death to the aspirations of organizations which fail to win. Moreover, the definition of the unit substantially affects the resulting bargaining structure. For example, the bargaining units might be statewide or the units might correspond to the various operating departments or even to sections of those departments. Both the employer and the management structure for bargaining obviously will have to be responsive to these alignments.

Supervisory Employees

Another problem encountered in determining bargaining units is what to do about employees having supervisory status. The NLRA defines supervisory employees very broadly and denies them statutory protection with respect to organization and collective bargaining, with the result that they may be included in a bargaining unit only with the employer's consent.[10] In the *Fordham University* case the University argued, on the basis of the NLRB definition, that the entire tenured faculty, who are members of the faculty senate, should be excluded from the bargaining unit in view of the varied responsibilities of the faculty regarding curriculum, appointments, promotions, grievances, supervision of graduate students and research assistants, and the like; and in view of the faculty senate's other collective managerial responsibilities in decision-making.

The argument did not prevail. Difficult questions are involved here, nonetheless. Should the private sector concepts of "supervisor" control in the academic setting? Would the traditional collegial forms of faculty participation in academic governance have to be scrapped to permit the introduction of NLRA-type collective bargaining? Should departmental chairmen, assistant deans, and

---

10. NLRA §2(11), 29 U.S.C. §152(11) states:
    The term "supervisor" means any individual having authority, in the interest of the employer, to hire, transfer, suspend, lay off, recall, promote, discharge, assign, reward, or discipline other employees, or responsibly to direct them, or to adjust their grievances, or effectively to recommend such action, if in connection with the foregoing the exercise of such authority is not of a merely routine or clerical nature, but requires the use of independent judgment.

members of departmental executive committees be included with the regular faculty in an appropriate bargaining unit or, state law permitting, should they be accorded bargaining rights but in separate bargaining units?

Legislative Guidelines for Unit Determination

A survey of state statutes and the federal executive orders yields a variety of approaches to the definition of an appropriate unit. Some state legislation contains language similar to that of the NLRA, providing minimal legislative guidance and leaving the standards for determining appropriate groupings of employees to the discretion of the administering agency. Other states have tried to provide specific guidelines. The Hawaii statute,[11] effective July 1, 1970, definitively prescribes bargaining units to be used statewide:[12]

All employees throughout the State within any of the following categories shall constitute an appropriate bargaining unit: (1) Nonsupervisory employees in blue collar positions; (2) Supervisory employees in blue collar positions; (3) Nonsupervisory employees in white collar positions; (4) Supervisory employees in white collar positions; (5) Teachers and other personnel of the department of education under the same salary schedule; (6) Educational officers and other personnel of the department of education under the same salary schedule; (7) Faculty of The University of Hawaii and the community college system; (8) Personnel of The University of Hawaii and the community college system, other than faculty; (9) Registered professional nurses; (10) Nonprofessional hospital and institutional workers; (11) Firemen; (12) Policemen; and (13) Professional and scientific employees other than registered professional nurses.

Other states have not yet set such specific guidelines for bargaining units, but have indicated some preference in terms of general principles or policies. The Pennsylvania statute[13] directs the agency to avoid an over-fragmentation of bargaining units to the extent feasible, thus recognizing a problem of serious proportions.

---

11. Session Laws of Hawaii, Act 171, 1970.
12. Id., §6.
13. 43 Pa. Stat. Ann. §1101.101 et seq. (Purdon 1970).

The Scope of Negotiations

The legally permissible and desirable scope of subject matter for collective negotiations is a critical issue. The answer, of course, depends on the applicable statute and how it is interpreted.

Some state statutes are modeled after the NLRA, stating the duty to bargain "in good faith with respect to wages, hours, and other terms and conditions of employment." The NLRB and the courts have developed a substantial body of interpretations implementing those provisions. Will the state administrative agencies and the state courts tend to apply the same kinds of principles?

Some state legislatures consider the scope of bargaining in the public sector to be such a serious problem that they have attempted to exclude some subjects from the bargaining process. The Hawaii statute has the following provisions:[14]

> Excluded from the subjects of negotiations are matters of classification and reclassification, retirement benefits and the salary ranges and the number of incremental and longevity steps now provided by law, provided that the amount of wages to be paid in each range and step and the length of service necessary for the incremental and longevity step shall be negotiable. The employer and the exclusive representative shall not agree to any proposal which would be inconsistent with merit principles or the principle of equal pay for equal work pursuant to [another statute] or which would interfere with the rights of a public employer to (1) direct employees, (2) determine qualification, standards for work, the nature and contents of examinations, hire, promote, transfer, assign and retain employees in positions and suspend, demote, discharge, or take other disciplinary action against employees for proper cause; (3) relieve an employee from duties because of lack of work or other legitimate reasons; (4) maintain efficiency of government operations; (5) determine methods, means, and personnel by which the employer's operations are to be conducted; and take such action as may be necessary to carry out the missions of the employer in cases of emergencies.

Other statutes use different language, either mandatory or permissive.

---

14. *Supra*, note 11, §10.

Management Functions

An alternative approach is to require that certain stated functions be retained by management. Thus, federal Executive Order No. 11491 states in Section 12:

> Each agreement between an agency and a labor organization is subject to the following requirements . . .
>
> (b) management officials of the agency retain the right, in accordance with applicable laws and regulations—(1) to direct employees of the agency; (2) to hire, promote, transfer, assign, and retain employees in positions within the agency, and to suspend, demote, discharge, or take other disciplinary action against employees; (3) to relieve employees from duties because of lack of work or for other legitimate reasons; (4) to maintain the efficiency of the Government operations entrusted to them; (5) to determine the methods, means, and personnel by which such operations are to be conducted; and (6) to take whatever actions may be necessary to carry out the mission of the agency in situations of emergency; . . .
>
> The requirements of this section shall be expressly stated in the initial or basic agreement and apply to all supplemental, implementing, subsidiary, or informal agreements between the agency and the organization.

Some state statutes include similar restrictive provisions which have the effect of circumscribing public sector negotiations far more narrowly than is true in the private sector.

Conflicting Legislation

Another tough legal problem arises in administering public sector legislation where the bargaining obligation is expressed in general NLRA-type terms. A determination must be made as to the extent the bargainers are free to negotiate to finality on matters specifically covered by preexisting legislation. A state law may provide for a state-administered pension plan, or create a state-administered system of teacher tenure, or provide specific hours of work for firemen. Municipalities operating under home rule charters adopted pursuant to state constitutional authority may establish pension plans or civil service systems or otherwise deal specifically with other terms and conditions of employment regarding some or all categories of city employees. A serious question arises in these contexts: Does the enactment of legislation which states the bargaining obligation in general terms override preexisting legislation and home rule charters which have set terms and conditions of employment? These problems have already arisen, with varying results, and will continue to plague the administering agencies, the courts, and the parties to bargaining.

Some state legislation has sought to meet this problem, but the provisions are often difficult to interpret. The New York statute, for example, includes the following provision:[15]

> Any written agreement between a public employer and an employee organization determining the terms and conditions of employment of public employees shall contain the following notice in type not smaller than the largest type used elsewhere in the agreement:
>
> > It is agreed by and between the parties that any provision of this agreement requiring legislative action to permit its implementation by amendment of law or by providing the additional funds therefor, shall not become effective until the appropriate legislative body has given approval.

The appropriate legislative body for statewide or state employees, I would presume, is the legislature itself. The appropriate legislative body at the school district level, at least in Michigan, would be the district school board and at the municipal level in both New York and Michigan—if Michigan had the provision—the city council or a similar legislative body.

Perhaps this kind of restriction does not pose a great problem at the municipal level, since municipal government can only become bound or provide funds by appropriate legislative action, but an important technical distinction should be noted. Provisions such as those stated in the New York statute (or like provisions in the Pennsylvania statute[16] and elsewhere) may mean that the local legislative body has two bites at the apple. In statewide bargaining relationships where the bargaining is done by a subordinate agency of the state, as it certainly must be, the provision would appar-

---

15. N.Y. Civil Service Law §204-a (McKinney 1969).
16. 43 Pa. Stat. Ann. §1101.901 (Purdon 1970).

ently mean that the labor relations act does not necessarily circumscribe the field of negotiations. Anything could be negotiated, including pension plans covered by a state law, but the resulting agreements would lack finality. The parties would have to take the further political step of seeking confirmation from the legislature. That situation presents an enormous problem not faced in the private sector.

The Bargaining Obligation

What kind of bargaining or negotiation obligation is imposed by state provisions or by President Nixon's 1969 federal Executive Order 11491? The executive order and some state legislation directs that parties "meet and confer" with respect to wages, hours, and other terms and conditions of employment. The language of the NLRA, copied in many state acts, states an obligation to "bargain collectively" with respect to wages, hours, and other terms and conditions of employment. Are these obligations identical?

Presumably the use of the "meet and confer" language represents a deliberate attempt to impose a bargaining obligation less strict than the traditional obligation to "bargain collectively in good faith." I do not purport to deal here with the full ramifications of the distinction. The basic theoretical difference is that meeting and conferring, unlike the stricter bargaining, does not mandate that negotiations be carried to an impasse. It neither requires nor permits the administering agency to pass judgment on the bargaining process as minutely as the NLRB has customarily done. The NLRB examines the negotiations, often in great detail, to determine whether bargaining positions have been taken in good faith. Such examination goes substantially beyond inquiry into whether the parties have simply met and conferred.[17]

The bargaining structure is an extremely important aspect of the total bargaining process, and structure is greatly affected by de-

---

17. Under the Los Angeles City Ordinance (GERR, No. 388-F-1; Jan. 1971), it is an unfair employee relations practice for either management or the union "to refuse to meet and confer in good faith at reasonable times, places, and frequencies . . . or to refuse to consult upon request . . . on matters which are within the proper scope of representation." "Meet and confer" is defined as the obligation "to meet and confer within a reasonable period of time in order to exchange freely information, opinions, and proposals, and to endeavor to reach an agreement on matters within the scope of representation."

termination of the appropriate bargaining unit. As fragmentation of units increases, so does the problem of conducting collective bargaining. This problem is serious in the private sector but even more serious in the public sector. What one unit gets other units will want, and probably more—a roadblock hampering the negotiation of a complete set of agreements. Unfortunately, highly fragmented bargaining units have emerged under some state laws. Other state laws encourage the establishment of broad units, with particular sensitivity to the special problems collective bargaining faces in the public sector. It is to be hoped that future legislation will follow the latter course.

The bargaining structure is in some respects a practical rather than a legal problem. In theory, most legislation is formulated to prevent one side from interfering with the internal structure adopted by the other side. However, the good faith requirement can be a basis for the claim that each side should have bargaining teams possessing genuine authority to negotiate—a matter of internal structure. The size and makeup of a bargaining unit will have considerable bearing on how such authority and structure are designed.

A faculty senate or other similar decisionmaking body in a college or university conceivably could become the faculty's bargaining agent. Certification of an outside agent or an AAUP chapter would raise the critical question of what should be done with any existing decisionmaking or consultative apparatus.

The Strike Issue

In the private sector the accepted orthodoxy is that there can be no genuine collective bargaining without the right to strike. The possibility of withholding services is supposed to be the catalyst which helps to produce agreement. The employer's ability to lock out employees theoretically plays a similar role. On the other hand, the prevailing view reflected in state statutes is that strikes by public employees are illegal.

The statutes of Hawaii and Pennsylvania do not impose an absolute prohibition on all strike action, but they do provide that strikes which critically affect the public welfare are not permitted. The same is true of the Vermont statute with respect to municipal employees. Hawaii and Pennsylvania also prohibit strikes before the statutory impasse procedures have been exhausted. Pennsylvania prohibits strikes by guards at mental hospitals or prisons, by personnel necessary to the functioning of the courts, and by police and firefighters.

The state legislatures have stated the strike prohibition in various ways and with various kinds of supporting sanctions. Michigan and some other states provide no specific sanction, but the employer may take disciplinary action or seek a court injunction. In other states specific, and in some instances severe, sanctions are indicated. The New York statute mandates that injunctive relief be sought, that strikers have probationary status for one year, and that a deduction be taken from the worker's pay of an amount equal to twice his daily rate of pay for each day of violation. Further, a union in violation of the act forfeits its right to have dues deducted for a period of time to be determined by the public employment relations board; and the union may be fined for contempt of an injunctive order in an amount fixed by the court.

Injunctive relief, where available, is not necessarily automatic. The labor organization, countering with a charge of bad faith bargaining or the like (as in Michigan under the *Holland*[18] decision) may defeat or delay the issuance of an injunction.

Impasse Resolution

Public sector legislation emphasizes impasse resolution procedures. The usual pattern is mediation followed by factfinding with nonbinding recommendations. Six states[19] have provided for binding arbitration of disputes with police, firefighters, or other groups.[20] Nevada recently adopted a statute giving the governor authority to direct, before submission of a dispute to factfinding, that the recommendations on some or all issues be final and binding. The Maine and Rhode Island statutes provide for compulsory arbitration of some, but not all, issues.

The results of strikes by public employees vary with the state of the labor market, the kinds of sanctions authorized, and whether such sanctions are imposed. However, many people believe that we must concentrate not on the strike issue but on developing suitable dispute settlement mechanisms.

---

18. Holland v. Holland Education Ass'n, 380 Mich. 314, 157 N.W.2d 206 (1968).
19. Maine, Michigan, Rhode Island, South Dakota, Vermont, and Wyoming.
20. Michigan's experiment with compulsory arbitration will expire in June of 1972 unless the legislature elects to extend it.

As compared with mediation and factfinding, compulsory arbitration is not yet extensively used. Its use raises some interesting questions. What kinds of decision standards should be applied? How important are limitations on budget or revenue sources in determining wage issues and other money issues? In effect, does arbitration involve a dangerous reallocation of governmental responsibility and authority? Does it have an adverse effect on collective bargaining? Is it desirable in part on the ground that it may substitute rationality and equity for the relative power positions of the parties to collective bargaining?

I have tried to provide a capsulized survey of the legal structure and of some of the problems underlying public sector unionism at the federal and state levels, with some comparative references to the private sector. It should be obvious, even from this limited discussion, that private sector legal and structural models have strongly influenced the nature of public sector legislation and practices. That influence may lessen with increased efforts to take into account the problems peculiar to the public sector, efforts especially needed in considering how to handle the unionization of college faculties.

CHAPTER 2

Perspectives In
Public Sector Bargaining

*Robert G. Howlett**

The Background in Michigan

The Michigan Public Employment Relations Act (PERA)[1] was enacted in 1965, after the passage of the Wisconsin law.[2] Our law, enacted the same summer as statutes in Connecticut and Massachusetts, covers all public employers and employees in Michigan except the state itself and its employees. A constitutional provision vests power with respect to state employees in the State Civil Service Commission, a constitutionally created body.

Following the enactment of our law, some of the state universities contended that they and their employees were not subject to the statute because in Michigan the state universities are constitutional bodies. Decisions of the Michigan Court of Appeals and the Michigan Supreme Court have ruled against the universities, holding that nothing in the constitutional grant of power deprives the legislature of the power to enact labor relations legislation applicable to the state universities.[3]

The Michigan act, closely following the National Labor Relations Act (NLRA), establishes a representation procedure to determine whether employees wish to be represented by a bargaining agent

---

* Chairman, Michigan Employment Relations Commission.
1. Act 336, P.A. 1947, as amended; Mich. Stat. Ann. §§17.455(1)-17.455(16) (1968); M.C.L.A. §§423.201-423.216 (1967).
2. Wisconsin Municipal Employment Relations Act of 1959, Wis. Stat. 111.70. State Employment Labor Relations Act of 1965, Wis. Stat. 111.80.
3. Board of Control of Eastern Michigan University v. State Labor Mediation Board, 384 Mich. 561, 184 N.W.2d 921 (1971), aff'g 18 Mich. App. 435, 171 N.W.2d 471 (1969); Regents of University of Michigan v. State Labor Mediation Board, 18 Mich. App. 485, 171 N.W.2d 477 (1969).

in an appropriate unit. There is one significant difference between the Michigan legislation and the federal legislation. The Michigan Employment Relations Commission (MERC) held, and the Michigan Supreme Court affirmed the decision, that supervisors are covered by the Michigan statute but must be in separate bargaining units.[4]

The Michigan statute has an unfair labor practices provision regarding employers, including a requirement that the public employer bargain in good faith. Unfortunately, the act does not explicitly deal with unfair labor practices by unions, but it does define collective bargaining as a mutual obligation of the employer and of the employees' representatives. Thus, the union and the employer have the same legal obligation to engage in good faith bargaining. The obligation of a union to bargain may be enforced through the circuit courts rather than by MERC.

Both our private and public sector laws, enacted in 1939[5] and 1947[6] respectively, are primarily mediation statutes. We have an effective mediation service, using twenty-one staff mediators. Although it is true that the first duty of the mediator is to resolve the impasse, the supposition that the mediator does not care what result bargaining achieves is inaccurate. Mediators frequently tell the parties, separately as a rule, what they believe the result of bargaining should be and what is in the public interest. Occasionally, they give public recommendations, as the state and federal mediators did recently in the long Consumers Power strike in Michigan.

Our first petition for representation filed by an institution of higher education came from the Henry Ford Community College teachers in November, 1965, shortly after the law went into effect. Our first petition for a faculty at a four-year college—the first in the country—was the Central Michigan University petition in June, 1969. Since the law was enacted, we have held fifty-five consent elections in higher education institutions—fourteen among faculty;

---

4. Hillsdale Community Schools, 1968 MERC Lab. Op. 859, aff'd, 24 Mich. App. 36, 179 N.W.2d 660 (1969), leave to appeal denied, 384 Mich. 779 (1970); School District of City of Dearborn v. State Labor Mediation Board, 22 Mich. App. 222, 177 N.W.2d 196 (1970).
5. Act 176, P.A. 1939, as amended; Mich. Stat. Ann. §§17.454(1)-17.454(31); M.C.L.A. §§423.1-423.31.
6. Supra, note 1.

forty-one among nonfaculty. We have ordered eleven elections—two faculty, nine nonfaculty.

Bargaining Units

As is true of most state boards and commissions, it is our responsibility to determine a bargaining unit. We apply three general tests: (1) the largest feasible unit to effectuate the purposes of the act; (2) the community of interest; and (3) the differentiation between proposed units. We were advised by our supreme court in the *Hotel Olds*[7] case, involving private sector employees, that a primary objective of the commission is to constitute the largest unit which, in the circumstances of the particular case, is most compatible with effectuation of the law, and to include all common interests in a single unit.

Consistent with that advice, we have attempted to avoid the fragmentation of units. In 1966, in a case involving the City of Warren,[8] we applied the community of interest test. We said that to establish the appropriateness of the units sought by the petition two conditions precedent are necessary. First, a community of interest between the employees in the unit sought by the petitioner should be established. Second, it must be shown that there is a differentiation in the community of interest with respect to the employees comprising the units proposed by the petitioner, the employer, and any intervenor.

We have applied these rules to universities. In a case in which professors of University College at Michigan State University[9] sought a unit for themselves, we dismissed the petition, holding that a unit comprised of faculty members in one college was not appropriate.[10] We also dismissed a petition by student employees in two departments of Wayne State University, holding that the proposed bargaining unit was inappropriate, since the community of interest of these two departments of student employees is not functionally distinct from that of other student employees.[11] We

---

7. Hotel Olds v. State Labor Mediation Board, 333 Mich. 382, 53 N.W.2d 302 (1952).
8. 1966 MERC Lab. Op. 25.
9. University College is a two-year college in which all Michigan State University freshmen and sophomores are required to enroll.
10. 1970 MERC Lab. Op. 1029.
11. 1969 MERC Lab. Op. 670.

have not yet had a case concerning the dividing line to be set in universities. In two cases now pending, the faculties of Wayne State University[12] and Eastern Michigan University[13] are seeking bargaining units.

Representation cases are customarily heard by a trial examiner who, after the hearing, prepares a draft opinion for the three members of the commission. The commission members read the record and make a decision which may follow the trial examiner's proposal, modify it in some respects, or completely change it. In the pending cases involving Wayne State and Eastern Michigan, I am reasonably certain that the commission will decide to hold oral argument and invite participation of representatives from all interested organizations and the other state universities.

Previous rulings suggest that we will probably make some division among faculty. In the case involving The University of Michigan interns and residents,[14] the commission excluded from the bargaining unit the pharmacy and dietetic interns, the trainees in physical and occupational therapy, and the nurse-anesthetist trainees. Upon petition of pharmacy employees at The University of Michigan,[15] the commission ordered a unit of all pharmacists in the hospital and student health service, excluding pharmacy interns and residents as inappropriate members of the unit. In the nonteaching units in the colleges and universities, we have ordinarily included all employees other than those whose work is in direct support of the educational process.

The Scope of Bargaining

What subjects are acceptable for bargaining? Before the enactment of the Michigan statute, some academicians prophesied that

---

12. Case Nos. R71 B-58, R71 B-75, R71 B-79, and R71 C-137. On February 4, 1972, MERC ordered an election and held the unit to include academic staff, teaching faculty, and the College of Medicine. Department chairmen were excluded, however.
13. Case Nos. R70 K-407 and R71 A-2. On February 4, 1972, MERC ordered an election and held the unit to include assistant, associate, and full professors; instructors; librarians of faculty rank; lecturers who are employed six hours or more for two or more consecutive semesters; academic advisors; counselors; and residence hall head advisors. Deans, directors, department heads, and other supervisors are excluded. Eastern Michigan University will appeal MERC's decision.
14. 1971 MERC Lab. Op. 270. The Michigan Court of Appeals reversed the MERC order creating a bargaining unit, Jan. 21, 1972, No. 11524.
15. 1971 MERC Lab. Op. 337.

public school teachers and other public employees would attempt to dominate policy. Frank Zeidler, a former mayor of Milwaukee who had relevant experience in Wisconsin, noted that since the term "conditions of work" is a broad phrase, it can be interpreted to permit employees to challenge work assignments, policies on what services the government will perform, and any other activity of government. The National Education Association (NEA) said in one of its publications that negotiations should include "all matters which affect the quality of the educational system."[16] In 1963, a *New York Times* article reported "mounting evidence that teachers are no longer content to rule only the classroom to which they are assigned. They want a hand in the assignment and a voice in the policy that controls their professional lives."[17]

North Dearborn Heights

In view of such reports, we were not surprised when, in 1965, we received our first public school case, filed by the North Dearborn Heights School District.[18] The teachers' organization had asked to bargain on fourteen separate issues and were met with refusal of the school board to bargain on any of them. The teachers' organization filed an unfair labor practice charge. The case went to a MERC trial examiner. (Members of the commission decide unfair labor practice cases only after the filing of exceptions to a trial examiner's decision.) The trial examiner held that all fourteen of the issues were bargainable. The issues included curriculum and classroom schedules, class sizes, selection of textbook materials and supplies, planning of facilities and special education, establishment of in-service training for teachers, procedures for rating the effectiveness of teachers, and the establishment of a self-sustaining summer school program.

Michigan school board members and superintendents reacted predictably. The governor's telephone was hot. Friends castigated commission members for this terrible thing we had done to the

16. National Education Association, *Guidelines for Professional Negotiation* (1965), pp. 21-22, quoted in M. Lieberman and M. Moskow, *Collective Negotiations for Teachers* (Chicago: Rand McNally, 1966), p. 225.
17. *New York Times,* Jan. 16, 1964, p. 88; quoted in J. Steffensen, *Teachers Negotiate with Their School Boards* (U.S. Department of Health, Education and Welfare, Office of Education, 1964), p. 1.
18. 1966 MERC Lab. Op. 434, 445.

educational process. Of course, the commission members had not done anything; our trial examiner had made the decision. One of the Detroit newspapers published an accurate account of the event, but the headline read, "State Mediator Rips School for Bad Faith Bargaining." Our mediators were understandably disturbed, as they had done no such thing.

The case was ultimately settled, and we dismissed it as moot. Since then we have not had one case involving the refusal of any school governing body to negotiate on a "policy matter," as that phrase is generally used.

Policy Matters

Perhaps we should not have been surprised to find that teachers are "people" and were primarily interested in money. In the initial years, bargaining tended to revolve around salaries and fringe benefits, with virtually no interest shown in policy matters.

That situation has gradually changed. As the salaries of Michigan teachers rose from fourteenth in average salary in the country to third, behind only Alaska and California, teachers became more interested in policy matters. The school boards, often with the aid of the mediators, have become able to accommodate to the changed situation. Policy matters are discussed, with the mediator sometimes altering the thrust of a particular discussion if it seems overly concerned with policy. Many items now included in collective agreements would have been opposed vigorously by school boards six years ago.

I suggest that including policy items has merit. Certainly some elementary and secondary teachers are better qualified to determine school policy than are some school board members.

Whether this is true with respect to university and college professors vis-a-vis members of university and college governing boards will need to be explored. The university situation is different from that in the secondary and primary schools. Universities and colleges have senates, councils, and advisory committees, and each of these may have a voice in determining conditions of employment and matters of policy.

In two cases,[19] we held that the departmental advisory commit-

19. Michigan State University, University College, Department of Social Science (Hildebrand), 1971 MERC Lab. Op. 728, and Michigan State Uni-

tees of Michigan State University are not labor organizations but are set up by the board of trustees of the university, are part of its governing system, and were not established to represent employees in their dealings with the administration.

The expression "scope of bargaining" may refer to the subjects normally discussed by employers and unions in bargaining, or it may refer .to the subjects which are bargainable under the applicable statutes.

The scope of bargaining will receive substantial consideration in the public sector, since public employees generally have a greater interest in discussing policy matters than private sector employees. The National Labor Relations Board (NLRB) and the courts have been attempting for more than thirty-five years to draw a line between what is bargainable and what is not. They are still working on it, so one cannot expect the public sector agencies to determine the matter overnight.

Bargaining Limitations

Most of the state statutes have followed federal language in providing that there must be bargaining, or meeting and conferring, over wages, hours, and working conditions. A number of states have limited the issues subject to bargaining.

Four limitations, not generally present in the private sector, are present in public sector bargaining. First, a statute may provide only that employer and employees "meet and confer" or that public employees may present proposals—language which does not authorize collective bargaining. Second, a statutory "management functions" or "management rights" clause places a limitation upon bargaining. Third, a limiting factor is implicit in any conflict between PERA and other statutes, such as the civil service and teacher tenure acts. Fourth, limitations arise because of the inherent differences between the public and private sectors.[20]

In 1970, the Federal Advisory Commission on Intergovernmental Relations recommended in its model statute the enactment of a management functions provision which would provide that:

---

versity, University College, Department of Natural Science (Van Tassell and Murray), 1971 MERC Lab. Op. 750.

20. R. Howlett, "Address delivered at an FMCS Seminar," (Atlanta, Georgia, January 23, 1969), 70 LRR 258, 286 GERR B-4, E-1; R. Howlett, "The Right to Strike in the Public Sector," 53 *Chicago Bar Record* No. 3, p. 108 (Dec. 1971).

Nothing in this act is intended to circumscribe or modify the existing right of a public agency to:

(1) direct the work of its employees;

(2) hire, promote, assign, transfer, and retain employees in positions within the public agency;

(3) demote, suspend, or discharge employees for proper cause;

(4) maintain the efficiency of governmental operations;

(5) relieve employees from duties because of lack of work or other legitimate reasons;

(6) take actions as may be necessary to carry out the missions of the agency in emergencies; and

(7) determine the methods, means and personnel by which operations are to be carried on.[21]

Most of the states that have adopted public sector legislation[22] have, in part, followed the commission's recommendation. Some states borrowed the language quoted above, which is taken directly from private sector collective bargaining agreements.

I question the wisdom of placing either government or government employees in the straitjacket of such a statutory management functions clause. The world has changed explosively in recent years and is still changing. Subjects which were not bargainable in the private sector ten or twenty years ago are often included in the total package today. If the statute excludes certain issues from bargaining, the parties cannot legally bargain about them, even though both might be willing to do so. If the statute stipulates that specified power is to be retained by public management, it is likely that a taxpayer's suit challenging a contract covering such an excluded item would be successful. Moreover, a public employer could refuse to comply with a contract provision on a prohibited subject and the employees could do nothing about it.

There is a significant omission in the statutory management functions clause suggested by the Advisory Commission on Intergovernmental Relations report. In private sector contracts, the

21. Model statute drafted by Advisory Commission on Intergovernmental Relations, May, 1970, as amended in 1971, GERR RF 51:219.
22. Alaska, California, Connecticut, Delaware, District of Columbia, Hawaii, Idaho, Kansas, Massachusetts, Minnesota, Montana, Nebraska, Nevada, New Hampshire, Pennsylvania, Vermont, Virgin Islands, Washington, and Wisconsin.

clause always includes a proviso that the powers retained by management are subject to the other terms and provisions of the collective bargaining agreement. In the public sector statutes, the proviso is missing. The limitation is thus absolute. This is unfortunate. For example, if the school board has complete power to determine methods, means, and personnel, there would appear to be no right to bargain on the school calendar, preparation periods, transfers from one school to another, or the questions of teachers performing lunchroom duties or patrolling the halls.

Another example is a 1967 decision of the Wisconsin circuit court which held that the school calendar is a mandatory subject of collective bargaining because it directly affects wages and working conditions.[23]

The Hawaii statute[24] directs that the public employer has the right to determine the qualifications, standards of work, and the nature and content of examinations; and the right to hire, promote, transfer, assign, and retain employees in positions. Under such a limitation, a union could not insist on bargaining over work standards, bidding procedures, promotion, or the transfer and assignment of employees to various types of jobs. The process of bargaining should not be preempted by setting such narrow limits.

Conflict Between Statutes

What about the conflict of public employment relations acts with constitutional provisions, other statutes, home rule charters, and the like?

Arbitration

Our first experience with this conflict involved the Oakland County Sheriff's Department.[25] The Michigan statute governing county sheriffs[26] vests broad power in the sheriff to appoint one or more deputies, to revoke such appointments at his pleasure by instrument in writing, and other similar powers. The Oakland County Sheriff's Department, represented by the county, refused to bargain on arbitration as the terminal point in a grievance pro-

---

23. City of Madison v. Wisconsin Employment Relations Board, 65 LRRM 2488 (Dane County Cir. Ct., No. 121-135, April 26, 1967).
24. GERR RF 51:2014.
25. 1968 MERC Lab. Op. 1.
26. Michigan Sheriffs' Act, Mich. Stat. Ann. §5.861 et seq.

cedure and union security. We held unanimously that in Michigan arbitration as the terminal point in the bargaining procedure is legal and a mandatory subject of bargaining. The Wisconsin Supreme Court, in the *City of Rhinelander*[27] case, a landmark decision, had previously taken the same position. Shortly after our decision, the Supreme Court of New Hampshire upheld arbitration as the terminal point in a grievance procedure.[28]

Agency Shop

The question in the *Oakland County Sheriff's Department* case with respect to union security was an interesting one. The NLRA,[29] which prohibits employer discrimination to encourage or discourage union membership in hiring or tenure, includes a proviso that an employer and union may enter into a contract including the limited union security specified in the act. It was argued that because the Michigan statute lacks the proviso, all types of union security are illegal.

MERC held that only the agency shop is legal in Michigan. One of my colleagues held that, except for maintenance of membership, all union security is legal in Michigan; my other colleague held that no union security is legal; I held that the agency shop, and only the agency shop, is legal. This became the prevailing opinion.

Our circuit courts, in cases involving both civil service and teacher tenure acts, have affirmed MERC's position that the agency shop is legal. The judges have pointed out that the purpose of both civil service and teachers' tenure is to protect employees against arbitrary administrators and politicians; and that the agency shop, which simply requires that the employees pay for the service which the bargaining agent is legally obligated to render, has nothing to do with tenure or protection against political or administrative pressures.

The Michigan Court of Appeals assumed the validity of an agency shop, but held that:

. . . the validity of this agency shop provision hinges on the relationship between payment of a sum equivalent to the dues

27. Local 1226, Rhinelander City Employees, AFSCME, AFL-CIO v. City of Rhinelander, 35 Wis. 2d 209, 151 N.W.2d 30 (1966).
28. Tremblay v. Berlin Police Union, 108 N.H. 416, 237 A.2d 668 (1968).
29. 29 U.S.C. §158(a)(3).

of SEA, MEA and NEA and a non-member's proportionate share of the cost of negotiating and administering the contract involved. If that payment is greater than or less than that proportionate share, the agency shop provision is in violation of M.C.L.A. §423.210. [The provision comparable to Section 8 (a) (3) of NLRA.][30]

Home Rule Charter

Another interesting case decided by MERC involved the home rule charter of Flint, Michigan.[31] The charter provides uniform standard wage rates for the several classifications of all municipal employees. The union representing the municipal hospital employees wished to bargain over wages. The city administration said, in effect, that it would not bargain unless all the other employees were brought in with their representatives; alternatively, that the city would bargain, and if an agreement were reached which conflicted with the charter, a recommendation would be made to the voters that the charter be changed. The union filed a charge; a complaint was issued. MERC held that the position taken by the city was a refusal to bargain, concluding:

Were the Respondent's position to prevail, the Home Rule City could diminish the scope of, and even eliminate, the requirement of PERA to engage in collective bargaining, by adopting, through vote of the electorate, charter provisions detailing terms and conditions of employment ordinarily found in collective bargaining contracts. The Legislature, by the enactment of PERA, authorized public employees to select a bargaining agent to engage, for them, in collective bargaining for wages, hours and working conditions. The concept for which the City of Flint contends could reverse the intent of the Legislature as expressed in PERA.[32]

The *Flint* case was appealed, but the appeal was withdrawn because the same issue was pending on appeal in *Sloan v. Warren*

---

30. Smigel v. Southgate Community School District, 24 Mich. App. 179, 186, 180 N.W.2d 215, 219 (1970), *leave to appeal granted,* 384 Mich. 772 (1970). The case has been appealed and is now pending before the Michigan Supreme Court.
31. City of Flint and Hurley Hospital, 1970 MERC Lab. Op. 348.
32. *Id.,* at 349.

City Civil Service Commission.[33] In the *Sloan* case, the court of appeals held that a city civil service commission, established by ordinance pursuant to the authority granted by the state constitution to cities to establish and regulate a merit system, had jurisdiction to determine the seniority rights of employees in layoffs. Hopefully, the supreme court will not agree with the court of appeals. If it does, it will substantially damage collective bargaining. There must be, and there will be, accommodation between public employment relations acts and conflicting law.

Arvid Anderson has aptly pointed out:

> It seems that the advent of collective bargaining will have an impact on the merit system. But an accommodation can be found by which the essentials of the merit system with respect to the recruiting, examination, hiring and the establishment of standards for promotion and training will be preserved. It seems likely, also, that accommodation will be developed between grievance procedure under civil service and grievance procedure as it is known in private employment. A greater potential conflict seems to lie in the area of job classification and job evaluation and in the general area of salary and pay plan proposals. The latter deal with basic subjects of collective bargaining.[34]

The Public and Private Sectors

Whether collective bargaining is sufficiently different in the public and private sectors to warrant separate treatment is a question frequently discussed.[35] Several differences have been suggested.

First, some point out that the right to strike is a weapon ordi-

---

33. 26 Mich. App. 555, 182 N.W.2d 815 (1970), *leave to appeal granted,* 384 Mich. 806 (1971).
34. Arvid Anderson in K. Warner and M. Hennessy, *Public Management at the Bargaining Table* (Chicago: Public Personnel Association, 1967), p. 289. He is chairman of the Office of Collective Bargaining, New York City. See his 1969 and 1971 articles listed in the Bibliography and his contribution to the 1969 *Michigan Law Review* symposium (Russell Smith, *et al.*).
35. R. Howlett, "Address delivered at an FMCS Seminar," *supra,* note 20; R. Howlett, "Arbitration in the Public Sector," *Proceedings of the Southwestern Legal Foundation 15th Annual Institute on Labor Law* (New York: Matthew Bender, 1969), p. 253ff.

narily prohibited to public sector employees. However, public employees have used the strike effectively. I think the right to strike will be extended further within the public sector, while restrictions will be placed on the right of private sector employees to strike in enterprises that have even greater impact on the public than do public institutions. Neutrals will be used more in both sectors to resolve impasses. Public sector bargainers are always aware of strike power, which, as in the private sector, is greater in some bargaining situations than in others. There is also the possibility of a lockout by the employer. In Michigan, we have had nine lockouts by school boards. I suspect that the lockout has the same legal status as the strike, though the Michigan statute is silent on the question.

A second difference often noted is that decisions in the public sector are political rather than strictly economic. This difference is overstated. Government is big business, now performing many services formerly furnished by private enterprise. Moreover, in 1970 a private business was awarded a contract to run the Banneker Elementary School in Gary, Indiana. A first in the country, the four-year, $2.6 million contract allows the contractor complete authority to hire teachers, select and implement the system of instruction, and provide learning materials. If this mixture of public and private sectors works in Gary, the arrangement could spread to other systems.

A third, and perhaps the most significant difference, is that public institutions must live within budgets limited by tax monies. But companies have budgets, too, and must live within their means. They are similarly limited in the extent to which they can raise prices or increase efficiency. Thus, this difference is also smaller than some people think.

Our mediators in Michigan have found that the basic desires of the public and private employees are the same at the bargaining table. Teachers and other public employees want more compensation, just as executives, lawyers, and doctors do. I expect the same will be true of college professors. Likewise, the negotiating techniques used are the same.

It is urged that public employees have a greater degree of interest in policy matters than private employees. But private sector unions exert pressure both politically and at the bargaining table on subjects involving social security, welfare provisions, foreign trade, pricing systems, productivity, the decisions and efficiency of management, ecology, and minority group rights.

The distinction in policy, including the right to strike and interest arbitration, between the private and public sectors should be made on the basis of the impact of the bargaining situation on the economy and on people. A division grounded solely on the fact that employers and employees are public on the one hand, and private on the other, is unrealistic and not in the public interest.

I predict that during the next decade the means of resolving impasses in the two sectors of the economy, including the right to strike and interest arbitration, will become closer; and that the use of the strike will increase in the public sector, and the use of interest arbitration will increase in the private sector.

CHAPTER 3

Faculty Bargaining:
Practical Considerations

*William F. McHugh**

Based upon my experience as special university counsel in the State University of New York (SUNY) negotiations, I shall discuss six interlocking issues with respect to collective bargaining: the implications of the *Fordham University*[1] case, budget considerations, information exchange in bargaining, subjects for negotiation, student participation in bargaining, and some general observations on faculty unionism.

Fordham University

The National Labor Relations Board (NLRB) first asserted jurisdiction over private institutions of higher education in the *Cornell University*[2] case. Moreover, the NLRB ruled that the bargaining unit could appropriately represent all nonacademic employees of Cornell University at any university facility in New York. In defining a statewide comprehensive unit, the board rejected the request of certain employees in the School of Industrial and Labor Relations, New York City office, for a separate bargaining unit in New York City. This decision has some significance for all private institutions with multicampus arrangements, extension divisions, or other off-campus facilities, because it suggests the possibility of favoring larger units. However, the board did say it would utilize

---

* Formerly Special Counsel, Employment Relations, State University of New York; presently Associate Professor of Law, American University Law School, Washington, D.C.
1. 193 NLRB 23. A petition for reconsideration was filed the following day, September 15, 1971. See Appendix F for text.
2. 183 NLRB 41. See Appendix D for text.

the same tests applied to multiplant unit problems in industry.

In the *C.W. Post*[3] case which followed, the NLRB reasserted its jurisdiction over faculty in private institutions. It held that faculty members have the usual incidents of employment relationship and are therefore entitled to collective bargaining under the National Labor Relations Act (NLRA). Full and adjunct faculty were put in the same unit with counselors, librarians, and other support staff. Department chairmen, however, were excluded as supervisors. Apparently, the multicampus unit question was never raised by the parties. Long Island University has three campuses, two of which were organized at the time of the hearing—the C.W. Post Center and the Brooklyn Center.

In the *Fordham* case the full and adjunct faculty were grouped in a single unit. The NLRB reasserted that faculty members are not supervisors and enjoy the usual incidents of the employment relationship and are therefore entitled to collective bargaining rights under the NLRA if they so choose. Further, the board ruled that department chairmen were not supervisors and were to be included in the employee unit with faculty. The *C.W. Post* decision, excluding department chairmen from the bargaining unit, had not been released when Fordham prepared its brief. The *Fordham* decision indicates that the NLRB is going to proceed in an ad hoc fashion on the question of whether department chairmen are supervisors and are, therefore, to be excluded. Thus, each institution will be separately analyzed to determine whether or not department chairmen are supervisors—a fundamentally sound approach to this most difficult question.

The *Fordham* decision held that the law faculty of the university should constitute a separate unit. The board made several points in support of that holding: (1) none of the employee organizations involved in the proceeding argued that the law faculty should be in the unit; (2) the law school occupies a separate building; (3) it operates on a different calendar; (4) there is very little interchange between the law faculty and the undergraduate faculty (which could probably be said also of extension agents and the graduate faculty); and (5) law faculty salaries are higher than most (true also of medical faculties). The board noted that the courts regulate the admission of lawyers to the bar, emphasizing

---

3. 189 NLRB 109.

that outside agencies are closely linked to the academic requirements of the law profession. (This is applicable to the medical
profession, social workers, and others in the sense that outside
agencies are also involved in administering standards for admission into the profession.)

It is noteworthy that the *Fordham* decision to separate the law
faculty is different from some state decisions, notably New York,
which have included law faculty with other faculties. *Fordham* suggests that larger units will not necessarily be as favored by the
NLRB as they have been by many state boards. The ramifications
for multiprofessional or multicampus units are far reaching. If
faculties are significantly split up in separate units, the door is
open for unmanageable fragmentation from an administrative point
of view. We will have to wait and see the effect of the *Fordham*
decision on multipurpose private institutions with faculties located
away from the main campus. It seems clear that universities will
find it hard to justify to the NLRB not having a separate unit
for faculties of law or medicine.

Bargaining and the Budget Process

What will be the impact of collective bargaining on the budget-
making process? There will certainly be greater involvement by
government officials in the collective bargaining process of public
institutions. The principal motivation here will be a concern for
cost and budget control which will be accompanied no doubt by
pressures for trade-offs of money items for noneconomic academic
concessions. This may project government officials into the internal operations of the public college or university. Unfortunately,
the dividing line between academic and economic issues is indis-
tinguishable in many cases. Experience in New York at both the
community college and state university levels indicates the need
for meshing governmental-fiscal authorities into the bargaining
process in order to assess the budget implications of bargaining
and to cost out the various proposals made by employee organizations. This may threaten traditional academic autonomy.

At the same time, bargaining will increase faculty participation
in the broader financial affairs of their institutions. Any persuasive
arguments concerning salaries, work loads, fringe benefits, sabbaticals, or tenure will have to be hinged upon the total fiscal

picture of the institution. In general, I believe that the existing faculty governance machinery does not really provide a disciplined system for resolving budget allocation problems. Collective bargaining will change that by its potential for providing such a means. Because of the very nature of the bargaining process, the bargaining agent will have to be concerned with the overall budgeting process. Some contracts already provide opportunities for faculty to become more fully involved in the budget process.

The New Jersey State Colleges contract[4] expressly provides that the bargaining agent may participate in the public budget hearings —i.e., those provided by the governing board and presumably hearings before legislative bodies. The St. John's University contract[5] contains a rather detailed provision for representation of the bargaining agent and the faculty on various universitywide committees, the work of which directly affects the budget.

In the City University of New York (CUNY) contract, article eight deals with exchange of information and specifies that major fiscal studies and such other matters relating to the fiscal conditions of the institution will be available to the bargaining agent. Article ten requires consultation with the chancellor and campus presidents, and access to the board of trustees.

Similar consultation provisions are included in the SUNY contract, which the faculty ratified on August 31, 1971. The bargaining agent—a faculty senate association affiliated with the New York Teachers Association (National Education Association)—has the right to receive a copy of the board agenda at least two weeks in advance of its submission to the board, with an opportunity to discuss anything on the agenda with the chancellor. Theoretically, the bargaining agent could present comments at some point to the chancellor or perhaps even make a formal presentation to the board of trustees relating to budgetary matters and allocations. Whether the various contracts will in fact be administered to permit involvement in the budget process is not yet clear because of limited experience.

Information Exchange in Bargaining

If the bargaining process is to work, a full exchange of budgetary information is required. I have observed at some institutions

---

4. Art. 4, 3i. See Appendix J—Contracts.
5. Art. 4, pp. 5-9. See Appendix J—Contracts.

almost a built-in reluctance among administrative and fiscal officials to give faculty information relating to the financing of certain academic programs. I fear that some administrative functionaries look upon information control as a major fulcrum of their authority and therefore seem reluctant to share it with faculty except upon a piecemeal basis. Whatever the explanation, administrators must come to realize that the free and candid exchange of fiscal information is absolutely essential during the bargaining process. Certain information might tactically be withheld for awhile, only to be made available at a later stage in bargaining. But in the main, there has to be a free exchange. Thus, computers will have to be utilized to recover complex data quickly. Presently, at some institutions, asking a basic question as to the number, age, and salaries of associate professors in the university raises all sorts of logistical problems. But such information is essential to negotiations on such matters as shortening the probationary period for tenure, rank ratios, and projecting future costs. Indeed, this type of information and data is essential to intelligent management of the institution apart from collective bargaining; but collective bargaining makes it imperative. Thus, sophisticated information systems will be needed to analyze the cost of various proposals. Bargaining representatives must know the cost implications of longer or shorter sabbatical leaves. Some suggest that such matters should be left to the department to decide, but that is not enough to gauge institutional cost factors. Even provisions for office space and chairs have significant cost implications. For example, I doubt that anyone has tried to determine the cost of lengthy tenure review hearings. Effective bargaining depends upon specific information relevant to demands. The bargaining process accelerates the need to make careful studies in anticipation of demands. In complex institutions, sophisticated information systems relating the budget process to collective negotiations will be imperative.

A system for establishing priorities is essential, especially in a financial crunch. I believe collective bargaining will provide a useful means to accomplish this end. Existing programs will need to be evaluated and joint studies made to determine how programs will be financed. Joint faculty-administrative study committees established during or after the bargaining process will facilitate such efforts.

A view of budgetary and allocation problems seen only from the myopic view of departmental or school budgetary considerations is self-defeating during a fiscal crunch when severe priorities are essential. The institutional perspective required by bargaining is essential and desirable.

A key budget official is an indispensable member of the administration's negotiating team. Some budget people are wondering whether, under collective bargaining, their role will be taken over by the employment relations staff. Nothing could be further from the truth. The budget official should be involved at every stage of the bargaining process; indeed, some aspects of his role will increase in importance.

The collective bargaining process is costly in terms of time. The number of man hours invested, especially the first time around, is very high. The first negotiation in the smaller New York community college lasted somewhere between three to six months. The bargaining agents set up weekly meetings at first; somewhat later the number of meetings in a week increased to two or three; and near the end of negotiations frantic around-the-clock sessions became the pattern. I do not know precisely how much time was spent in preparation, but I would estimate the figure to be at least equal to the time spent in actual sessions— a tremendous investment of personnel time when one considers that bargaining was going on in twenty-two community colleges.

Subjects for Negotiation

The scope of negotiations also has marked budget implications extending beyond simple expenditures for salaries and fringe benefits. In the SUNY case, Israel Kugler, president of the United Federation of College Teachers (AFT-AFL/CIO), testified that the following subjects would be included in the negotiations:

> Merit increases, number of students, promotion, compensation for extracurricular activity, TV and radio tape residuals, research staff office space, secretarial services, travel funds, academic calendar, evening and extension assignments, sabbatical leave, leaves of absence, maternity and sick leave, tenure policy, grievance procedures, general regulations pertaining to campus affairs, consultation on educational matters, curriculum, admission, student activities, choice of administrators including deans, chairmen and presidents, pensions, health benefits, life and disability insurance, salary policy, moving

expenses, tuition waiver for dependents, central faculty authority, master plan formulation, educational policy governing the entire university, establishment of new campuses, intercollege agreements, and finally, but not least, selection of the chancellor and other central administrators.[6]

Certainly acceptance of this definition of scope would have a far-reaching effect on preparation of the budget, on the establishing of priorities, and on the general fiscal commitment of the institution.

Student Involvement in Bargaining

So far there has been relatively little student participation in the collective bargaining process. I speculate that when students realize the implications of faculty unionism, they are going to want to become involved in the process. I do not believe that students should be included in the entire span of negotiations. Their presence, either to observe or to comment, would be appropriate on certain issues, especially those proposals which would require a substantial raise in tuition. There is an excellent opportunity for student involvement in faculty-university study committees and other committees created for the purpose of defining issues and gathering facts.

Why not put students on the bargaining team? The simple reason is that they do not necessarily align themselves with either side. To secure their own interests on a given issue, however, I can anticipate students trying to organize their resources to challenge university policy or to influence negotiations themselves in areas of special importance to them. Perhaps students will enter arbitration proceedings in an amicus curiae capacity. Conceivably, they could assert some sort of third-party beneficiary theory with respect to the failure of either the administration or the bargaining agent to apply particular contract provisions clearly related to their interest.

It seems unlikely to me that undergraduate student bodies will organize into student unions, elect a bargaining agent, and go through the formal bargaining process as we now know it. There is not a sufficient community of interest nor available financial re-

---

6. The list is drawn from my own brief in the case. See also Appendix K—Bargainable Issues.

sources or staff. On the other hand, teaching assistants may try to organize for collective bargaining, as suggested by the experience at the University of Wisconsin and The University of Michigan.

Faculty Unions

Administrative people often ask me whether faculty unionism is a good thing or not. It really depends upon the institution in question. For some institutions collective bargaining can be a positive and stabilizing force. The effectiveness and creative potential of collective bargaining depends greatly upon the people involved.

We are witnessing a significant movement toward collective bargaining in certain types of institutions in higher education—a movement which is augmented by substantial social forces. We have been conditioned by a decade of confrontation. Interest relationships seem to be superseding status relationships, perhaps an inevitable consequence of the move toward large and complex urban institutions. We have practically institutionalized conflict. To hear someone decry the adversary relationship between administration and faculty, which is implicit in the bargaining process, is almost ludicrous in the wake of the confrontations of the sixties and where existing conflict resolution machinery is almost nonexistent. The adversary relationship frequently exists and we ought to recognize and accept it as a given and promote methods for stabilizing it.

In some institutions, indiscriminate tinkering with faculty governance machinery has led faculty members to promote their interests through collective bargaining. I agree that in some instances students and other nonfaculty groups appear to be taking control of matters that properly belong to the faculty. Without defining those matters, it is important for faculty to have a separate forum where they can express themselves, influence institutional policy, and exercise their unique responsibilities unencumbered by nonfaculty.

The democratization of the university is in some measure manifest in the younger faculty members who want greater influence in their departments and various faculty councils. Perhaps collective bargaining affords this opportunity in a way the traditional senate does not.

Other factors influence the trend toward faculty unionism, including public attacks on the professoriate and a growing sense of public dissatisfaction with the academy. Bills have been introduced in state legislatures to eliminate or restrict tenure, to increase work loads, or to exercise disciplinary proceedings which appear punitive to faculty.

The scarcity of faculty positions now makes job security a major consideration. The pending economic crunch and the eroding fiscal condition of many institutions is arousing talk of academic program retrenchment. There is a slowing down of salary increases. Educational experimentation—e.g., open admissions, off-campus study, degrees by examination, greater use of technology—will also affect the interests of faculty.

State governments are placing increasing pressure on their institutions to harmonize the educational enterprise with the purposes of government. This is manifest in the increasing involvement of the state and local fiscal authorities and other governmental officials in the fiscal matters and other areas of internal academic policy. All this is bound to affect the nature of educational programs and directly affect faculty interests. The passage of public employment relations laws will increase the impetus to organize the faculty as public school teachers have already done.

We in higher education, faculty and administrators alike, must be sensitive to the question of how the bargaining process can be improved to serve the best interests of our society. This means adapting the process to the unique character of the particular institution concerned. It means pulling administrative heads out of the sand. It means seeing to it that the collective faculty gets the best leadership in its organizational structure, not fourth-raters. It means restraint in the uses of power and developing methods in the process which will promote goodwill and compromise, minimizing needless conflict and narrow self-serving attitudes. You start this by understanding the process, its limitations, and its potential.

Part II
Institutional Differences

CHAPTER 4

Collective Bargaining in Public Institutions

J. David Kerr
Kenneth M. Smythe

THE PROCESS

J. David Kerr*

Collective bargaining is a process by which decisions are made. The process of public sector collective bargaining in Michigan is similar to that in at least fifteen other states and follows the basic approach set forth in the National Labor Relations Act (NLRA). Thus, I intend to use the Michigan experience to indicate how several basic decisions may be made in these contexts. Since technical rules vary from state to state and since such rules may also differ depending on which employee group is in question, expert assistance is needed to deal with these matters in specific terms.

Petitioning for an Election

Interest in a collective bargaining agent is expressed through a petition requesting an election for such an agent. The petition can be either typed or handwritten, and the signatures can be placed individually on cards or collectively on long sheets of paper. It should clearly state that the purpose of the petition is to have an agent designated as a representative to bargain on rates of pay, wages, hours, or other conditions of employment—or whatever may be bargainable under the relevant state laws.

---

* University Attorney, Central Michigan University, Mt. Pleasant.

In Michigan, 30 percent of the people within the initially-proposed bargaining unit must sign the petition; 10 percent must sign a different petition for each additional proposed agent (called an intervenor) to get on the ballot. Any petitioning organization must be a union—i.e., it must purport to represent members of the unit for the purpose of collective bargaining. It may not include people such as supervisors or administrators, who under Michigan law (unlike NLRA provisions) may form a separate bargaining unit.

Once the governing body of the institution is aware of a petition for election or recognition, it has several choices. It can recognize the bargaining agent without an election, saying, "Yes, you have the right kind of showing; we agree that you represent a majority of the proposed bargaining unit." However, if the agent is simply recognized, until a contract is reached there is not subsequent protection against raiding by some other agent. In other words, another agent could appear with a 30 percent showing and petition for an election in the midst of the bargaining process between the recognized unit and the employer. A successful election acts as a bar to other agents petitioning for an election for a twelve-month period after certification of the agent. A contract acts as a bar to an election for the period of the contract (not to exceed three years), except for a period extending from the 150th day to the 90th day before the end of the contract. (Under the NLRA it is from the 90th to the 60th day.)

Institutions of higher education should exercise caution when offered the opportunity to view cards or petitions unless they desire a collective bargaining agent. Members of the faculty have been known to sign a petition for the purpose of bringing an issue before the university community and then voting against the proposal. Yet the institution may be held to be acting in bad faith if it insists on an election when the petition or cards which have been seen by agents of the institution show that over 50 percent of the people in the proposed unit have signed. Usually it is best not to look at the petition or cards.

If the institution does not recognize the proposed collective bargaining agent, the state employment relations commission will arrange an informal conference between representatives of the institution, the petitioner, any intervenors, and an officer of the commission. The purpose of the conference is to see whether agreement on the issues can be reached without hearings or other formalities. The petitions or cards will be checked by the commission officer against a list of employees furnished by the institution setting forth the names of persons in the proposed bargaining unit. The officer will check the two sets of names against each other to determine if the 30 percent showing of interest has been made by the petitioner and the 10 percent required of any intervenor. If the question is raised, a check will be made to determine whether the petitioner and intervenors meet the definition of a collective bargaining agent (union) and to determine whether the parties agree that the proposed bargaining unit is appropriate. Three choices can then be made by the institution: (1) recognition of the agent without a vote, (2) consent to an election, or (3) referral for hearing on any areas of dispute such as the appropriate makeup of the bargaining unit or a determination of whether a given petitioner or intervenor is a collective bargaining agent.

In Michigan and in most other states allowing public collective bargaining, hearings are conducted by hearing examiners who take testimony and write opinions which are referred to the state employment relations commission for decision. Bargaining unit questions are often crucial in these hearings. After consent to an election or after hearings before the employment relations commission, the election is held.

Many decisions reached through faculty collective bargaining affect the entire institution. Both faculty and administration should therefore be aware that people other than the bargainers have an interest in the proceedings. Such people include: students; professional, technical, and supervisory staff; clerical staff; and the food and maintenance staffs. Decisions which adversely affect these other groups may cause them to react and to bargain in areas which the faculty may feel interfere unreasonably with the academic areas of the university.

The traditional description of bargainable areas covers wages, hours, and other conditions of employment. Faculty have also bargained on policy issues crucial to the institution. Such areas include rights and responsibilities of faculty in institutional government and faculty organs for deciding or making recommendations in the areas of hiring, promotions, tenure, and nonreappointment.[1]

1. See Appendix K—Bargainable Issues.

The college or university community will have to work out which areas of decisionmaking should be in collective bargaining and which areas should be left to other organs in the institution, such as the faculty senate.

In systemwide bargaining, the legislature may have some type of representative in the process. In Michigan, the legislature has not been active in the faculty collective bargaining process. When the American Association of University Professors (AAUP) went on strike at Oakland University, both the legislators and the press treated the matter much like a strike in a K-12 school system. Sometimes legislators resist increasing appropriations after laws have been established requiring collective bargaining. Administrators are told by legislators to bargain hard and tough. They are warned that the legislature will not bail them out if they agree to too much. In public education, relations with the legislature during collective bargaining can become a major issue, one deserving as much consideration as any other single factor.

The individual faculty member's relationship to his bargaining agent is an important one, often overlooked. A collective bargaining agent represents; it has the power to bargain and then to bind faculty members to a contract. Once power to make certain decisions has been granted by a majority of the agency's local membership, or the majority has approved a given decision, that view prevails, even to the extent of determining who gets the money. A large junior faculty with a majority vote could perhaps arrange for dollar amount increases instead of percentage increases—thus making their salary increases proportionately larger than those of the higher-paid faculty. Or, they could decide that no faculty members would be paid more than $25,000 and reallocate the remainder to lower-paid faculty. As long as the majority of the bargaining agency members approve—not even the majority of the bargaining unit, unless they are all members of the agency—this is the way it is going to be.

Ratification of Contracts

Which faculty members may vote on ratification? To deal with this question we must first recognize the distinction between a bargaining unit and a bargaining agent. The bargaining unit consists of the people who are represented by the bargaining agent. The people in the unit may or may not be members of the bargaining agent, e.g., the National Education Association (NEA) or the American Federation of Teachers (AFT). The bargaining agent determines who shall decide on ratification of the contract. Some of the forms for determining ratification chosen by bargaining agents are: (1) vote by all persons in the bargaining unit, (2) vote by members of the bargaining agent only, and (3) vote only by an executive board or other committee within the bargaining agent. At Central Michigan University the bargaining agent (the NEA) allowed all members of the bargaining unit to vote. However, at Oakland University the agent (the AAUP) has only allowed members of the agent to vote. This is legal. The agent may provide for its own method or ratification in its own internal regulations.

Most faculty bargaining agents provide for some type of majority rule for decisionmaking. Faculty members who select collective bargaining but do not take part in the affairs of their bargaining agent leave decisionmaking to other members of the faculty, who may or may not share their concerns. Such a course leads to trouble regardless of whether 70 out of 300 or 500 out of 3,000 run the show. If collective bargaining occurs, faculty should be active in the process since that is the only way they can be assured of a voice in the decisionmaking. Unfortunately, my experience is that very few people take an active part. If collective barganing is to succeed in colleges and universities, I feel that a majority of the faculty must participate in the process.

Impasse Resolution

Several impasse resolution procedures, such as mediation, factfinding, and arbitration, are available when bargaining breaks down. Mediation through an officer of the employment relations commission attempts to get both sides together, regardless of what the resulting agreement may be. In factfinding, documents and testimony are presented to a factfinder, who makes a written finding about the facts in the situation and usually makes a specific written recommendation for settlement. In Michigan, factfinding is advisory; the parties do not have to follow the recommendation. Most people mistakenly think of arbitration only as binding arbitration—where the arbitrator sets the terms of settlement. There is also advisory arbitration, which is essentially only a recommendation like that in factfinding. In Michigan, mediation and factfinding are required by laws affecting colleges and universities. Binding arbitration has been required for certain police and firefighter disputes.

Decertification

When persons in the bargaining unit no longer wish to have a bargaining agent, what can they do? In Michigan, 30 percent of the bargaining unit members may petition for a decertification election. They can petition when a contract is not in effect, when a contract expires, or within 150 to 90 days before the end of the contract period (90 through 60 days under the NLRA). Election procedures are similar to those used for the original election of a bargaining agent and may be followed either to discontinue having any bargaining agent or to replace the first one.

THE PARTICIPANTS

*Kenneth M. Smythe**

In June, 1971, the American Association of University Professors (AAUP) asked the National Labor Relations Board (NLRB) to issue general rules in order to define four areas of concern in higher education bargaining units: (1) supervisors, (2) types of organizations that may form bargaining units (e.g., whether faculty senates or other faculty bodies would be appropriate), (3) the status of teaching fellows and research associates, and (4) the status of part-time teachers. The NLRB turned down the petition. (See Appendix H)

One reason for the board's reluctance was its lack of experience with higher education. In the period ahead, both the NLRB and the state agencies may be expected to move cautiously, feeling their way into this area on a case-by-case basis. They are going to make mistakes—chiefly, I think, with respect to determining the bargaining unit.

The Appropriate Bargaining Unit

To be appropriate, a bargaining unit must reflect a community of interest—a similarity of wages, fringe benefits, hours, working

---

* Office of the General Counsel, Wayne State University.

conditions, and the like. On this basis, then, the question is posed as to whether a unit should combine both the teaching faculty and the traditional academic support people—the counselors, librarians, academic advisors, registrars, program planners, and other service officers.

During a three-week hearing before the Michigan Employment Relations Commission (MERC) on the Wayne State University petition for recognition of a proposed bargaining unit, the Wayne State Board of Governors argued that there were two appropriate units. One was the teaching faculty, which we called the "pure unit"; the other was the academic support personnel. A determination of the matter has not yet been made by MERC.[1] Long Island University made a similar kind of presentation before the NLRB and lost.[2]

Whether Wayne State wins or loses, important issues have been raised. It is significant, for example, that the three national teacher organizations involved took two very different positions. The AAUP and the National Education Association (NEA) joined in support of the pure faculty notion. The American Federation of Teachers (AFT) asked for a broad academic unit covering all teaching faculty and academic support people. Generally speaking, the law is that the appropriate unit is the largest unit with a community of interest. Faculty, we believe, tend not to have regular working hours and often do not work for the same salary or under the same working conditions as the academic support people. The latter group usually works a scheduled forty-hour week on a different wage scale and may have different fringe benefits.

Bargaining unit determinations almost always turn on the facts under the community of interest test. What roles and functions do people actually perform? If they are similar, and if there is significant interchange between these groups in the discharge of their duties, they will probably end up in one large bargaining unit. This appears to be the NLRB trend, but what state labor boards will do is difficult to determine.

Part-time Employees

The NLRB decisions to date generally hold that regular part-

---

1. On February 4, 1972, MERC ordered an election and held the unit to include academic staff, teaching faculty and the College of Medicine. Department chairmen were excluded, however.
2. Long Island University, 189 NLRB 109.

time employees share a community of interest with full-time employees. The status of the part-time person who teaches one class a year is not settled, however. One who regularly teaches two classes for two or three successive terms would appear to share a community of interest with full-time people.

A teaching assistants unit was recognized at the University of Wisconsin, but MERC[3] denied the right of teaching fellows at The University of Michigan to be represented by a bargaining unit.

Professional Units

The concept of professional craft severance has been followed by the NLRB for a number of years. Generally speaking, skilled tradesmen are not grouped in units with production or maintenance employees. The question arises, then, whether a law or medical school faculty belongs in the same unit with sociology professors. The Wayne State University medical school faculty filed a separate petition in our bargaining unit case.

Generally, colleges and universities should resist application of the craft severance principle. If the principle prevails, we will see separate units pulling at the administration from different directions, all arguing for different fringe benefits and privileges. This will be an exhausting and costly process.

Department Chairmen

The question of department chairmen seems to appear in every case. The universities usually claim that a department chairman is supervisory because he has the power to hire, fire, promote, discharge, or effectively recommend such action in the interests of his employer. In Michigan, the rulings have gone both ways. Again, it is a question of fact. If the department chairman has such power, he is excluded. If he does not, he is not considered a supervisor and is included in the faculty unit.

What happens if the chairman of a large department is clearly supervisory, while the chairman of a small department is at most a group leader? Group leaders have always been included in the general bargaining unit because they do not have supervisory authority. One or two cases indicate that with a legitimate job classification, such as department chairman, all members of the class

3. 1971 MERC Lab. Op. 754.

will be excluded from the bargaining unit, even though a few members do not exercise supervisory authority. Where is the cut-off point? If 45 percent supervise and 55 percent do not, is the entire group in or are the 45 percent out? There are no clear answers at this time.

In the *Long Island University*[4] case, academic deans and department chairmen were excluded from the academic bargaining unit. The parties agreed to exclude nonacademic deans. The supervisory status of associate and assistant deans was not determined, but they were permitted to vote subject to challenge. At Wayne State University, we got an agreement with all of the organizations to exclude deans and assistant deans. On the facts, the Wayne State argument is correct, but the issue will continue to be decided on a case-by-case basis. How the NLRB rules this week will probably determine how the state boards are going to rule next week.

Election Rules

In the industrial area, campaign propaganda promises are involved in an election. An employer has a constitutional right to talk and communicate with his employees, but he may not coerce them or threaten their jobs if they join or vote for a union. The relevant cases are confusing, but they do suggest that the employer had better be very careful about what he says. The NLRB wants to protect the employee and will require the employer to bend over a bit to make sure the employee has a free choice. Rules such as the one against campaigning twenty-four hours before an election are fitting where the employees are production and maintenance people, but faculty members are highly educated people and administrators should be able to take the wraps off to some extent. A tenured full professor surely will not feel coerced by anything the administration says about a collective bargaining unit. I expect some modification in the NLRB's attitude in this area.

In an industrial election, management usually provides a single polling location for stated hours during all shifts. If the employer has more than one location, there may be a floating ballot box. This traditional method of voting presents a problem for colleges and universities, because some faculty members will be on sabbat-

---

4. 189 NLRB 109.

ical or off-campus on any given day. Under such circumstances, a one-day election is unfair.

At Wayne State University we are more than happy to have faculty join a union and we will bargain with them in good faith, but we want to be sure that the majority really want a union. In our hearing before MERC we demanded a mail ballot at the outset. In traditional terms, three thousand mail ballots which must be sent out and opened is an abhorrence, but it must be done. Wayne State covers a broad geographic area and employs people who do not come to work every day at regular times. Some full-time faculty members teach only at night.

CHAPTER 5

Private Institutions
and the NLRB

*Tracy H. Ferguson**

Cornell University

Background

Many state collective bargaining statutes do not apply to private institutions of higher education. Rather, the primary reference is the National Labor Relations Board (NLRB), which has assumed jurisdiction in private colleges and universities whose gross operating budget is a million dollars or more. This "million dollar" rule[1] came into existence a bit later than the *Cornell University*[2] case, but it is tied directly to that case.

In 1968, while researching an article[3] on collective bargaining in colleges and universities, I noticed that many state laws did not seem as fair as the National Labor Relations Act (NLRA). Therefore, I raised the rhetorical question of whether it would not be wise for a private university faced with an organizational campaign to ask the NLRB to take jurisdiction. I posed the question in the face of the 1951 *Trustees of Columbia*[4] case, where the NLRB clearly stated it would not take jurisdiction over a nonprofit educational institution unless the unit in question involved a commercial aspect of the school. The NLRB position made it clear

---

* Bond, Schoeneck & King, Syracuse, New York. Member, National Board of Directors, American Arbitration Association.
1. 186 NLRB 153. See Appendix E for text.
2. 183 NLRB 41. See Appendix D for text.
3. T. Ferguson, "Collective Bargaining in Universities and Colleges," 19 *Lab. L.J.* 778 (1968).
4. 97 NLRB 424.

that blue collar people on campuses, if they were not covered by state law, had no legal procedure for getting representation except through voluntary agreement with their administration. Harvard and other larger schools have had such voluntary contracts with labor unions for many years.

In 1969, when my firm was engaged by Cornell University, the rhetorical question raised a year earlier became a practical question. New York had amended its labor relations act to place private state colleges and universities under the jurisdiction of the state labor relations board, throwing these institutions into the pot with industrial plants.

For several years the Civil Service Employees Association (CSEA) at Cornell had circularized the blue collar workers, but it had never lodged a formal demand against the university. In 1969, however, the CSEA filed a petition with the state labor relations board seeking an election to achieve representation in a campus-wide unit at the Ithaca campus. At the same time, the librarians filed a petition seeking a separate unit as an in-house group not affiliated with the CSEA. An extension group of the Industrial and Labor Relations School located in New York City filed a similar petition on behalf of both its professionals and its secretarial staff.

At this point, Cornell University decided to seek jurisdiction under the NLRB. The basic reason for that decision was the inadequacy of New York labor law. The New York statute has no counterpart to the federal provisions concerning unfair labor practices. The NLRA prevents employers from interfering with, restraining, or coercing employees in the exercise of their rights to organize and to obtain representation. It also provides that both parties must bargain in good faith. The New York law, like many other state laws, places no such requirement on the unions, although it does require the employer to bargain in good faith.

The Cornell position was not extremely popular with some of our colleagues. The state colleges of California, which did not have a state act or a board to uphold any obligation to bargain, filed briefs in opposition. Joining with them were the New York State Labor Relations Board, the Georgia Association of Independent Colleges and Universities, Baylor University, California Institute of Technology, the Illinois state colleges and certain other colleges in Illinois, the University of Miami in Florida, the University of

Mississippi, Southern Methodist University, and the National Association of State Labor Relations Agencies.

Briefs supporting the Cornell position came from Boston University, Colgate, Dowling College, Fordham, Hamilton, LaSalle, New York University, Rochester Institute of Technology, the University of Rochester, St. John's, Wheaton, Yale, the AFL-CIO, and the Legal Defense and Educational Fund of the National Association for the Advancement of Colored People. As is apparent, academia was not exactly unanimous in its views before this landmark decision was made.

The NLRB Decision

The NLRB's decision was addressed solely to nonacademic employees. In fact, not one word is said in the opinion about an obligation to bargain with academics. A statistical reference is made to the number of teachers in public and private institutions, but nothing indicates that Cornell University is obligated to bargain with its faculty. That fact was called to my attention after the decision came down. In presenting the case, nothing was said about faculty bargaining. The main concern was blue collar workers and librarians, some of whom were professionals, and the professionals and secretarial workers in New York City. The major issue, however, was jurisdiction. Because the result on that stands fast, we are talking about faculty bargaining in private institutions today.

The question of unit was also an issue. At that time, Cornell had fifty-seven different facilities in the state. Some were two- or three-man operations in the agricultural department or in a scientific survey program. Some three hundred people worked in New York City and Geneva, New York. But the bulk of Cornell employees, about four thousand in the categories of primary concern, were on the main campus.

The CSEA eventually accepted the university's definition of the broad unit. It protested the inclusion of the librarians and the New York unit, but the university felt they had such a community of interest with Ithaca and professionals that it did not want them fragmented. There was also a very practical reason for that position. Industrial experience shows that employers get whipsawed when there are many separate units. Each unit wants the same as the rest or more. A broader unit facilitates effective dispute resolution.

Fordham University

The decision in the *Fordham University*[5] case, handed down September 14, 1971, included in the bargaining unit all professional employees of Fordham University including full-time and regular part-time members of the teaching and research faculty, department chairmen and assistant chairmen, division chairmen, members of the faculty senate, and faculty members serving on university committees as faculty representatives. There was a battle royal over department chairmen. Stewart Rothman, who represented Fordham and had formerly been general counsel of the NLRB, argued in his brief that faculty were not employees within the meaning of the NLRA and that department chairmen clearly had "managerial" functions.

Those of us brought up in the labor field are used to an industrial experience. We cannot automatically transfer our labor relations experience in private industry to this kind of industry. Educational institutions present a different milieu—different circumstances and different relationships. Some basic tenets carry over, of course, but old labor pros have trouble shifting gears to deal with the vastly different functions in the educational setting.

The clergy at Fordham—a Jesuit school—are included in the unit with the lay people. Nonsupervisory professional librarians and language informants are also included. The president, vice presidents, deans, associate deans, assistant deans, graduate assistants, teaching fellows, and guard personnel are excluded. The law school faculty is also excluded. The Association of American Law Schools had filed an extensive brief enumerating differences between themselves and other faculty members. They emphasized that law schools, in part, come under the aegis of the American Bar Association, that the law faculty determines its own curriculum, and that the law school has its own calendar. (See Appendix G for the text of the brief.)

The Fordham University administration sought a broad unit. Extensive testimony was adduced to show a community of interest

---

5. 193 NLRB 23. Petition for reconsideration was filed the next day, Sept. 15, 1971. See Appendix F for text.

among all professors. It was argued that the professorial role was the same throughout the faculty, despite the differences inherent in the various disciplines.

A footnote in the *Fordham*[6] decision stated that many of the reasons for finding the law faculty to be an appropriate separate unit are equally applicable to Fordham's other professional schools. The NLRB observed, however, that since no party contended that any other such school be a separate unit, "we need not pass upon the appropriateness of any such separate unit."

Consider political factors. The present NLRB chairman, Edward Miller, is a Republican appointee with a conservative management background. His predecessor, Frank McCulloch, was an acknowledged liberal. Miller and Howard Jenkins, a liberal Republican, held with the union. The dissent was filed by Ralph Kennedy, a new appointee from the West Coast, who formerly was a regional director.

What will happen to the Fordham petition for reconsideration? The customary procedure would be to return it to the original panel unless another board member asks for a consideration en banc. But there is currently one position open on the board. So my guess is that the petition will go back to the three-man panel and will be denied.

Working with the NLRB

The NLRB has twenty-nine regional offices, with subregional offices in some larger cities. When a proposed faculty unit moves to organize, it has two alternatives: it may file a petition—either on its own or through a union—with the nearest NLRB office, or, it may forward a demand for recognition to its college or university administration and the latter files a petition stating that a demand has been made. If the academics file the petition, they must also submit signed cards showing interest from at least 30 percent of the proposed unit. The employer does not view the cards, but it may indicate whether it wants an election.

The first legal clash may appear at this stage of the proceedings. If, for example, law school professors propose a unit for themselves, the administration may insist that the entire faculty is the appropriate bargaining unit, not the law faculty alone. If the

6. 78 LRRM 1181 n.11.

conflict persists, a hearing will be held and a decision will be made by the regional director upon recommendation and findings of the hearing officer. The NLRB, upon request filed by any interested person, may then review the decision of the regional director and will make the final determination.

Yale University

The NLRB has not decided what is *the* appropriate unit, but what is *an* appropriate unit on a case-by-case basis. Even in an industrial setting, the appropriate unit is chosen on the basis of a showing of a community of interest among employees. The *Yale University*[7] case was the next nonacademic case following the *Cornell* decision. Here the unit included both professionals and some white collar secretarials in the epidemiology department. The NLRB dismissed the petition, holding that this unit was too small and that there were people of like interests in other departments.

The *Yale* case dealt with a department connected with a hospital. There are currently four cases before the NLRB involving hospitals faced with bargaining demands from blue collar workers and, in one instance, from a group of interns. Will the board take jurisdiction? It has taken jurisdiction over colleges and universities, but the NLRA explicitly excludes nonprofit hospitals under section 2. Although the school may own the hospital, the board may say that since the hospital is a nonprofit institution, perhaps even with a separate or intermingled board of directors, the NLRB is precluded by statute from taking jurisdiction.[8]

Long Island University

The next NLRB development concerned the companion cases of the C.W. Post Center and the Brooklyn Center of Long Island University.[9] The question here was whether the faculty members were "employees" or "supervisors" within the meaning of the NLRA. The NLRB concluded that they were employees and an election was directed. The unit as described in the decision included:

---

7. 184 NLRB 101.
8. The NLRB has now so held in two cases: Duke University, 194 NLRB 31; and Loyola University Medical Center, 194 NLRB 30. No decisions have yet been published in the other two cases.
9. 189 NLRB 109-110.

All professional employees employed at the Employer's C.W. Post Center, Brookville, Long Island, New York, including professors, associate professors, assistant professors, instructors, adjunct professors, adjunct associate professors, adjunct assistant professors, lecturers, professional librarians, guidance counselors, and research associates; but excluding all other employees, student assistants, instructors who are hourly paid serving on an in-residence basis, laboratory managers, laboratory assistants, stockroom technicians, machine shop technicians, denier animal trainers, graduate students, admissions counselors, academic counselors, deans, division chairman, department chairman, guards, and supervisors as defined in the Act.[10]

Some categories, such as student assistants and graduate students, were explicitly excluded. The decision is significant, but it cannot be assumed that this will be the ruling of the NLRB in every college case. There were some stipulations of agreement in this case that led to the result quoted above.

The NLRA purports to define "supervisors" as those who have the right to exercise managerial authority to make effective decisions.[11] This is easily understood. But then it goes on to say that persons may be regarded as supervisors only if they can "effectively recommend" discipline with respect to so-called managerial policies, particularly in areas where judgment is necessary. What does "effectively recommend" mean?

In the industrial sector, clarification comes down on a case-by-case basis. For example, if an assistant foreman went to his foreman and said, "I think Don Jones on this floor isn't worth much—you ought to fire him," and if the foreman acted accordingly, then the assistant seems to fit into the category of supervisor. But suppose the foreman testifies at a hearing: "Yes, I take the word of my assistant when I make such decisions—and of a lot of other people on the floor as well." Is the assistant then a supervisor? If the foreman is asked whether he pays more attention to his assistant's judgment than the judgment of others, and if he replies: "Of course, I give great weight to what my assistant says,

---

10. 77 LRRM 1005.
11. 29 U.S.C. §152(11).

even though I don't rely on his judgment entirely," then (as the NLRB has ruled) that assistant foreman is a supervisor.

Presumably, decisions about department heads in libraries would be made using similar criteria. In the *C.W. Post* case the chairmen were seen to act more on their own initiative and were excluded, whereas at Fordham, where their relation is more strictly collegial, they were included.

CHAPTER 6

Collective Bargaining in Community Colleges

*Karl J. Jacobs**

The Community College Faculty

Community colleges share five characteristics not common to other institutions of higher education. These differences appear to impel a large proportion of community college faculties toward collective bargaining.

One striking difference is the general lack of academic tradition. Many community colleges were formed virtually overnight, and the faculties were gathered rather suddenly from many quarters. For better or worse, the organizational structure and the mutual accommodation of diverse faculty members have not had the usual mellowing of years.

A second difference is the predominance of former secondary school teachers in such colleges. They bring the distinctive public school experience with them, particularly the recent tendency toward collectivization. In fact, many community colleges were formerly part of a K-14 system.

Third, the personnel policies of the colleges are often patterned after the secondary school system, especially in the matter of adopting a salary schedule. The approach of many local governing boards to community college problems is similar to that of a local school board, since many of their members have served on public school boards. The ineptitude and unfairness of some boards and administrations have prompted many faculties to seek collectivization because they saw no other way to attain the more effective

---

* President, Rock Valley College, Rockford, Illinois.

communication and influence enjoyed by faculty in four-year institutions.

Fourth, there is still no clear working definition of a community college faculty. As a result, these people are not quite sure where they fit in the overall scheme. Their comparative situation is changing, but traditionally community college faculty have not been accepted as full partners by their four-year colleagues. This unstable situation was aggravated by efforts of the American Association of Junior Colleges to win a distinctive place for these colleges without being explicit about what that place should be. The corresponding public attitude has been that community college faculty members have an inferior role because they belong to institutions created, as it were, for the less competent student.

The fifth difference is the relative lack of professional mobility among community college faculty. A prevalent but somewhat unrealistic view of four-year professors is that they are academic entrepreneurs, able to move when new opportunities present themselves. Thus, they gain upward mobility, at least in terms of status institutions, if not always in terms of salary. Normally, if community college faculty do not shift to the four-year college, they move either laterally or into administration. They see their identities and their careers in connection with a single institution.

Like secondary school teachers, such faculty are more likely to view themselves as part of a proletariat rather than as members of the managerial or entrepreneurial class. I must, therefore, take exception to the analogy Mr. Smith drew to the white collar worker. Currently, white collar workers tend to see themselves as becoming part of the managerial class. In fact, that distinction almost serves to define their position. Except for an isolated few, however, community college faculty do not see themselves progressing in this direction. To a lesser degree, this is probably true of many four-year college faculty.

Bargaining and Decisionmaking

The current pattern of collectivization in community colleges reveals that in large urban areas the community has generally accepted unionization as a political reality. Community colleges in Michigan's Wayne County and Illinois' Cook County, for example, were among the first to organize. Of course, Michigan's rural colleges were also quick to organize, but in Michigan unionization is an accepted way of life. From 1965 to 1968, collective bargaining appeared in almost every public school district in Michigan.

The progress of collective bargaining in community colleges has differed greatly from that in the secondary schools, chiefly because college faculty activities are not so precisely structured. The college teaching schedule is unevenly spread over an entire day; a secondary school teacher is confined to certain blocks of time. Office hours of college faculty are irregular and, as a practical matter, difficult to enforce. Faculty members generally define their own use of time apart from the scheduled teaching hours.

The pattern of decisionmaking in community colleges inevitably breeds conflict between demands for flexibility and goals of standardization. Any attempt at innovative programming may collide with a master agreement and accompanying bargaining arrangements which have been patterned after those in the public schools. The primary variable often turns out to be the amount of judiciousness and flexibility within the bargaining agency itself.

The Administration and the Board

One of the most acute problems which may arise in a district where collective bargaining organization is underway is the psychological impact on board members. In Illinois, which has no public employees act, many board members find the whole idea of faculty organization extremely distasteful.

What is the actual responsibility of the board and the administration regarding faculty? A fair, effective administrative procedure for setting priorities is very important, along with effective vehicles of communication. Many boards and administrations do not have this. Misunderstanding often results, even though both parties may be acting in good faith.

Community college boards ought to involve faculty in decisionmaking, with a mutual and clearly defined understanding of their respective roles. The knowledge of budgets and priorities ought to be shared. A fun-and-games approach to competitive salaries and fringe benefits does not sit well with employees, either. Public sector employers must realize that there is a marketplace and that it is a moral marketplace as well as a labor marketplace. Even if there is no employee relations law, there ought to be a frank, fair-minded discussion with the faculty on these matters. Outside consultants should be brought in to discuss the implications of organizing and to suggest alternatives to formal union bargaining.

We should keep away from emotional, simplistic arguments like "It's unprofessional," or "You are betraying the best interests of the students." These alleged consequences are heard all too often. Such arguments have proved to be untrue in Michigan community colleges and elsewhere.

What can be done to prepare the board and administration for bargaining? Hold workshops. Train a member of the administration to understand and work with unionization so that someone will be sophisticated enough to avoid emotional catharses between board members and administrators on the evil characteristics of the faculty. Subscribe to union literature and collect a basic file of information, starting with the comprehensive bibliography in this volume. Institutional research should graph salaries and fringe benefits over a five-year period, relating them to basic cost of living indexes. Know specifically what has been done for all the employees, and do not rely on impressions.

Selecting the Bargaining Team

Once board members and administrators have gotten beyond the initial feelings of threat and betrayal, they can get down to the business of bargaining in good faith. The board should first organize its team. It should not allow any employee group to tell it who is to sit on the management team and who is to act as its chief negotiator. The National Labor Relations Act is very specific on that, and I think it is a basic guideline.

In Rockford, Illinois, under their contract the teachers union exercised a veto power over any proposed member of the management bargaining team. There is an old bargaining axiom that whatever mistake you agree to, you will have to pay to get it out of a contract. No one is going to let you get out of it for nothing. The Rockford board finally had to pay a great deal in meeting the union's counterdemands in order to reclaim a prerogative that in my opinion is inherently theirs.

Neither the college president nor a board member should ordinarily be on a bargaining team. Some board members really like a "piece of the action," but they are not trained in this area. Even if they have the time to sit on the team, it is not their role as members of a collective board. One of the worst collective bargaining agreements I have ever seen was rammed through by a well-meaning board member. The president and the board should act as the court of last resort. If a board member or the president says no, where can negotiations go after that? The negotiator, after doing his dog-and-pony show, should be able to back off gracefully by saying, "The board has agreed to this provision on the basis of such-and-such." The negotiator is not supposed to have any personal feelings about it. If he is wrong and he acted in good faith and the board reversed him, the negotiating team understands. In fact, they are hoping that his "no" will become a "maybe" and that "maybe" will eventually lead to what they want.

The Chief Negotiator

A lawyer acting as a chief negotiator will be more expensive than a person trained from the college staff. (There are exceptions if the college is relatively small.) However, the ultimate cost of having an inexperienced person should be examined. It is probable that the initial cost of engaging the most competent person you can find will be far less in the long run. Do not hire a general practitioner in law with absolutely no experience in labor relations. It is far better to hire a labor lawyer with a reputation in the field or a competent labor consultant.

There are a number of ways to put together a negotiating team. The business manager or the personnel director will probably be a good chief negotiator. Some consulting firms recommend this, but there are problems in having the business manager. He may already be one of the most overworked people in the college. Another difficulty is that his role as custodian of the budget may have impaired his credibility with faculty.

If an attorney is chosen, be sure that he understands community colleges. If he tags you too close to the secondary system you will have difficulties in the negotiations. Moreover, the attorney should be prepared to move beyond the industrial model or he will create innumerable problems.

To a large extent, bargaining is a political specialty. Legal expertise is less important than personality structure, an understanding of the situation, and negotiating skills. The chief negotiator should have a detailed and intelligent grasp of the operation of the college. He must have enough political sensitivity to know when to say no and when to consult. Negotiation is an art, and not every attorney has the necessary skills.

The Contract

It would be ill-advised not to consult with an attorney when the contract is written, but be careful not to let the attorney handle the writing. Write out exactly what you want and have the words adapted or modified to say in legal terms what you mean. It takes an attorney to understand our first Flint contract, which is simply not a document for lay use on a day-to-day basis. I do not blame the attorney who did the drafting because the job was inappropriately foisted on him. However, the result is a contract that is simply not functional.

Some boards unwisely refuse to listen to the advice of their attorneys. This is asking for trouble, because the attorney can make sure that the contract is legally correct and that it is clearly understood by the two parties. Too many serious quarrels arise between employers and employees as a result of simple misunderstandings.

In opposition to Mr. Smith's assertion, I believe that the first contract is crucial. Experience shows that problems arising from an inadequate or ambiguous first contract will not always be solved later. Make sure the first contract is the best you can get, because you will pay dearly for those initial mistakes.

Be mindful always that a contract is binding on both parties and that each is obligated to live up to its terms. An amazing number of people fail to grasp this basic truth, assuming that a "reasonable request" not covered in the contract should be granted. In some situations there is sufficient mutual trust so that things may be worked out within the context of a contract. A hasty exercise of administrative prerogative may be disastrous in the face of contract language that is not the administration's own phrasing. A contract always gives away managerial rights, because the board is the only one with something to give. One must be careful not to bargain away the right of management. In the Chicago master contract agreement in 1971 and in prior contracts it was shown that because of substantial erosion of the board's managerial rights the Illinois legislature was considering a bill[1] in 1971 setting minimum and maximum hours on teaching loads. A board must be especially careful to retain its legally granted powers. It has no authority to give those away. Moreover, it is not fair to the faculty, particularly as a settlement relates to the financial integrity of the college, even though they may temporarily see the matter in a more parochial way. If a board lets its local prerogative slip away, outside controls may impose severe consequences on faculty as well.

General Trends

What lies ahead? Indulging in a bit of crystal gazing, I see increased collectivization of all employees, including those in four-year colleges. There will be more legislation or federal court interpretations affecting the public sector nationwide.

There will be increasing state involvement in traditional academic decisionmaking. This is already happening in Michigan, where the legislature set minimum and maximum teaching loads for faculty of public institutions.[2] The same trend is evident in private enterprise. The ideology regarding government involvement had been "hands off" until private corporations found themselves in poor positions competitively and looked to state and federal legislation to protect them. It could happen in higher education, especially if governing boards handle collective bargaining ineptly.

Nonacademic employees in community colleges will increasingly be brought under general civil service provisions. There is already some indication of this in Illinois, where the civil service commission appears eager to include these people.

Virtually intolerable pressures will be placed on boards to increase productivity. There will be a squeeze from the top—from the governor's office, from the bureau of the budget, from state coordinating boards, and from the state legislature—to increase productivity in order to decrease costs. At the same time, pressures will increase from the bottom up—from employee groups wishing to extend benefits while resisting increases in productiv-

1. H.B. 790.
2. Mich. Pub. Act No. 122, §19 (Sept. 29, 1971). This provision was ruled unconstitutional by Judge Marvin J. Salmon in Regents of The University of Michigan v. State, No. 7659-C (Ingham County Cir. Ct., Dec. 6, 1971).

ity. As a result, we will see a greater turnover of college presidents. I fear we will also see an increasing reluctance of competent people to stand for election to board positions at community colleges because of the abuse and unpleasantness arising from the community pressure that surrounds collective bargaining.

The national unions will undoubtedly increase their interest in the public sector. In the process there will be some clumsy attempts to adapt industrial practices to the academic setting. Probably there will be mergers among the teachers unions. The American Association of University Professors will have to clear up its current organizational schizophrenia.

Finally, I would expect a gain in that special sensitivity which is essential to the art of bargaining. It is a little like when you were a young man. When do you kiss the girl good night? You just seem to know, don't you? Those that don't know don't get the kiss.

CHAPTER 7

Institutional Differences:
Questions and Answers

Kenneth M. Smythe
Tracy H. Ferguson
Karl J. Jacobs

Addressed to Mr. Smythe

Q. Will agency shop provisions supersede traditional tenure rules?

Smythe: A final answer cannot be given now, but the pattern followed in twelve Michigan decisions would allow discharge of a faculty member who fails to pay the union service fee in an agency shop situation, even though he has tenure. The same principle has been applied in Michigan, with fair consistency, to secondary school teachers under the K-12 teacher tenure statutes. The most recent court of appeals case[1] took a different tack, however, refusing to approve an agency shop provision requiring payment of a service fee equal to the union dues, saying the evidence had not established that the members paying the service fee **actually received** services from the collective bargaining agent worth that amount.

Q. Does a contract won through bargaining increase the pressure to retain the untenured faculty member who shows only mediocre performance or potential?

Smythe: The bargaining determines the practice. Usually construction and maintenance people have a one- to three-month probation-

---

1. Smigel v. Southgate Community School District, 24 Mich. App. 179, 186, 180 N.W.2d 215, 219 (1970), *leave to appeal granted,* 384 Mich. 772, Oct. 26, 1970.

ary period. Colleges and universities tend to have six-year probationary periods for faculty during which they can discharge without cause at the end of a specific contract term providing they put in some kind of notice. This matter is difficult to predict, but I think there will be efforts to increase security for lower echelon faculty members. Some arrangement short of tenure may have to be made rather early in the person's employment, or the probationary period may be shortened. Normally, colleges and universities would seem to prefer the flexibility that attends a long probationary period and to keep decisions on tenure and promotion in the hands of colleagues. A major bargaining issue will surely revolve around retaining enough flexibility to keep out or remove the less able people.

Q. Will collective bargaining tend to reduce salary differentials between disciplines?

Smythe: Experience indicates that natural scientists have to be paid more than most social scientists or they will leave. Likewise, economists tend to get higher faculty salaries than historians. At first most agreements will probably reduce the differences, but some spread will creep back in if institutions are to compete on the market. At Oakland University in Michigan and elsewhere, faculty representatives have attempted to negotiate a superstar clause which would permit paying highly distinguished faculty off scale. I believe contracts should include different scales for different disciplines.

Addressed to Mr. Ferguson:

Q. In a decision handed down in February, 1971, the National Labor Relations Board (NLRB) certified a bargaining unit at Monmouth College, West Long Beach, New Jersey, and excluded part-time faculty at the request of the full-time faculty. Why were part-time faculty included in the unit certified at Fordham University and excluded at Monmouth?

Ferguson: The difference is that Monmouth had a consent election. In the Long Island case there were consents to some of these classifications. Fordham unsuccessfully contested the inclusion of part-time faculty. The part-time people said they felt they were an integral part of the faculty, and the NLRB takes very seriously how people regard themselves. Not everything in the labor relations field is decided on the basis of objective fact—nor should it be. How people feel can be terribly important.

Q. How might the NLRB view the claims of a faculty body that has traditionally met and conferred with administration and has shared in the decisionmaking at a university?

Ferguson: If the practice has been codetermination (to use the German concept), it is collective bargaining, no matter what it may have been called. Under such circumstances, the board will take into account the past history of collective bargaining. Whom did faculty sit down with? Were the faculty members who met and conferred representative of every discipline or school, or was it usually a matter of separate disciplines? Were the decisions made jointly, in a process of give and take, or only upon advice of faculty? If the role of faculty was basically advisory, no collective bargaining took place. In industry, I have seen instances where the results of hard bargaining were issued under the heading "company announces new policy," as if the decision had been made unilaterally. What is done matters more than what is said about such processes.

Q. Many nonteaching personnel in various supportive or research functions are full professionals, have advanced degrees, perform related skills, and have the same fringe benefit program as teaching faculty. Would this have any bearing on an NLRB decision about the bargaining unit?

Ferguson: Probably not. You will get nowhere before the board if you merely rely on the concept of professional training. The fact that someone in the finance office has a Ph.D. is irrelevant. Even though they have the same fringe benefit program and the same salary rate structure, my best guess is that nonteaching people would be excluded because of the difference in their work. Production and maintenance personnel in industry are placed in one unit if the departments agree to this procedure, but in many plants the two are completely separated. While the set-up men on the machines belong in the production unit, the electricians and tinsmiths are considered to be maintenance personnel. If administrative personnel in universities want to be excluded, I think they can easily make a case on the grounds of separate function. Research activities, on the other hand, will be likened to teaching.

Admittedly, the professor does not just teach. He does many other things that nonteachers do—personal counseling, committee work, and other institutional chores. Moreover, parts of other job classifications might also be thought to qualify as teaching. But it is an open question whether teaching and nonteaching personnel will be included in a single unit on such grounds. Institutions should certainly not rely on previous unit determinations. If they feel they have special considerations, they should bring these before the board. ·

Addressed to Mr. Jacobs:

Q. Should a dean be a member of a bargaining team?

Jacobs: It depends on the situation. There is a risk of compromising the dean's effectiveness outside the bargaining process. Although it would be a useful learning experience for the dean, nevertheless I must opt for keeping the dean off the team. He should never be the chief negotiator.

Q. Is it beneficial to have the state board for community colleges involved in collective bargaining?

Jacobs: Such boards have not offered good leadership. If the board members are appointed, they are too political to be effective in bargaining. In Illinois, the state board for junior colleges has not managed to define its own role, and it has been in existence five years. If the board should try to establish guidelines for collective bargaining, it would be troublesome and impractical, especially in Illinois. The Chicago and Cook County problems are far removed from the situation at Carl Sandburg College in Galesburg, for example.

Q. Is there any way to avoid the damaging adversary relationship between faculty and administration which is likely to occur in collective bargaining?

Jacobs: The faculty may become the adversary during negotiations, but they are not the enemy. The first psychological barrier that a president must overcome is to educate and reinforce his people, including the board, to remember that the faculty members are the same fine, responsible people they were before the issue of collective bargaining arose. Faculty members often see collective bargaining as a great emotional cause. The initial bargaining may be similar to the pattern of revolution. Crane Brinton outlined this pattern very well. Revolutionaries are consumed by the movement. They want to give political speeches and are very difficult to negotiate with. Administrations would be well advised to let them go through their act. Listen to their personal experiences and nod sympathetically about the division chairman who has been abusive. No doubt you will hear the same complaints many times.

In the second wave of negotiations, the practical people will start coming forward and you will be getting down to the gut issues, because the faculty members will have evaluated the initial accomplishments. Thinking back to my own union activity, I remember a tendency to underestimate the subtlety of the faculty's power, giving more attention to the overt instruments of power—strikes and binding arbitration. I believe that faculties have enormous persuasive power which they can learn to use in bargaining with boards and administrators.

Q. Should strikes be permitted?

Jacobs: Strikes do not frighten me. I could work very well in my office while people are walking around outside. I went on strike in Dearborn and it was one of the most therapeutic things in my life. My wife was pregnant. We walked together, and we felt we were part of the great unwashed masses. It was a tremendous thing for us. Still, I think faculty can generally accomplish more by exercising their considerable persuasive powers instead.

CHAPTER 8

Cases at
The University of Michigan

*William P. Lemmer**

I will discuss the problem of medical interns and residents, teaching fellows, teaching assistants, and research assistants. I have found only one court decision directly related to these categories—a recent circuit court decision[1] in Dane County, Wisconsin. That case involved questions of access to confidential information. The court ruled that the teaching assistants' association had no right to scholarly activity reports concerning outside consulting activities of faculty members—confidential reports done by faculty members as part of a statistical study in budget preparation. In itself the decision is not very significant, but it raises controversial issues and shows the power concept in play.

As my discussion is entirely within the context of Michigan's Public Employment Relations Act (PERA), some statements will not be applicable to other states or the National Labor Relations Act (NLRA). As a University of Michigan attorney, I have been dealing with two cases which may serve to highlight some of the issues. One case involves an association of interns and residents; the second, an association called the Teaching Fellows Union. Both can qualify as labor organizations under Michigan law.

The Interns-Residents Association

The organizing of interns and residents is a structured national movement. They distribute organizing literature similar to any

---

* University Attorney, The University of Michigan, Ann Arbor.
1. No. 132-401 (Dane County Cir. Ct., July 12, 1971).

AFL-CIO manual, setting out the ground rules, including rules for strikes. They have had at least one national conference.

In April, 1971, The University of Michigan's Interns-Residents Association submitted a petition to the Michigan Employment Relations Commission (MERC) seeking to represent "all residents, interns and fellows employed by the employer possessing the equivalent of a minimum of an M.D. or D.D.S. degree, excluding postdoctoral fellows in the basic sciences and all other employees." After four days of hearings before the trial examiner in June and July of 1970, along with the unusual procedure of oral argument before commission members, MERC issued a finding on March 16, 1971. In a rare 2-1 split decision, it declared that the unit was appropriate for collective bargaining and directed an election.[2] The case then went to the Michigan Court of Appeals. The court denied a motion to stay the election but agreed to review the split decision. The court issued an order after the election, which resulted in favor of representation, staying all proceedings until the court ruled on the matter. The case was argued in October, and on January 21, 1972, the court reversed MERC in a 2-1 decision.[3]

The issues raised in this case were ones of first impression for MERC, although in four cases in 1969 and 1970 the New York State Labor Relations Board found units of interns and residents appropriate for purposes of collective bargaining.[4] To my knowledge, not one of the New York cases was appealed to the courts. Our intermediate appellate court has thus made the first appellate ruling in the country on this issue, subject, of course, to further appeal on leave granted by the Supreme Court of Michigan.

The Philadelphia Experience

On December 6, 1971, the Pennsylvania Labor Relations Board denied a petition filed by the Philadelphia Association of Interns and Residents for recognition as a bargaining unit at four Philadelphia hospitals: Albert Einstein Medical Center, Wills Eye Hospital,

---

2. 1971 MERC Lab. Op. 270.
3. No. 11524 (Mich. App., Jan. 21, 1972). The University of Michigan Interns-Residents Association has voted to appeal the decision to the Michigan Supreme Court.
4. Brooklyn Eye and Ear Hospital, 32 NYSLRB No. 21 (1969); Long Island County Hospital, 33 NYSLRB No. 320 (1970); Bronx Eye Infirmary, Inc., 33 NYSLRB No. 41 (1970); and Albert Einstein College cf Medicine of Yeshiva University, 33 NYSLRB No. 86 (1970).

Temple University Hospital, and Pennsylvania Hospital.[5] The board held that the hospitals were public employers but that the interns, residents, and clinical fellows were not public employees. The board found that they "render extensive and valuable services to the hospital," but services which are "integral to and inseparable from the educational process"; and "the ultimate responsibility for their actions rests with the chief of the department and with the attending physicians." The board also found that they are transient employees who will sever their connection with the hospitals upon completion of their training. Therefore they lack the "continuing relationship" the statute was enacted to protect. Compensation, it noted, is of relatively little importance in the selection of their postgraduate training in medicine.

The fundamental issue in this kind of case is whether interns, residents, and postdoctoral fellows in medicine or dentistry are employees covered by the labor law. Neither the Interns-Residents Association nor MERC has denied that individuals in these categories are students; nor has any organization, including The University of Michigan, denied that the individuals perform a service. Herein lies the rub. For what purpose is the service performed?

Defining Who is an Employee

The MERC decision noted at the outset that virtually no factual dispute existed, the issue centering on differing interpretations of the legal impact of the facts. In concluding that interns, residents, and fellows are employees and thus subject to PERA, MERC may have confused interpretations with facts. MERC's syllogism was simple: major premise—employees provide services for an employer; minor premise—interns, residents, and fellows provide a service for the employer in terms of patient care and research; conclusion—interns, residents, and fellows are employees. It seems logical, but the dissenting member of MERC encountered semantic difficulties and reached a contrary conclusion with which the court of appeals agreed.

---

5. 1971 PERA R-237-E, R-239-E, R-243-E, R-253-E. A brief for Temple University had focused on four arguments: (a) that interns, residents, and clinical fellows are students and not employees, that if they are found to be employees, they are (b) only temporary, casual employees (c) in a supervisory role, and (d) that forming a unit of such a composition would violate PERA's prohibition against over-fragmentation of bargaining units.

The legal questions that have arisen are intriguing. For example, let us start with MERC's major premise but change the minor premise to read, "interns, residents, and fellows are engaged in their own personal medical education programs at an institution of higher education, which education requires service to patients as an inherent part of that education." The logical conclusion is that interns, residents, and fellows are not employees. We can state it another way: students study and learn at institutions of higher education; interns, residents, and fellows study and learn at institutions of higher education by providing patient care and doing research as an inherent part, really the heart, of their studies; therefore, teaching residents, interns, and fellows are students. The court found that the educational and employment aspects of their relation to the regents are "inextricably mixed." The court observed that had the legislature intended graduate students to be public employees covered by the statute, they would have clearly indicated that intent.

MERC noted, as did the dissenting opinion of the court, that there was a one-year agreement for service. The university contended that such a document merely confirmed that the individual had accepted an appointment as an intern or resident in one of the university's advanced medical education programs and that he was going to participate in that program. The agreement could have been written to avoid terms used in employment relationships. All the university needed was some notice that the person was going to show up and participate in the program. The court did not speak directly to this point but did argue that "if the interns, residents and postgraduate fellows associated with the University Medical Center were to be classified as herein requested, the assistants in all other departments, working part-time at their trade or profession for a small stipend, would, in order to avoid discrimination, conclude that they were entitled to the same treatment. Such a result could well wreak havoc upon the very ability of the Regents to control and arrange the educational affairs of the University. It is further noted that the legislature, itself, considers interns and other assistants as students rather than employees for the purpose of determining the amount of annual appropriations made to the University."

MERC also found, as did the dissenting member of the court, that interns and residents do not participate to any significant degree in classroom activities, but are engaged in clinical work in the hospital. The university, on the other hand, contended that the hospital is the classroom and that until somebody devises a better way to teach medicine, that is the way medicine will be taught.

MERC relied on the fact that the hospital, although connected with the university and its medical school, has its own role as a facility for providing medical care. The university contended that it is a teaching hospital, with the primary purpose of providing the best possible circumstances for a medical education, not a community hospital staffed by private practitioners. If it were not a teaching hospital, there would be no reason for a faculty that in number approximately equals the complement of interns and residents.

Salary or Stipend?

The interns and residents call the money they receive salary; the university calls it a stipend. The university also provides them with the health and life insurance and other benefits available to its employees. If the process for payment of the stipend had been structured differently, the university might have avoided the disagreement and the complications. The federal government provides a substantial part of the money to pay interns and residents, pursuant to a national policy to encourage advanced training in medicine. The critical question is whether the level of financial assistance converts the money received into salary, warranting the conclusion that the service rendered is that of an employee. The majority opinion of the court did not regard the level of compensation as a critical factor in determining employee status. The dissenting opinion disagreed on the ground that the compensation is not tax exempt.

Hindsight suggests that perhaps fringe benefits should not have been provided. Some teaching hospitals have not done so. However, I believe the university would have continued its present policy regardless of the consequence. Fringe benefits afford some protection to the individual while he is pursuing his education and encourage him to continue.

MERC agreed that the relationship of interns and residents to the hospital is unique because the services provided are "intimately related to and flowing from the very nature of their studies." The university pointed out that were these individuals found to be employees for the purposes of collective bargaining, the entire educational program would be subject to bargaining. To illustrate: as part of the program, an intern or resident may be assigned to certain tasks for specific periods at other hospitals with which The University of Michigan has agreements. Is this a working condition or part of the educational program, or both? MERC suggested that such assignments may constitute a real problem, and told us that if the problem arises and has not been settled in advance through collective bargaining, somebody will probably file an unfair labor practice suit. In Michigan only unions can do that. MERC would then decide whether the activity was a matter of education or of working conditions.

Control of Educational Programs

At the present time, changes in the educational programs of interns and residents are the responsibility of the various departments or specialties within the medical school. Such changes are taking place rapidly today. Under a collective bargaining arrangement, program changes would no longer be permitted, if the right to do so had not been retained under the agreement. A basic fact of collective bargaining is that employers can no longer deal directly with individuals. Communication is through the collective bargaining agent. Frequently a medical student and his faculty counselor decide upon a change in the student's program. Unless that procedure were preserved in the collective bargaining agreement, it would not be permitted.

MERC carefully pointed out that in applying Michigan law to interns and residents, the commission need not be tied to previously adjudicated unit determinations or employment concepts. On the other hand, MERC also applied the traditional labor relations pigeonhole defining casual or temporary employment when the university argued that if the relationship with interns and residents is to be termed employment, such employment is at best temporary, for fixed periods of time. In traditional labor relations, temporary means sporadic and irregular. But in this unique situation, where there is a constant changeover in members of the bargaining unit, it would seem difficult to achieve a stable collective bargaining relationship, which is what collective bargaining laws are supposed to be about. The court agreed with the university's views.

Teaching Fellows Union

On March 19, 1970, the Teaching Fellows Union at The University of Michigan petitioned MERC for designation as a bargaining unit. In the first public employment relations board decision in the country on the matter, MERC dismissed the petition on December 6, 1971.[6]

The student employee question is relevant to this case also. Unlike interns and residents, many of the teaching fellows are required to teach as part of a degree requirement. The university argued that if an employment relationship were found, the teaching fellows would comprise an inappropriate unit because, like most universities, Michigan has research assistants and other kinds of assistantships (e.g., counselors, advisors, librarians, and psychologists). These appointments provide a source of financial aid to students and the appointees provide a service. The appointments are frequently used interchangeably. For example, an individual may teach for one semester, do research the next term, and the third he may be on a scholarship for study alone.

MERC found that the unit sought was inappropriate because it did not include all graduate assistants. As this finding was sufficient for dismissal of the petition, MERC did not consider other issues. The commission found, however, that there is a community of interest among graduate assistants with respect to the graduate student pool from which they are drawn, their eligibility for and method of appointment, their basic working conditions, salary schedules, method of payment, requirement of maintaining student status, and relationship to faculty as supervisors. It also found that the various assignments within the group are often interchanged and that the bulk of graduate assistants are involved in classifications related to the process of education.

The University's Constitutional Status

Closely related to all of these considerations is the critical ques-

---

6. 1971 MERC Lab. Op. 754. See 1971 *Wisconsin Law Review* no. 1, "Collective Negotiations in Higher Education: A Symposium," on the University of Wisconsin's Teaching Assistants Association. A consent election was held in this instance. Thus, the Wisconsin Employment Relations Commission made no decision on the appropriateness of the unit. See also the article by the Wisconsin Chancellor Edwin Young, a labor economist, "Management and Collective Bargaining on the Campus," 13 *AGB Reports* no. 3, 17-23 (Nov. 1970).

tion of the constitutional status of The University of Michigan as an institution of higher education. As a constitutionally established institution, the university has customarily had autonomy in educational matters. Presumably, recent attempts by the Michigan legislature to assume control will be applicable also to other similarly constituted universities.

On December 6, 1971, Ingham County Circuit Judge Marvin J. Salmon held that The University of Michigan, Michigan State University, and Wayne State University do indeed have autonomous authority in several crucial areas.[7] Judge Salmon stated that the legislature can require these schools to furnish an annual accounting of income and expenditures, and it can continue to review capital outlay requests (chiefly for construction of campus buildings). The legislature cannot dictate credit-hour teaching load of faculty members, the number of out-of-state students enrolled, and fees. It cannot dictate that state appropriations are not to be used to pay an employee or educate a student who has been convicted of a charge of university disruption; or for construction not authorized in legislative line-item funding. The legislature cannot deduct from the appropriations amounts equal to any excess in anticipated student fees. Judge Salmon held that the legislature can, however, appropriate money on a line-item basis, require reports to be submitted with budget requests (the state budget director being allowed to withhold allotments to the universities if they fail to comply), and require prior planning information on capital outlay requests (since the legislature is not constitutionally required to fund building construction).

Judge Salmon also ruled that the Michigan State Board of Education lacks the authority to require the universities to obtain its approval before they establish or expand programs, departments or branch campuses.

Several aspects of the Ingham County decision are favorable to the universities' contentions, but the struggle over autonomy is not ended. Nor is the situation likely to be as stable in those institutions without constitutional status.

---

7. Regents of The University of Michigan v. State, No. 7659-C (Ingham County Cir. Ct., Dec. 6, 1971).

Part III
Alternatives To
Collective Bargaining

CHAPTER 9

Alternatives To Bargaining
And Traditional Governance

*Charles M. Rehmus**

The Traditional Company Union Model

The range of possibilities for resolving faculty-administration conflicts is somewhat larger than the simple dichotomy between the
traditional model and the trade union bargaining model.

Many university and college faculties have developed a system
of professional relationships giving them a high degree of autonomy and self-direction coupled with regularity and security in the
employment relationship. In the traditional theory they are organized as a community of scholars. The faculty dominates educational policy matters and often exerts a major influence in deciding college organizational structure. It controls the education and
certification of those entering the profession, thus obtaining, to a
degree, the same kind of control over the labor market that members of the legal profession have enjoyed for many years. Faculty
members make decisions on the selection, retention, and promotion
of other faculty members and, in some cases, heavily influence
the selection of their supervisors.

Faculties supported by the three basic concepts of academic
freedom, professional courtesy, and job tenure have, in effect,
created a kind of professional self-government which, if it works,
can be one of the best of all worlds for an employed professional.
At least, so goes the tradition; the actual practice varies widely.
A faculty is usually organized into some kind of campuswide repre-

* Professor of Political Science, The University of Michigan, Ann Arbor,
and Co-director, Institute of Labor and Industrial Relations, The University of Michigan-Wayne State University.

sentative body which has no ties to any external organization. Officially such a body possesses only advisory powers, but it can function as a major decisionmaking center. It may even influence the distribution of funds, to a degree. This traditional academic model strongly resembles a company union. Typically, a company union consults with management on matters of concern, often receiving concessions; but it is heavily influenced by management thinking and attitudes and shows little or no capacity for revolt if the decisions made are not to the employees' liking.

Faculties in many colleges and universities are beginning to challenge the efficacy of the company union model. If they are not self-governing communities, faculties have become increasingly dissatisfied with administrative control of curricula and promotions and with the rigid application of daily work rules. Economic discontent has compounded the dissatisfaction to such an extent that acceptance of collective bargaining is on the increase. Some faculties have opted for union representation but rejected the notion of forming an academic senate or representative assembly. Others have formed both a union and a senate organization, but have found the delineation of their respective domains to be an almost impossible task. Moreover, the assumption of a community of interest between faculty and administrators is gradually declining throughout the country.

The Trade Union Model

An increasing number of faculties are rejecting traditional academic governments, looking instead to the trade union model of organization. For our purposes here, I define trade union as simply another model by which employees intend to govern, or have a share in governing, their working life. A trade union, whether it is called an association, a league, a guild, an organization, or a union, has three distinct characteristics.

(1) It is grounded on the belief that a fundamental and permanent conflict of interest exists between managers and the managed. Unions on campus have not denied that there are legitimate institutional goals. They have not denied that there is a community of interest shared by the institution and the faculty. But they have emphasized that the goals of the system and of the faculty may differ widely and that conflict will inevitably arise as the generalized goals of the institution are translated into decisions on

operation and policy. Hence, the role of the union is to make sure that actions taken reflect the interests of the faculty. The union normally emphasizes that even professional employees must be prepared to exercise militant pressure to get the results they believe necessary.

(2) Exclusivity is a fundamental element of the trade union. A professional group or society which begins to talk about needing an organization solely for lay professionals, excluding administrators, who may also be well-qualified professionals, is thinking of embracing the union model. This is happening in education, in nursing, in engineering—wherever professionals assume a basic separation of interests. The result is exclusivity. In labor law the concept of exclusivity is embraced in the phrase "exclusive bargaining unit."

(3) A trade union primarily regards itself as a service organization for the individual employee, while the traditional professional association or academic governing body is concerned with work standards for the profession generally and the faculty as a whole. In a general way, the professional association is also concerned with standards of employee compensation and fringe benefits. Except in rare situations, however, it will not concern itself with individual grievances. The union, on the other hand, is normally willing and able to regulate working conditions and to police their day-to-day effect on the employee.

No matter what it may call itself, an organization is a union if it has these three elements: the assumption of conflict between those who are employed and those who administer; the acceptance of exclusivity; and the willingness to protect the individual or a small group of individuals. Increasing numbers of faculties are beginning to accept these elements as necessary characteristics of their organizations.

Many professionals fear the trend toward trade unionism. The word "union," as applied to themselves, inevitably disturbs them. They perceive their personal role in different terms and they dislike bringing certain aspects of trade union behavior into institutions of higher education. But many faculty members have come to believe that, in the long run, unionization will result in greater professionalism. They argue that pressuring for more professional autonomy or for higher salaries is essential to insure professional services of high quality. They also argue that unified action is the only way to achieve the basic appurtenances of professionalism where educators have not been treated as professionals.

An Alternative Model

What alternatives to these two extremes are possible? A bilateral decisionmaking model provides several workable alternatives. This model presents a strictly interior pattern in which substantially all important decisions are jointly made by administrators and faculty. If there is mutual agreement on wages or the terms and conditions of work, for example, joint recommendations can be made to the governing body, or, wherever appropriate in a public institution, to the legislature. For such a model to work, the administration has to want substantial involvement of faculty in decisionmaking. Moreover, the administration must be willing to modify its own ideas regarding work loads, working conditions, fringe benefits, and salary structures. It must be willing to seek greater faculty input to solve problems jointly, ridding itself of the notion that faculty involvement necessarily challenges administrative authority.

What budget research pattern would be appropriate to the bilateral model? Presumably the administration would establish the initial framework within which negotiations would proceed. The faculty would first present information on their items of concern, including salary and fringe benefits. Both parties would depend upon rational presentation and argument as opposed to making "demands" in order to effect reallocations in the proposed budget. Where faculty and administration disagree, careful and extensive study of the budget might reveal items which can be reduced to release funds for the disputed proposals. This hypothetical decisionmaking apparatus has seldom been used, but I suggest that it is a practical intermediate approach which could become increasingly popular.

The Bilateral Model in Operation

How might this third pattern be put into operation? First, a faculty or a selected representative body composed of faculty members would appoint a negotiating committee. Second, the administration and the governing body would voluntarily recognize the right of such a committee to negotiate for the faculty. In return for this voluntary recognition, the faculty would probably have to give up the right to strike or to use other disruptive pressures to achieve its goals. Third, the faculty committee would need financing, probably by dues from faculty members. An administrative subventure might be used, though this seems to me an inappropriate source of funds. Fourth, the committee would have to be given access to any relevant information it may seek. In other words, all information available to the management (administration) side of the bargaining table would be available to the faculty committee.

Under this procedure I think most noneconomic issues could be resolved with little difficulty. The faculty negotiating committee would present its economic proposals and the administrative committee would be obligated to respond with specific answers to questions framed by the faculty committee and with counterproposals. In effect, both sides would have equal responsibility for developing the entire budget, not just the salary and fringe structure of the institution. If the negotiating process results in agreement, the agreement would become a joint recommendation of the faculty committee and the administration to the governing body. If the negotiating process does not result in agreement, a number of alternatives could be pursued.

Impasse Resolution Procedures

Within the federal government an elaborate system for collective bargaining has emerged; it works reasonably well, usually without resort to strikes or other pressure. The federal experience suggests four possibilities for resolving an impasse in faculty-administration negotiations. The first is a stipulation that the governing body will make the final decision, after the two committees have had equal time to present their cases to that body. I do not believe this is the best solution. The second possibility is mediation by some person, not necessarily a professional or government mediator, who is acceptable to both groups. The third solution is to go to factfinding by a skilled and experienced neutral who will make nonbinding recommendations for resolving the disputes. The fourth method is binding neutral arbitration—a solution for which I have some bias, as a sometime arbitrator.

The model I have been discussing hypothesizes a whole negotiating structure in which there is no reliance upon existing labor laws—a structure which would normally operate without need to resort to strikes or other pressure tactics to resolve impasses.

The University of Scranton

Will it work? It has worked at the University of Scranton, where such a faculty committee was recognized voluntarily, negotiated with the administration, had difficulties, and reached agreement. The faculty committee was then responsible for selling the terms of that agreement to the entire faculty. Moreover, the two parties achieved agreement that there would be no strikes and that the parties would not be subject to the jurisdictional procedures of the National Labor Relations Board (NLRB) or any other agency. The pattern worked and President Hanley stated the following conclusions:[1]

> The advantages of a professional negotiating team have become obvious to me. It affords the faculty real representation; it allays fears and creates confidence; it affords a new input for the faculty into administrative and financial decisions, an input which can improve our day-by-day workings. It avoids the dangers which I associate with unionization of faculty inasmuch as the matters to be dealt with are specified by mutual consent and the team retains its academic interests.

Grievance Procedures

Whether or not faculties adopt collective bargaining or a bilateral decisionmaking model, one aspect of the union model would be appropriate for all institutions of higher education. I refer to a regularized grievance procedure culminating in neutral arbitration —one of the major contributions of the American union movement to working life. Such a grievance procedure brings important elements of due process to the employment relationship. All employees should have available to them a routine and expeditious appeal from supervisory decisions adversely affecting them. Such a procedure is commonly lacking in institutions of higher education.

The keynote of the grievance process is the possibility of review of administrative decisions by qualified and independent neutrals.

---

1. Dexter L. Hanley, "Issues and Models for Collective Bargaining in Higher Education," 57 *Liberal Education* no. 1, 14 (Mar. 1971).

Today the quality of working life in industry is fundamentally different from that of a generation ago. The reason lies in the changed standard by which management's actions vis-a-vis employees have come to be judged. Before there was a union, before there was a grievance procedure which included binding arbitration of grievances, the standard for judging management's actions was contrived by management itself, asking, "Do we think we were right and fair in our dealings with employees?" If the answer was yes, that was the end of the matter.

Today the standard is quite different. Now the question is, "Do we as managers think this is a decision so fair and right that we can prove it to an experienced neutral who does not work for this organization?" The use of this standard has fundamentally changed conditions of working life for the better. The grievance process which has proved so valuable in industry can surely apply in some way to colleges and universities. Whatever else we do, I think it is highly important for us to create this kind of grievance procedure in higher education.

Conclusion

Some may say, "All you are really talking about is negotiations without a union," and so I am. But there are many advantages to negotiating. The process tends to inform those who are uninformed and are, therefore, frustrated and dissatisfied. New ideas are developed. Problems are solved in a manner which involves the consent of all who participate in the decision. Felt inequities are usually remedied, though not invariably. In any event, assurance of equal treatment for all employees is provided without undue personal preference. While there is nothing about negotiations of any kind that creates money where there is none, good negotiations can frequently lead to mutual agreements about unproductive efforts or waste of resources. The resulting savings can then be used for many purposes, one of which is to alleviate the economic discontent of employees. Finally, negotiation is the best way I know for administrators to hear the truths as faculty members and their representatives see them. If these beliefs are not always true, they are, nevertheless, feelings—feelings that far too often get filtered out through the successive layers of executive committees, chairmen, deans, deans' committees, and a plethora of vice presidents. It is important for administrators to know these things. One of the greatest virtues of organizational negotiations is that people get told precisely what other people think. In too many institutions today the people at the top genuinely do not know, whether or not they care, what many in the faculty think.

Can such a model come about as an alternative to collective bargaining? I do not know. But I am reasonably confident of one thing—for the most part, faculties are committed to issues, not to organization per se. They are committed to results rather than revolutions. The future of administrator-faculty relationships thus depends less on faculty than upon those who have administrative positions and other positions of power. The future clearly does not lie with Edward Bellamy's looking backward. It is largely upon those who now have power, upon their willingness to share it, and upon the answers they will give whether the future will be 1984 or a New Frontier.

CHAPTER 10

Bargaining at the
City University of New York

*Belle Zeller**

Facts and Figures

Today, higher education personnel face this reality—not whether there shall be collective bargaining for the faculty and nonteaching staffs, but how and when. In my opinion, the sooner the better. The 1970s will witness a tremendous expansion of collective bargaining in higher education.

Collective bargaining agreements currently cover some fifty thousand employees[1] in about one hundred thirty institutions located largely in six states: New York, Michigan, Massachusetts, New Jersey, Pennsylvania, and Wisconsin. These figures exclude looser agreements which may or may not fall under collective bargaining per se. There are some eight hundred thousand persons in higher education teaching and nonteaching categories, with a 50 percent increase estimated by the end of the decade. Approximately two-thirds of these are now attached to public institutions.

Although community colleges account for less than one-sixth of the faculty in one-third of the institutions, three-fourths of the personnel now covered by collective bargaining agreements are in the community colleges. Even if the expansion in higher education occurs in the community colleges rather than in the four-year institutions, collective bargaining will indeed take a giant step forward. However, collective bargaining agreements now cover the faculties

* Professor of Political Science and Chairman of the Legislative Conference, City University of New York.
1. Figures include teaching and nonteaching staff, librarians, registrars, counselors, laboratory technicians, and fiscal officers.

of several universities, including the State University of New York (SUNY) and the City University of New York (CUNY), the second and third largest universities in the country. Furthermore, institutions in about ten additional states are scheduled for collective bargaining elections within the next six months.

Sixteen states now have comprehensive public employment relations statutes, popularly called Taylor Laws after the New York law of 1967.[2] These states permit collective bargaining for higher education personnel in public institutions. A number of other states have such bills under consideration. In 1970, the National Labor Relations Board (NLRB) issued a significant decision extending collective bargaining to private colleges and universities with a gross annual income of one million dollars.[3] This ruling affected about 80 percent of the schools.

Most of the contracts so far have been negotiated by three national organizations. The American Association of University Professors (AAUP) national council, apparently after much soul-searching and reluctance, decided to step up its bargaining efforts. The National Education Association (NEA) has vigorously moved into higher education. Long the leading teacher organization at the elementary and high school levels, NEA now recognizes the importance of a united professional teaching organization with an ever decreasing administrative input. The NEA, with a membership of 1.2 million teachers and an annual budget of twenty-nine million dollars, has set up a meaningful higher education structure to organize and serve college faculties. It is now actively campaigning to secure a more substantial part of the eight hundred thousand membership potential in higher education. The American Federation of Teachers (AFT) is also in the picture, especially in large industrial states and cities. Merger talks are much in evidence, especially because of the financial crises facing higher education, but mergers will probably not go very far at this time. Temporary transitional attempts at cooperation may be successful and should be encouraged.

The CUNY Experience

CUNY, the first of the larger university systems to enter collective bargaining, is an institution of some two hundred thousand

---

2. See Appendix A—Public Employee State Laws.
3. 186 NLRB 153.

students, including about forty thousand entering freshmen in the fall of 1971. The faculty, full-time and part-time, numbers fifteen thousand. We came to collective bargaining as a culmination of activities by the university's Legislative Conference,[4] founded in 1938. In those days there were only four units within the system, while today there are some twenty units. The Legislative Conference has had a de facto bargaining agent role all these years, though without a formal contract until the three-year contract was negotiated in 1969.

The Legislative Conference was not affiliated with any outside group until 1970. As a voluntary organization for almost thirty years, we supported ourselves entirely by voluntary dues, elected our own officers, and acted independently in protecting our instructional staff. This is far from being the company union we were sometimes accused of being. Before 1969, the Legislative Conference served as an agent to secure bread and butter benefits, particularly salaries and fringe benefits, for its members. Our greatest weakness was the lack of a regularized grievance procedure, which our most recent contract has corrected. Yet, during those first thirty years we achieved a state tenure law, higher salaries, and increased pension benefits on behalf of teaching and supportive staff. Most of our accomplishments required validation by state law; hence the name, the Legislative Conference of the City University.

Two Bargaining Units

Since 1969, CUNY has had two bargaining units which we requested of the State Public Employment Relations Board. The Legislative Conference, affiliated with the NEA and its New York State Teachers Association since 1970, represents the full-time instructional staff.[5] In a separate election the part-time people selected as a bargaining unit the United Federation of College Teachers (UFCT), a local affiliate of the AFT. The full-time instructional staff includes all ranks of teaching faculty and the entire supportive faculty—e.g., the library staff members who have professorial titles, the fiscal officers, the registrars, and the laboratory assistants. I think that combination is essential in an academic

---

4. See Appendix L—Bylaws: Legislative Conference of CUNY.
5. It now covers almost 9,000 instructional staff members.

institution that recognizes the importance of a supportive staff to its proper functioning.

The 1969 Contract

The contract negotiated by the Legislative Conference with the Board of Higher Education of New York City in 1969 was the first major collective bargaining agreement in American higher education. On the bread and butter issues we have one of the finest contracts in the country. It provides very high salaries for both the teaching and supportive staffs. However, a number of our fringe benefits, such as the retirement system, require state legislative action for validation. The contract also includes increased promotional percentages in the two highest faculty ranks, expanded pension and health benefits, $1.5 million annually for faculty research, $1 million annually for sabbatical leaves, a half million annually for travel funds, $250,000 annually for fifty distinguished professorships, increased faculty office space, secretarial help, and facilities. Above all, there is a detailed grievance machinery, involving a step one hearing at the college level, step two at the university level, and, finally, binding arbitration as step three. Some forty cases have been taken all the way to arbitration during the past two years. We have won a number of them. However, the university has not acceded to the arbitration awards in all cases and has gone into court out of concern that precedents were being formed too quickly. I think the chances of the courts overruling an arbitration award are slim.

We really have three administrative agencies to deal with. Initially, we make the contract with our board of trustees, New York City's Board of Higher Education. Since a substantial portion of our funds still comes from the City of New York, we also talk with the city administration. In addition, many aspects of our contract require a working relation with New York State.

Contract Implementation

Since the signing of the 1969 contract, the Legislative Conference has focused on its implementation. For this purpose, we have had to deal on a continuing basis with our peers at the department level, with administrators at the college and university levels, and with elected officials at the city and state levels. At all of these levels, the conference has attempted to solve problems professionally and, wherever possible, informally. We conferred with appropriate administrators as soon as issues arose and resorted to the grievance procedure only when informal negotiations broke down.

Throughout its thirty-three-year history, the conference has functioned alongside the college faculty councils and senates. These bodies have been retained within the twenty units of the university. Since the establishment of the university about six years ago, the University Senate has also been created. We still recognize the policy-formulating function of these bodies in academic matters, but we oversee the bread and butter contractual matters, academic procedures, and academic freedom.

I think the budget is the key to deciding which group takes responsibility for what. Staff salaries and fringe benefits cover a substantial part of the budget, and this is the responsibility of the Legislative Conference. During this transitional period, our faculty councils have functioned in the areas of academic standards, curriculum, granting of degrees, student relationships, and the like. As the bargaining agent, the Legislative Conference does not tell the faculties whom they are to promote, only that each year a certain increase in promotions is to take place in each rank under the terms of the contract. Likewise, the negotiating agent does not tell the faculties whom to appoint or not to appoint, but it has outlined procedures that must be followed. The contract stipulates that persons not reappointed must be notified as of a certain date. It spells out the procedures for evaluation of staff, but it does not empower the Legislative Conference to make academic policy decisions.

For example, recently the question arose as to whether we should have a university bachelors degree. Each institution has always given its own degrees (ten of the twenty units are four-year colleges and eight are two-year colleges at the present time). The Legislative Conference did not choose to pass on the merits of the issue but we did protest that, in violation of the contract, the administration prepared the program for a university degree without consulting the appropriate faculty bodies. Whether the present cooperative relations will continue, I cannot say. Thus far we have been able to maintain a fine working relationship with the faculty councils and the University Senate. Our contract has served to raise academic standards and has enabled us to recruit and retain highly competent faculty.

However, I think the time will come when the public institutions of higher education—possibly the private ones, too—will need greater political clout. This is one of the reasons we joined with the NEA. At a time when we watched our governmental agencies retrenching in the area of education, we found that without affiliation with a national organization we lacked the wide support necessary to exert adequate political pressure.

Advantages of Collective Bargaining

From our experience of the past thirty-three years, especially the last two under a negotiated contract, the Legislative Conference can cite the several advantages of collective bargaining listed below.

(1) One of the most fruitful results of affiliation with strong state and national organizations is the political power that comes collectively to the university and its instructional staff, particularly in stressful financial periods.

(2) Collective bargaining provides a more meaningful role for the faculty in the budgeting process, especially in setting priorities. In the public sector, it gives the faculty official stature in dealing with public officials.

(3) It provides shared responsibility, with accountability, for both administration and instructional staff. The adversary aspect of the relationship (which also exists without collective bargaining) can be reduced or eliminated entirely if there is a spirit of cooperation on both sides.

(4) Collective bargaining helps the administration as well as the faculty. Systematic procedures are set for the improvement and evaluation of nontenured faculty, and such procedures could be applied to tenured faculty, as well. Without collective bargaining, policies are all too frequently arrived at unilaterally by boards of trustees. With a contract, trustee pressure can be removed from university administration, and trustees themselves can more readily resist unreasonable pressures.

(5) Collective bargaining narrows the gap between the lower and higher academic ranks. It does not follow that benefits accruing to the lower ranks come at the expense of the higher ranks, as a perusal of the Legislative Conference contract will show. Note, as two examples, the salary schedules and the promotion quotas in the CUNY contract.[6]

---

6. See Appendix J—Contracts.

(6) The thrust of a collective bargaining organization (unlike a faculty senate) is to unite the university's staff. It includes the nonteaching instructional staff that is indispensable to the proper functioning of the university. It builds morale by narrowing the gap between faculty and nonteaching personnel. It attempts to establish parity and equity between the staffs at the senior and the community colleges.

(7) Collective bargaining does not lower standards. Judgment by one's peers can and does work to raise standards. Quality and equality can go hand in hand, provided adequate resources are provided. What is most effective in our contract is the fair and systematic machinery providing for the improvement, observation, and evaluation of nontenured faculty in our rapidly growing university.

(8) Financial crises facing states today have encouraged anti-intellectualism in our state legislatures. This is especially directed at college faculties. Collective bargaining agreements (whether under government sanction or not) can strengthen both faculty and administration in their efforts to prevent the erosion of standards and to resist the establishment of improper priorities.

(9) Collective bargaining can stimulate a larger input from students, at least in a consultative and advisory capacity. Responsibility shared by students adds strength to both faculty and administration and can build a viable united front dedicated to personal satisfaction, relevancy, and excellence in higher education.

CHAPTER 11

Panel Discussion

John W. Reed, moderator
Charles M. Rehmus
Russell A. Smith
Terrence N. Tice
Belle Zeller

Smith: Mr. Rehmus, is the bilateral decisionmaking alternative to collective bargaining that you suggested a codetermination system, a company union, or what?

Rehmus: The faculty senate today is really a kind of company union. I am suggesting a representative faculty committee with considerable power to negotiate short of entering the full-scale bargaining process. The bilateral model could avoid the divisiveness and conflict that many faculty members fear as a consequence of unionism, while assuring a candid discussion of the issues. It would allow an institution freedom to choose some aspects of collective bargaining, e.g., a grievance procedure, while rejecting others.

Smith: Then you do not regard it as an entirely distinctive model?

Rehmus: That is correct. I am not even sure that it would be a stable model. It might serve as a halfway house to unionism, or as a means of discovering improvements to the old mechanism.

Zeller: In some institutions the transitional step is necessary to assure faculty that they are not giving up their decisionmaking powers, particularly on the academic issues.

Reed: Could you specify exactly how your bilateral decisionmaking model differs from collective bargaining?

Rehmus: The chief difference is that the union model assumes a permanent conflict between administrators and employees. The other model does not. Conflict arises in the translation of the organizational goals of the academic community into day-to-day operating decisions. Many faculty members claim that this conflict already exists in their institutions. The union says the only way the conflict can be realistically managed is to accept it and fight. In the alternative model I propose, administrators voluntarily recognize the right of the faculty to join fully in budgetary determinations. Such a course requires informed negotiation by faculty representatives, based on their access to data and background information known to the administration. A voluntarily accepted procedure to resolve impasses short of strikes and other invidious pressure tactics should be created in advance of negotiations. Conceivably, adoption of the alternative model could allow faculty to move beyond their traditional advisory role without the relationship which usually arises in labor-management negotiations.

Tice: Would you discuss the sources for obtaining outside mediation?

Rehmus: Most states have a body of qualified government mediators. Their ability to learn rapidly the nuances and special requirements of any institution especially qualifies them to perform. Highly skilled and experienced mediators might also be available from neighboring faculties. Moreover, many capable professional mediators around the country would be acceptable to both faculty members and administrators.

Reed: Miss Zeller, do you find that the source of funds is not wholly or even significantly within control of the administration but lies with the legislature or private donors? How does this affect negotiations? Do you feel that you are dealing first with the administration, and then both faculty and administration make common cause in Albany?

Zeller: Usually we present a united front at Albany. Although there are preliminary discussions on program cuts and the like, we see eye to eye in asking for more funds. Over the years the administration has frequently asked the Legislative Conference for cooperation and has gotten it. But in my more than thirty years of going to the state capital I have never seen such an anti-education session as in 1971. Under our contract we have protection in some crucial areas, especially salary schedules. Grievances are tougher. The administration continues to assume that it can dismiss non-tenured faculty without giving reasons. We are going into court on that question, because we believe that a person kept for five years and then dismissed is entitled to an explanation. The administration has resorted to the courts in other grievances, even when we have won an award in an arbitration proceeding. Arbitration and judicial proceedings are expensive if for no other reason than the special legal counsel both sides must hire.

Reed: Would you please explain how the salary structure works at CUNY?

Zeller: At the time the contract was negotiated, 19 percent of our professorial staff were full professors and many more were qualified to move up. The contract includes a scale specifying that every year of the three-year contract each of the three professorial ranks shall be increased to a final 30 percent and instructors, 10 percent. But a contract is just a piece of paper until it is properly implemented, and that is where the collective bargaining agent has to be on its toes. We are constantly checking on the administration to see if the terms of the contract are being carried out. Work load has become a big bargaining item. All we hear now is increased productivity. What does this mean? We have taken the position that to increase the work load beyond what it was at the time we negotiated the contract is a violation of the contract. We believe a heavy work load will drive the most qualified faculty members from the university. Our public officials do not see it that way. To them, increased productivity means adding to the schedules of the faculty or increasing class size. We do not accept that interpretation.

Reed: Assuming the need to deal with conflict, we might also examine another alternative. Suppose an institution adopts a negotiating pattern based on seeking bilateral agreements on an issue-by-issue basis rather than covering all issues at once. These agreements could last indefinitely, whereas all terms expire at the same time with a master contract.

Zeller: I think the suggestion is retrogressive. It is what most institutions have had right along. Moreover, many of these problems are too closely related to one another to be treated separately. If a person is fired under some tenure provision, or lack of one, the question of grievance machinery comes up. The institution should be looking constantly at the bread and butter issues, including fringe benefits. Some of us are having trouble enough with particular subjects now. In 1971, New York legislators talked about rescinding the tenure laws because we now have collective bargaining, even though tenure-related protection and procedures are provided in our contracts. The CUNY contract also provided a million dollars a year for sabbatical leaves, but in 1971 the legislature passed a law declaring a moratorium on them, long before the president's wage-price freeze.

Rehmus: A system to negotiate indeterminate term agreements on specific subjects is not foreign to American industrial practice. This has been the practice in the railroad industry for many generations. Agreements can be reopened at the initiative of either party. I agree, however, that the complexity of interrelationships leads to the opening of many things at once. The union says, "We want to open on wages only," and the carriers reply, "That costs us money, and we can only afford it if we get some relief on the working rules." The whole ball of wax tends to appear, no matter what the negotiators started with. Another difficulty with the proposal is that the grist for trade may be lacking. In a pure world, perhaps each item could be dealt with strictly on its own merits, but the essence of the negotiating process is achieving concessions in one area in return for countervailing concessions in another. Finally, I suspect that those charged with administering long-term programs could not tolerate an obligation to negotiate on a moment's notice or, in some situation, even continuously. On balance I doubt that the arrangement would work or that it is likely to come about.

Tice: Either way, different terms could be placed on the various items of an agreement. They would not all have to be set for an indefinite period. A process for joint periodic review of certain policy decisions could also be developed, each with its own timetable. Institutions that are not currently moving toward either collective bargaining or consultative negotiations ought in any case to be developing the processes for joint discussion and review of policy.

Smith: I wonder whether the faculty senate and its committees must be put on the scrap heap if collective bargaining is adopted. Perhaps the virtues of existing processes can be incorporated into the total representation process along with the certification of a union as a collective bargaining agent.

Rehmus: Possibly. Previous governance procedures have been preserved at CUNY.

Zeller: That is true, but frankly I do not know how long they will last. The question of overlapping, of what is a proper matter to come before a faculty council and what is not, has arisen several times.

Rehmus: The experience in the community colleges I am familiar with is also not very encouraging in this regard. In some cases community colleges having no faculty senate refused to create one. In others, they retained a senate and attempted to define the respective jurisdictions of each group. This simply did not work because the union tended to be more aggressive, arguing that almost every falling sparrow was its concern. Eventually the faculty senate atrophied. At San Francisco State College the faculty senate chose to be the bargaining agent and also created a union as a gun behind the door in case the senate did not get satisfactory settlement. For a complicated set of reasons, including difficulties in race relations, this bimodal kind of control was later destroyed. The experiences so far indicate that in such a dual situation the authority of the faculty senate will decline, unless the faculty negotiating body or the union is willing to circumscribe its own areas of interest very narrowly.

Reed: An argument against binding arbitration in the public sector has been advanced on the reasoning that a legislatively created and empowered board of trustees may not give away its statutory responsibility to govern by permitting a third party, such as the arbitrator, to substitute its judgment for that of the board. Will this argument hold up?

Rehmus: As a general rule, the courts and attorneys general have held that binding arbitration of a grievance is not a derogation of power. On the other hand, a considerable body of opinion holds that interest arbitration—that is, binding arbitration of the terms of agreements—is a proper delegation of power only if there is specific enabling legislation.

Smith: The latter point is quite definite.

Zeller: But isn't the board a party to the agreement? And what is binding arbitration, anyway? We get an award from an arbitration group, then the board of trustees goes into court seeking to have it reversed, and yet we say we have binding arbitration.

Smith: In a sense, binding arbitration is simply a situation where the employer who loses takes it gracefully.

Rehmus: Actually the arbitration award can be beaten in court only on certain grounds. Eventually more precise rules will be made to define the areas in which arbitrators can make binding awards. This should lessen substantially the time and money unions spend in court defending an arbitration award.

Smith: We have a number of arbitration statutes now in the public sector. So far as I know, they do not include teachers. If and when they are included, binding arbitration would be applicable to them, subject to the statutory limitations, including court review.

Reed: Miss Zeller, why does CUNY have a separate bargaining unit for the part-time faculty and supportive staff?

Zeller: We are not all in favor of the separation. Why did we ask the state agency for it? It was just a case of arithmetic. If we had combined all the part-time people with our full-time faculty in one unit, the part-time staff would have outnumbered the full-time personnel and the Legislative Conference would possibly have lost the election. The situation in our schools of general studies, where most of the part-time people are found, was deplorable. They had legitimate grievances. We realized that we needed more time to work on these people. Many of the part-time staff teach only one or two evenings a week and would have been entitled to the same vote as a full-time professor in the day session. Further, a number of the part-time faculty are full-time high school teachers who are members of the American Federation of Teachers, the bargaining agent for the other unit. Some also believed that the needs of the full-time career faculty and the part-time staff were so different that each would be better served in separate units. For myself, I do not think it is desirable to have two units, and I hope that before long we can agree on a merger. We are talking about it. Perhaps the ideal situation for all concerned would be two units with one organization representing both units.

Reed: The New York experience may not be an apt example for other institutions because of CUNY's size and the long experience of the Legislative Conference. Nevertheless, it would be interesting to know whether the first bargained contract actually infused a large amount of money into the system or whether the money was simply allocated differently so that the faculty got a larger share of the pie.

Zeller: The university received a great deal more money as a result of the negotiations, chiefly from New York City, and not only for salaries. The fact that Mayor Lindsay was running for reelection that year helped our cause. We brought our two-year colleges up to the same salary levels as those in the four-year colleges. We also wrote into the contract $1 million dollars annually for sabbaticals, much more than we had before, $1.5 million for research grants, a half million for travel grants, and some other items. Fortunately, we did not have to depend on the state legislature for most of these amounts.

By the way, we seem to have been assuming in our discussion that all administrators object to collective bargaining. I am not at all sure this is true. There are advantages in it from their standpoint, too, and this should be pursued further.

Tice: It is useful to recognize that there is something of a love-hate relationship between some faculty members and administrators. Sometimes this occurs because administrators have come out of faculty, sometimes because they have not. Whatever models are used—collective bargaining or alternatives—we must find ways of dealing with this love-hate relationship and with conflict in general. I do not think totally serene relationships can be expected. In this connection, I should like to make four observations that touch on issues which many in academic life feel rather deeply about today.

First, in the coming years "adhocracies," to use Alvin Toffler's term,[1] will not be sufficient to handle needs within the campus community. We can continue a little while with commissions by presidential or faculty senate appointment and with other ad hoc arrangements, but over the long run we will need procedures for long-term planning. Whether or not we get into collective bargaining, I believe it is in the interests of the faculty and the entire academic community to secure such procedures as soon as possible.

Second, individual faculty commitments will have to include some involvement in organization. Studies show that this is something faculties are traditionally not terribly eager to do. Most faculty members like to spend their time teaching and doing research. They often resent long hours of committee work. This difficulty will have to be overcome if we are to deal realistically and efficiently with our problems. Partly because of faculty reticence and partly because top administrators have the responsibility to lead, I agree with Mr. Rehmus that much of the initiative for such changes will have to come from the administration.

Third, in view of turbulent campus events in the past two or three years, students and the supportive staff need to be involved with faculty and administration in matters of priority, budgeting, and long-term planning. The basic reality here is simply power and the attendant kinds of planning the entire academic community is willing to do together. We need to do more thinking about how alternatives to collective bargaining could include students and supportive staff.

Fourth, the entire community must make some arrangement to move rapidly toward new habits and manners of working for legislative reform. The history of collective bargaining in two- and four-year public institutions does not clearly show that the simple fact of bargaining improves the posture of the institution in the state or its capacity to deal with legislators. Within each context people will need to weigh the extent to which collective bargaining could improve the capacity of an entire campus community to press for legislative reform in education or the extent to which collective bargaining itself would provide the wedge required.

---

1. Alvin Toffler, *Future Shock* (New York: Random House, 1970).

Part IV
Faculty Organization

CHAPTER 12

Should Faculties Organize?

This chapter records the separate opinions of four persons well-qualified to speak to the question posed by the chapter title and their frank interchange of views in a panel discussion. John W. Reed, Professor of Law, Director of The Institute of Continuing Legal Education, and Chairman of the Senate Assembly's Committee on the Rights and Responsibilities of Faculty Members at Michigan, moderated the discussion. All of these men are involved in the lively issues arising from faculty attempts to answer this critical question.

In Chapter 13, Terrence Tice, Assistant Professor of Philosophy, School of Education, and editor of this volume, analyzes the reasons for and against faculty collective bargaining. He writes from the vantage point of his considerable study and his experience as Assistant Chairman of the Senate Assembly's Committee on the Rights and Responsibilities of Faculty Members at Michigan.

Grace W. Holmes
Consulting Editor

Alfred D. Sumberg*

Several pressures are causing faculties to organize. Among these are limited financial resources for compensation and academic programming, the advent of collective bargaining by nonacademic employees or by faculty members in nearby institutions, and the changing power relationships on campus. In addition, many legislatures have, in effect, mandated collective bargaining as the future employer-employee relationship for the public sector, primarily to curtail the lobbying efforts of public employee organizations, not because of any desire to extend similar rights to public and pri-

---

* Associate Secretary, American Association of University Professors.

117

vate sector employees. Once the necessary statutes have been passed, legislatures tend to disclaim any further responsibility for the details. Their watchword appears to be: "If you want something, negotiate for it."

Thus far, public employment legislation has not crippled academic institutions. Generally, the boards are equitable in their bargaining unit determinations, and there has been little interference with the traditional or constitutional autonomy of institutions.

The new public employment laws are usually patterned after state or national labor relations acts governing private employment relationships, but it does not follow that the academic community must pattern its organizations after industrial unions. Public school teachers who organized in the early 1960s made this fundamental error and have had to live with the consequences. The laws provide an opportunity for constructive negotiations in areas of college and university governance, grievance procedures, academic freedom, and compensation. Faculties should regard collective bargaining as a means of putting into effect the goals of the past fifty years.

Since the standard industrial interpretation of managerial rights is virtually irrelevant to the situation of academic communities, why bother with it? Why not apply and further develop the standards of governance already existing in the academic community? Administrators and trustees will likely apply industrial interpretations to negotiations at first, but they must be quick to learn and to accept academic traditions in order to reach collective bargaining agreements truly reflective of academic interests.

In many schools the substantial pressure to organize is now accompanied by little desire for collective bargaining. I expect this view to prevail for some time. Differences in these institutions can best be resolved by a representation program of shared responsibility—one patterned after the provisions in the statement of the American Association of University Professors, the American Council on Education, and the Association of Governing Boards of Universities and Colleges issued in 1966,[1] with improvements. If this fails, collective bargaining would be the chief alternative. If neither works, chaos may ensue.

---

1. "Statement on Government of Colleges and Universities," 52 *AAUP Bulletin* 375 (Dec., 1966).

A faculty which still has the choice between shared responsibility and collective bargaining should make its decision only after studying the goals and interests of the faculty and of the institution. Faculties must improve their ability to look ahead in both areas. Two simple truths should also be kept in mind. First, collective bargaining in higher education is a far more complex process than the proponents of industrial-style unionism sometimes suggest. It needs to be explored in relation to the needs of both faculty and institutions, with a thorough awareness of the structural complexities. Second, the needs of each institution must be closely studied. No generalization can yet be made about the specific applicability of either collective bargaining or shared responsibility. Community colleges, state colleges, multicampus institutions, and private schools have developed very different characteristics.

Should faculties organize? Only after thorough investigation has revealed good reason to do so. Then, and only then, is it time to consider the kind of organization.

Allan F. Smith*

The bargaining agreement, whether or not it is modeled after industry agreements, is a difficult instrument for describing professional relationships. Speaking as an administrator, I agree with Mr. Sumberg that we must examine the results that may or may not be achieved from collective bargaining. The real question for examination is what can be achieved by organizing.

The struggle over curriculum is not between deans and the administration or the regents and the faculty, but between faculty and students, who are pressing faculty to make the curriculum responsive to the current needs. If there is to be a lack of faculty power regarding curriculum development, it will not be because an administrator says no. It will be because students (and faculty) find the curriculum unresponsive.

What are the most important elements of faculty freedom? What is it that makes a faculty member enjoy his work and his life? The answer lies in the power to choose colleagues and declare work assignments. Perhaps a third element is the power to determine the content and functions of the courses he teaches. If these

---

* Vice President for Academic Affairs, The University of Michigan, Ann Arbor.

are the principal aims of a faculty member, are they now being threatened? If so, by whom are they endangered? How can collective bargaining change the professional relationship that operates to deal with these problems? I do not know.

Frankly, I am conditioned by twenty-three years at The University of Michigan as a faculty member, law dean, and vice president. It is a massively decentralized institution where departmental decisions largely determine colleagues, curriculum, and work assignments. These issues are not subject to the external direction of either the university or the state. Mr. Sumberg suggested that public employment relations laws serve as a mandate which should be taken up as a matter of course. As a rule, we do not regard highly the legislative wisdom directed at higher education, so why should we expect this particular declaration to be either intelligent or humane?

Is there a basic conflict of goals? I would find it hard to place much value on a goal established by trustees or any other group if it is contrary to a goal formulated and agreed to by faculty. Although the legislature may disagree, no collective bargaining contract presumes that kind of relation. I would hate to think that The University of Michigan administration represented the legislature and I am sure the legislature would not choose us as its representative. In fact, we have been engaged in suing the legislature for unconstitutional invasion of the prerogatives of the university.[2]

Ultimately, the decision as to whether faculty should organize will be determined by an assessment of the gains and losses in faculty power. Collective bargaining ordinarily seems to bring an immediate economic gain to teachers in the public schools. This may also occur in the higher education arena. It is always possible to rearrange the economic relationships within an institution. But one cannot bargain exclusively on economic relationships forever. Surely the other side of the table will want something in return for the money. This will involve trade-offs in the matters of work load, choice of colleagues, work assignments, and curriculum. I really do not want people other than faculty members to control those conditions.

---

2. Regents of The University of Michigan v. State, No. 7659-C (Ingham County Cir. Ct., Dec. 6, 1971).

Malcolm G. Scully*

With some reservations, I believe academic professionals should organize because, unlike many professionals, they are employed by institutions. Their goals and those of the institution may sometimes differ. Such divergence can be expected to widen as institutions enter into the next period of fundamental change—a period Clark Kerr calls "climacteric two."[3]

The first climacteric, Kerr indicates, occurred in the nineteenth century. The coming one will be a period marked by doubts about the kinds of services universities should provide to the government and individuals, by suspicion directed at science and rational thought, by conflict between campus and society, and by divisiveness within the academic situation itself. In Kerr's view, a tremendous struggle for power over some of the crucial issues in higher education will ensue.

In a power struggle of such dimensions, I think that groups which are not organized collectively will probably lose out in the struggle. Mr. Kerr predicts that higher education will move from its traditional model of layered responsibility (with trustees responsible for investment, faculty responsible for curriculum, and students responsible for extracurricular activities) to the "quasi-public utility model." What he means by that phrase is not entirely clear, but it would seem to be a model requiring some form of collective organization.

One major trend Kerr notes is a more careful examination of the "cost effectiveness" of operations. If this is not done internally, it will be done externally by the new experts working for legislatures and governors. Thus, many fiscal decisions of public institutions will be made off campus—in the state financial office or the state board of higher education. Faculties may have to organize to deal with those offices.

Many observers believe that centralization of state systems of higher education has tremendously increased the pressure for faculty unions. A recommendation of the first Newman Task Force[4]

---

* Formerly Assistant Editor, *The Chronicle of Higher Education*, Washington, D.C.
3. Clark Kerr, Speech delivered at the Annual Meeting of the American Association for Higher Education, Chicago, Ill., March, 1970.
4. F. Newman, et al., *Report on Higher Education* (Office of Education, March, 1971).

that the trend toward massive centralized state systems of higher education be reversed was partly based on the assumption that the trend increases the prospect of collective bargaining, which the task force opposed.

Numerous other forces are gradually removing authority and autonomy from campus. Among them are court decisions like the *Roth*[5] case in Wisconsin, which tends to break down the distinction between tenured and nontenured faculty members. The federal government has shifted from an emphasis on grants for basic research to contracts for applied research, a fact which may reduce the autonomy of research people.

In short, all the trends point to a power struggle on campus. I think professionals should organize to compete in the struggle. It may not be pleasant and it may not always be collegial, but it will be necessary.

We are entering into a period of tremendous flux in higher education and the outlook is not all positive. Faculty unions, for example, could become a highly conservative force. The experience in some elementary and secondary schools, and possibly in some junior colleges, indicates that faculty unions could become powerful advocates of the status quo.

The real issue is not whether, but how, professionals should organize. Faculties must move to protect what is rightfully theirs from forces which are trying to take over some of their power and responsibilities. But they must not move in ways which will rule out experimentation and change. Involving students and the rest of the academic community is important and presents a challenge that will have to be dealt with in many contracts, or the unions will assuredly become an extremely conservative force in higher education.

It is worth noting that the National Student Association and the Association of Student Governments, at their joint meeting in the summer of 1971, agreed to start discussions about forming a national student union. These discussions may be unrealistic, but they certainly illustrate an upswing in student power. If a national student union does arise, as it has in some other countries, the faculty unions will have to take students into account in ways they are not considering right now.

5. Roth v. The Board of Regents of State Colleges, 310 F.Supp. 972 (W.D. Wis. 1970), 336 F.Supp. 751 (W.D. Wis. 1971), 446 F.2d 806 (7th Cir. 1971), *cert. denied*, 40 U.S.L.W. 2292 (U.S. Oct. 26, 1971).

Robert T. Blackburn*

Donald Bylsma and I have recently completed two reports on our study of the effects of collective bargaining in two-year colleges.[6] Presenting some of the first data available, the reports show that faculty participation in the governance of those institutions has been significantly advanced by collective bargaining. Traditionally, faculty in the two-year colleges have had virtually no say in most of the essential policy decisions of their institutions, even those closely affecting their work and welfare. Arguments pointing to an ideal of faculty participation in "mature" universities and liberal arts colleges often seem to harbor the unstated premise that having an occasional faculty voice in decisionmaking is faculty power.[7] Our study does not bear this out—nor would a candid investigation of the ease with which individual faculty interests are frequently overriden by administrative fiat. Secretaries of faculty members are transferred without consultation or restraint. Recruitment efforts are supported, then dropped. Faculty productivity is measured by inconsistent criteria.

These and other bits of evidence simply add up to the fact that faculty power is a myth. The notion is a smoke screen covering where the real power resides—in boards and administrations. Whether collective bargaining will improve the lot of faculty over the long run remains to be seen. However, we do know that the chief items of private complaint may become items for collective negotiation. This is happening in the two-year colleges. I hope something like this will work, for many academic people—my principal subject of study—are threatened with a precarious future. Not only tenure but also long standing principles of academic freedom are under attack, matters which touch the very heart of higher education. In the face of such disheartening events, a contemporary Marx might well advise us: "Professors of the world, unite. You have nothing to lose but your impotence."

---

* Professor of Higher Education, Center for the Study of Higher Education, The University of Michigan, Ann Arbor.

6. "Changes in Faculty Governance and Faculty Welfare: Some Empirical Consequences of Collective Negotiations" and "Changes in Organizational Structure and in Locus of Decision Making: A Test of Theory in Community Colleges before and after Collective Negotiations." Both have been submitted for publication.
7. See Matthew W. Finkin, "Collective Bargaining and University Government," 57 *AAUP Bulletin* 149 (June, 1971); and 1971 *Wis. L. Rev.* 125.

Questions and Answers

Reed: There clearly is no simple answer to the question of whether professionals should organize. However, a number of important issues have been raised for discussion. I was particularly pleased that the question of student input was raised. Students have gotten into almost everything else, and certainly we can expect them to be interested in the matter of faculty working conditions.

Mr. Sumberg, would you respond to Mr. Smith's suggestion that faculty may lose out on some noneconomic concerns if they resort to bargaining?

Sumberg: I have often said that if collective bargaining is to be meaningful and constructive, it must deal with things faculties prize—things which they have achieved without bargaining. Negotiated agreements have already granted faculty authority to share responsibility in forming educational policy, to handle faculty appointments, and to participate in the selection of department chairmen and administrators.

I have been working in Pennsylvania, where the fourteen state colleges are about to hold an election. The State College and University Council of the American Association of University Professors (AAUP) is a contestant in the election.[8] Faculty members of these colleges are deeply concerned about deficiencies in the current system. Many now believe, as they might not have before Pennsylvania's employment relations law was passed in 1968, that collective bargaining is a more effective way to correct those deficiencies than continuing to operate under the principle of shared responsibility, without benefit of law.

Whether we leave such important matters out of collective bargaining largely depends on the desires of the faculty and the group that seeks to represent them.

Reed: Mr. Sumberg, you use the term "deficiencies" and Mr. Blackburn spoke of what he considered faculty "impotence" rather than faculty power. Mr. Scully, as a perceptive observer of the higher education scene, do you feel that Mr. Blackburn's characterization is accurate? Are faculty really that ineffective?

---

8. The AAUP affiliate lost the election in October of 1971 to the Association of Pennsylvania State College and University Faculties, an affiliate of the Pennsylvania Education Association.

Scully: No. I disagree with his position. I accept the Jencks-Riesman thesis of the professionalization of faculties.[9] Although individual cases of harassment certainly exist, departments are usually allowed to run their own affairs, as Mr. Smith indicated.

Blackburn: I agree with Mr. Smith that the primary concern of faculty is to have control over their work environment, academic activities, and choice of colleagues. Faculty get nervous when these prerogatives are invaded. Faculty supply is fantastically high now and will continue to be high. Some thirty thousand Ph.D. degrees were awarded this year, a 300 percent increase over ten years ago. There are not enough jobs. Administrations and foundations are clamping down on funds, and legislatures are specifying work loads and proposals to remove tenure. The freedoms faculty enjoyed in the past are simply disintegrating. I do not say that faculties should unionize, but I am worried about their work conditions. I do not hear many presidents coming to the defense of their faculties when they are under attack.

Sumberg: I find little evidence of faculty quiescence. The attacks on tenure, the squeeze on funds, the whole crisis of antieducationalism that Miss Zeller talked about this morning prompted faculty to take direct action in the legislative chambers. Faculties do not have to sit quietly while others take over their prerogatives. Trustees and administrations have often assisted them in their fight.

Scully: We must try to understand the nature of the changes occurring in higher education. A rise in professionalization took place during the era of expansion, but a reversal began in 1968 or 1969. Possibly Mr. Blackburn and Mr. Sumberg are referring to the signs of this rapid shift, along with probable dwindling enrollments in the future and growing dissatisfaction with our concepts of liberal education.

Reed: There are two kinds of problems here—internal and external. On the one hand, faculty, administration, and students have conflicting claims to power. Are faculties and administration going to bargain about the question of who has what power and leave

---

9. C. Jencks and D. Riesman, *The Academic Revolution* (Garden City, N.Y.: Doubleday, 1968).

the students on the sidelines? Students certainly will be heard from and the resulting internal conflicts will have to be dealt with. On the other hand, external pressures from legislatures and funding sources in private institutions are not likely to be answered simply because faculty and administration get together on a contract.

Smith: The external attacks on the value of higher education in the society are very real. In the past two or three years, state legislatures have been greatly interested in dabbling in higher education affairs through the imposition of external controls or the refusal of financial support. I know of no period in the past to match it, and we have not seen the last of it. The united effort of every constituency in higher education is needed to meet the attack. The external pressures represent one set of problems. The need for change in the internal governance and relationships is a very different question.

One wonders whether the size and diversity of an institution is relevant to a discussion about collective bargaining. In large, diverse institutions it is often difficult to know who is a true spokesman for the faculty. The University of Michigan has seventeen faculties. On many issues they speak with one voice, loud and clear, and their position is heeded. On other issues they differ. This fact presents problems for shared governance. At The University of Michigan, we have tried not to set very many academic policies centrally. If a collective bargaining group can manage to speak for a highly diverse group, it might be useful.

Sumberg: Collective bargaining has normally produced a greater formalization of the faculty-administration relationship. Perhaps it is a little stifling at times, but it is reliable. The principle of exclusivity requires the administration to talk only to the certified bargaining agent on a number of issues. The agent will certainly try to represent the views of his organization and often the entire faculty as well, advancing a unitary viewpoint.

The size of an institution has nothing to do with acceptance or rejection of collective bargaining. Other factors affect that decision. Rutgers, City University of New York, and St. John's are large universities engaged in collective bargaining. They are in the same boat with small community colleges and huge state systems. I am not even sure that traditions have much to do with whether faculty seek collective bargaining. Collective bargaining comes for very different reasons in different institutions, large or small.

CHAPTER 13

Pros and Cons
of Collective Bargaining

*Terrence N. Tice**

Academic Collective Bargaining Models

Many knowledgeable observers of the higher education scene are saying that collective bargaining is inevitable. Although they usually find difficulties with it, they believe it will soon gain the same prominence it has attained since 1965 in the public schools. I have no doubt that this decisionmaking procedure will be used at an increasing rate. I further believe that exciting new opportunities are thus presented, both to realign the purposes of higher education and to reconstitute the organs of faculty power. Nevertheless, there are cons as well as pros to consider.

A rational decision about collective bargaining requires a close weighing of the details. The decision should not be based on executive orders issued or legislative action taken without attention to the special needs and rights of higher education. It should not be made on the faulty supposition that because collective bargaining is becoming prominent it is therefore inevitable, or that because it is doing some good it is therefore desirable. Finally, the decision should take into account not only the various forms that collective bargaining may take but also the principal alternative forms for achieving change.

The administration in many colleges and universities has undeniably been at odds with faculty over wages, hours, and working conditions—the three basic interests served by industrial unions. In

---

* Assistant Professor of Philosophy, School of Education, The University of Michigan. Assistant Chairman, Senate Assembly's Committee on the Rights and Responsibilities of Faculty Members.

some of these, faculty have been moving into collective bargaining to redress their grievances. At other institutions, especially some major universities, faculty agencies and the administration have ordinarily cooperated on these matters. The administrations of public institutions have given the faculty strong support before the legislature. Less advantaged members, while they feel that their situation has been neglected and that their comparative economic status has deteriorated in recent years, frankly fear that collective bargaining would provoke a damaging adversary relationship with the administration.

The terms "shared authority" and "collegiality" represent values of long standing importance within the academic community. Faculty have fought hard battles to attain these values in the past. In the college or university setting, bargaining and collegiality may not be incompatible. A few contracts have already included statements intended to secure academic freedom, the rights of faculty senates, and consultative procedures. But restrictions on faculty autonomy and on the faculty's capacity to share in the process of formulating policy are almost bound to accompany negotiated agreements on faculty compensation. The two cannot be separated, if for no other reason than that faculty compensation comprises a major portion of the budget.

The typical collective bargaining model in industry says: "We'll take our part. You do what you want with the rest." Faculty at some institutions have recently been asking for a greater faculty role in planning, budgeting, and allocation of funds. They have acted on the belief that the academic concerns of faculty are affected by virtually the entire budget, not by salaries alone, and that the faculty has a responsibility to participate in setting institutional goals and priorities. The Faculty Reform Coalition, a voluntary group of faculty holding such views, was formed at The University of Michigan in May of 1970. At the time, students had begun to ask for a voice in setting university policy. Faculty were beginning to feel some pinch in the pocketbook and other areas, and to ask for greater representation. In addition, there was the memory of a rather violent-appearing episode earlier that spring over demands issued by the Black Action Movement and supported by a large number of faculty and students. In this painful situation many faculty came to believe that a more orderly process of gaining rapid reform should replace violent or adversary relationships.

As a rule, collective bargaining has fostered an adversary split between employer and employees. If cooperative effort in achieving reform is deemed important, a kind of model other than collective bargaining will probably have to be found.

The new model, whether formed through collective bargaining or otherwise, would perform two functions. It would enable faculty, collectively and individually, to press claims on matters of compensation and other matters of importance. It would allow faculty more effective participation in the governance of their institution.

Bargaining agreements may include provisions intended to preserve or promote designated faculty rights. But successive contracts could readily get into areas other than wages, hours, or working conditions—areas now generally thought to be the primary responsibility of faculty government or of administration. Rights themselves would then be subject to bargaining. Some informed observers have argued that once collective bargaining has settled in, the rights and influence of the faculty would be restricted primarily to internal affairs of departments or of schools and colleges—that is, to internal affairs not already covered in the negotiated contract. Successful efforts made in the past to strengthen faculty influence could be lost in a number of areas. Valued traditions of decentralized decisionmaking on internal budgeting, recruitment, promotions, scheduling, productivity, and even course offerings could be thwarted. Or, executive functions better achieved by administrative action than by bargaining would be subject to damaging curtailments and delays. Both are strong possibilities. They must be carefully weighed and assessed at each stage of development, but always before an institution enters the road to collective bargaining. Although the situation of disadvantaged faculty might initially improve—and this is by no means certain—overall salary increases could be more than offset by diminishing faculty rights. In some institutions, faculty have very few rights and responsibilities to lose. In such cases, faculty have to consider specifically which rights or responsibilities could be gained by collective bargaining or by some alternative development of faculty power.

Faculty Concerns and the Industrial Pattern

The basic concerns of faculty are markedly different from those of employees in the industrial sector and require a different kind of treatment. Among these concerns are such matters as academic freedom; professional tenure (including fair provisions for apprenticeship, for nonreappointment, for merit compensation, and for review of the work of tenured faculty); participation in policymaking; research facilities; professional and other supportive services; sabbatical and other leave provisions; relations with students; public service functions; curriculum innovation; and democratic procedures in numerous aspects of academic affairs. It is difficult to determine from the content and brief history of present contracts how many of these concerns can be met with collective bargaining, industrial style or otherwise, and how many are likely to suffer. It is also difficult to perceive how academic bargaining could differ markedly from industrial bargaining where state law makes no distinction between faculty and other employee groups, as in Michigan; or to determine whether the fact that the faculty situation is different would produce significantly different results.

Tenure and Faculty Performance

Attacks on tenure may cause faculty to consider collective bargaining a bulwark of defense. On the other hand, tenure could be abolished through collective bargaining as a trade-off for other things. Academic freedom is a highly valued tradition, and tenure policies have helped to secure its acknowledgement. Tenure could possibly be wiped out with or without collective bargaining, or modifications could be made in tenure policy to make for high level performance among tenured faculty. Whether such changes will be made seems to depend upon changes in economic conditions, legislative decisions, social needs (e.g., for people trained in the new technologies), and possibly in professional values, rather than upon collective bargaining. Nevertheless, the matter has to be considered.

Excellence in faculty performance may be discouraged in the process of gaining equitable treatment for all faculty members and using quantitative criteria for advancement. On the other hand, merit increases could be provided for, as has been done in some contracts. General excellence could be fostered by having policies more definite and equitable, by assuring economic security to a larger number, and by establishing review procedures to keep incentives high. It is important to realize, however, that the degree to which such goals could be achieved without collective bargaining is not known.

Through collective bargaining, faculty status could conceivably be improved in several areas—compensation and fringe benefits, teaching load, scheduling, class sizes, and facilities and services for faculty. All of these items have already appeared in some contracts. There have also been some clarifications of tenure and promotion routes. Improvements in nondiscriminatory employment policy and grievance procedures could be added. Advances could be made in sabbatical and other leave provisions, in selection of deans, in policy regarding use of adjunct faculty, and in support of professional travel and retirement policy. Such advances have been made in some places. On the other hand, all these matters are part of a total bargaining picture. Some of them cost money, which these days is more likely to come from increased faculty productivity than from anywhere else. Moreover, the considerable control faculty already have over these matters in some institutions could be increased and the situation of less-privileged faculty improved through structures already available but so far not used to their fullest value. In most institutions, the faculty senate has had a weak record and is certainly not a very impressive sign of faculty power. Representative faculty assemblies and groups have done much better. Their effectiveness could be greatly enhanced by moving closer to a negotiating role in areas of concern, especially those affecting economic policy, without giving up the collegial relationship with administration.

Productivity Bargaining

In the budget squeeze situation, where few incremental dollars are available, collective bargaining might at first succeed in getting salary improvement at the expense only of nonfaculty budgetary items. In time, however, the funds may be accumulated by reducing the numbers of faculty—fewer persons at higher pay, as in the public schools and elsewhere under collective bargaining— or by resorting to various forms of productivity bargaining. Such alternatives could have the salutary effect of forcing the faculty to reconsider its priorities and its methods of instruction.

Relations with the Legislature

No clear evidence has been found to show that any form of union organization will either help or hurt the faculty with the legislature. Nor does it appear that the lobbying position of a college or university would be harmed, even if all or most of the state's other college and university faculties were under contract to a single agency such as the National Education Association (NEA). It is highly plausible to predict that because of the NEA's additional commitment to employees at the K-12 levels, employees in higher education would get comparatively less strenuous advocacy in the state capital, though the organization is currently working to secure relative autonomy for its higher education divisions. The actual state of affairs now appears almost surely to be one in which all three competing agencies—NEA, the American Association of University Professors (AAUP), and the American Federation of Teachers (AFT)—will have contracts with one or more institutions of higher education in a state, with legislators continuing to be approached from a variety of directions.

Gains by Disadvantaged Faculty

The majority rules in collective bargaining. Therefore, wide salary differentials that work to the detriment of hardworking, productive faculty in fields not competing with the outside market for personnel could be lessened or removed. Women and other faculty at the lower rungs of the promotion ladder could be protected against discrimination by "peer" evaluations. The record is mixed on this score. A standard salary scale has not always been included in bargained agreements. On some campuses the differentials between ranks or units have been reduced through bargained salary scales. A recent study shows that in eleven representative Michigan community colleges differentials have been increased.[1] At City University of New York, on the other hand, differentials have been significantly decreased, largely through a faster increase at the lower ranks.

What could younger faculty gain or lose through collective bargaining? This would depend on several factors: (1) present rank and professional standing, (2) the market for new faculty in the lower ranks, (3) whether the bargaining agreement is likely to bring across-the-board percentage gains or to lessen differentials, (4) what salary schedule standards are used, and (5) promotion and merit increase policies.

---

1. Christine Gram, "Impact of Collective Bargaining on Faculty Salary Structures in Michigan Community Colleges," (Ph.D. diss., Dept. of Higher Education, The University of Michigan, 1971).

(1) The first factor, that of rank and professional standing, is a purely individual matter.

(2) With regard to the second factor, this year younger faculty are in a buyer's market in most fields. If professional predictions of markedly lower recruitment rates over the next few years hold up, their situation is not likely to improve. If the average age of faculty goes up, as is also predicted, then there will be a proportionately greater claim for compensation at the higher ranks and there will be fewer assistant professors to pay. Of course, somewhere along the line the question may be raised as to whether salaries for younger faculty should be largely determined by the market. The consequence of any effort to deal with this question, inside or outside collective bargaining, is impossible to foresee at this point.

(3) The third factor is uncertain on the basis of present data. A decrease in salary differentials, however, cannot be counted on.

(4) Comparative salary standards are also difficult to predict. Under collective bargaining it would conceivably be more difficult to fire an assistant professor. It might also be difficult for him to get hired in the first place, or to move to another institution. In either case, it is by no means evident that his comparative economic position would be significantly raised. In 1970-71, The University of Michigan was ranked thirty-fifth in the country in average faculty compensation. The average compensation for its full-time assistant professors was $14,411, achieving a AA rating from the AAUP, while the average compensation of $22,227 for professors received only a B rating. Compared to the other Big Ten universities, The University of Michigan assistant professors ranked a close third in mean salaries but were last in proportionate increase over the past five years. Unless the "market" is to be regarded the prime determinant of salaries, with little attention to gross inequities within ranks and between units, it is highly questionable whether the statistical ratings of the AAUP provide adequate standards. Such comparative standards have nonetheless been the chief reference point for many years.

At the University of Wisconsin in 1970, the Teaching Assistants Association—acting as a separate group, not as part of the faculty —was able to achieve substantial gains in wages and working conditions through collective bargaining. Assistant professors, on the other hand, would not be able to organize separately. A change either in their relative position or in promotion policy is likely to depend more on an altered perspective within the faculty as a whole than on collective bargaining as such. Whether or not a collective bargaining situation will be needed to bring this about remains to be seen.

(5) Those who now receive the lower salaries in all ranks are likely to be affected most by changes in policy concerning promotion and merit increases, the fifth factor affecting gain or loss to younger faculty through collective bargaining. There is no clear evidence, however, that gains would be made in this area through collective bargaining, even though the greatest pressure may be felt here among the less privileged faculty.

If salary differentials are leveled off and freedom to respond to the market is lost, the capacity of departments and professional schools to compete for quality faculty may be diminished. Excellence within the institution largely depends on their maintaining this capacity. However, the value of market response must be weighed in relation to the value of achieving greater equity in compensation. Its importance partly rests on what policies other comparable institutions adopt and on the degree to which any given institution chooses to be a leader or a follower in changing compensation policies. One thing is clear: collective bargaining agencies are not likely to weigh market value more highly than equity.

Faculty-Administration Relations

Thus far, collective bargaining has occasionally served to stimulate faculty interest in the affairs of academic governance and to bring faculty leaders and administrators into unaccustomed close contact. In such situations, collective bargaining may actually be necessary before any significant change in faculty participation can be achieved. At other institutions, where faculty have had greater opportunity to exert influence, efforts to adopt alternatives to unionization could have a similarly positive effect.

In February of 1971, the Senate Assembly of The University of Michigan faculty appointed a Committee on Faculty Rights and Responsibilities. That committee accepted the following three principles governing faculty-administration relations. I believe they are essential criteria for weighing whether or how to enter collective bargaining, to improve current nonbargaining structures, or to form alternatives such as Charles Rehmus has outlined.[2]

(1) Professional standards of scholarship, expertise, academic freedom, autonomy, communication, and service may well be enhanced with greater faculty authority in university governance. Both professional standards and faculty authority can be expected to lessen as faculty take on a more restricted employee status. This lowered status must be strenuously avoided, whether or not collective bargaining is used.

(2) From an academic professional standpoint, the preferred model for relations between faculty and administrators comprises a collegial rather than a strictly hierarchical or adversary relation —one of shared responsibility and authority rather than one requiring competition, confrontation, or coercive sanctions. Professional standards of performance should be set by faculties, not by bargaining compromises or by decisions of state labor relations boards.

(3) Participation of both faculty and administrators in the governance of their institution should be organized so that the possibility of making decisions based on self-interest, poor judgment, lack of relevant information and values, or flimsy planning is held to a minimum. To avoid faculty errors of this kind, the administration should be accorded powers of overall leadership, coordination, planning and innovation, quality control, and business management, and should serve as a buffer between faculty and the governing board.[3] To avoid administrative errors, faculty should have wide powers of self-determination in professional and academic matters, an informed advisory role in all areas of administrative responsibility, and a share in making basic decisions that affect overall budgeting, allocations of funds, institutional development, and long-range planning.

---

2. This chapter is a thorough revision of draft materials I prepared for that committee, of which Charles Rehmus was also a member and John Reed the chairman.
3. An AAHE task force has recommended similar powers in its report *Faculty Participation in Academic Governance,* (Washington, D.C.: American Association for Higher Education, 1967).

Part V

The Bargaining Process: Problems and Procedures

CHAPTER 14

The Bargaining Process:
Problems and Procedures

Five attorneys speak to the specifics of the bargaining process in this chapter. Their statements reflect a wide range of experience in bargaining procedures in universities and colleges. The complexity of the problem is brought into focus in this confrontation of sharply differing views on the formal structure of bargaining, the impact of legislation on the process, and the kind of procedural model which is likely to emerge.

Grace W. Holmes
Consulting Editor

Harry T. Edwards*

Justice Holmes once said that the life of the law has not been its logic, but its experience. This observation seems particularly applicable to public sector labor law, at least to the present time.

Faculty groups in colleges and universities have held certain types of authority which have not typically been accorded industrial employees before or after collective bargaining. The question is whether administration groups will suddenly gain in power with the coming of collective bargaining. President Bowen of the University of Iowa has suggested that the greater the tendency toward coercive tactics in collective bargaining, the greater must be the authority of the president and the board of regents.[1] I think he is right. In the absence of coercion the institution can afford delega-

---

* Associate Professor, The University of Michigan Law School, Ann Arbor, and a state and federal arbitrator.
1. Howard R. Bowen, "University Governance: Workable Participation, Administrative Authority and the Public Interest," *Proceedings, 1969 Annual Spring Meeting,* Industrial Relations Research Association, pp. 517-528.

tion, wide consultation, and participation in decisionmaking. But when the game becomes a ruthless struggle for power, authority must be held firmly in the hands of the president and board. What is interesting about this claim is the tacit admission by the president of a large university that power really did not vest in his office before the coming of collective bargaining.

Another issue is the role of the employer. Who will fill that role in faculty collective bargaining? Will it be the president and his subordinates, the board of regents and its delegates, or the legislature and its delegation? At the school and departmental level, will it be the dean?

A related question is how the appropriate bargaining unit should be determined. Mr. McHugh raised serious doubts about the value of fragmentation. But I wonder whether fragmentation would always be a bad thing in the academic setting, especially if it should correspond to preexisting power structures. For example, if the power has always resided in the various deans, it surely makes good sense to let collective bargaining develop in a fragmented form with the dean acting as the employer and the faculty groups comprising the appropriate units. This is especially important where there is traditionally a weak administrator in a university. Could the administrator adequately fill the employer role in bargaining where there is a larger unit base?

Do statutory limitations on the permissible subjects of bargaining really make sense? I have always been amused by the limitations imposed by the National Labor Relations Act, which grants sanctity within the categories of mandatory, permissive, and illegal actions. For all practical purposes, such restrictions do not really make much difference at the bargaining table. The parties negotiate over any matters that are of consequence to them. When I sit across the table from union representatives and they raise a question that falls in the permissive or illegal category, my response is not: "Have you read *Jones v. Jones* where the National Labor Relations Board suggests this really is not a subject that we should talk about?"

I doubt that in the academic setting we should really worry about what is permissive or mandatory. Workers at General Motors have not traditionally been interested in the new car models. But in colleges and universities the product is education—something teachers are vitally concerned about. I suspect that the bargaining process will be hampered if we impose these absurd statutory definitions as to what is or is not an appropriate subject of bargaining within an educational institution.

R. Theodore Clark, Jr.*

I take exception to Mr. Howlett's suggestion that management rights provisions should not be included in statutes. As the bargaining relationship between public employers and employee unions emerges, it may be necessary to exclude certain matters from bargaining. The federal government has taken this route under President Kennedy's Executive Order No. 10988 (1962) and under President Nixon's revised Executive Order No. 11491 (1969).[2] There has been a gradual broadening of the collective bargaining process in the federal sector as the parties gain experience. This path may be applicable also at the state and local levels.

Management used to retain all rights not bargained away. In recent years, however, both the National Labor Relations Board (NLRB) and various arbitrators have assumed additional restrictions. In some instances they have held that management is obligated to bargain to the point of impasse before taking action in a given area, unless the right to prior action is set forth in the agreement. From a management viewpoint, having a rights clause in the agreement protects us from having to negotiate stated subjects and buttresses our case if a related grievance is taken to arbitration. On the other hand, I question the proposal that the administration has only those rights which are specifically stated in the agreement, whereas faculties retain whatever rights they have had in the past. This rule of interpretation is unfair, and I doubt that it will hold up in practice.

To a large extent, the choice of the bargaining model lies outside the control of the colleges and universities. Legislation adopted in a given jurisdiction substantially shapes the bargaining process in that state. The Michigan Public Employment Relations Act, for example, is largely drawn from the National Labor Relations Act. All bargaining processes in Michigan will, therefore, be related to that used in the private sector.

The labor organizations will also play a role. In Illinois we have been confronted with local affiliates of the American Federation of Teachers and the National Education Association. Both organiza-

---

* Seyfarth, Shaw, Fairweather & Geraldson, Chicago, Illinois.
2. See Appendix C for text of Exec. Order No. 11491.

tions have adopted a slightly modified industrial model for bargaining. Such a process is based upon conflict, using the strike as the ultimate weapon if agreement is not reached.

School administrators who face collective bargaining must learn how to cope with militant unionism. The concluding section in a Twentieth Century Fund task force report for 1970 observed:

> In government today, especially below the federal level, there is a paucity of experience in dealing with unions and administering labor contracts. Unless the costly and embittering mistakes made in industry at an earlier time are to be repeated in public employment, something must be done to provide those who act in government-as-employer and those who act for government employees with the knowledge and sophistication necessary to negotiate and administer labor agreements capably.[3]

There is considerable evidence that those who have represented public employers at the bargaining table have brought less than the desired degree of knowledge to the table.

In 1970, the Michigan Municipal League made a study of some 158 public contracts.[4] The results of that study show that over 25 percent of the contracts investigated contain either a union shop or a maintenance of membership provision, conditions illegal under Michigan law. Forty percent of the agreements lacked a management rights provision or had only a very brief statement. More than 40 percent of the agreements with grievance procedures either did not define the term "grievance" or defined it in broad terms. Some 35 percent of the agreements failed to include a no-strike provision, which in Michigan is virtually inexcusable.

The first bargaining negotiations between the employer and the employee representatives are of crucial importance. This initial meeting requires full knowledge and expertise, since it sets the course for all that follows. Any mistakes you make—any right, prerogative, or privilege that you give up—will be extremely difficult to recover in later negotiations. Chicago City College had a two-month strike in 1971. The central issue which triggered the strike was the effort of the board to gain back what it had given

---

3. Twentieth Century Fund, Task Force on Labor Disputes in Public Employment, *Pickets at City Hall: Report and Recommendations* (New York, 1970).
4. A. Smith and E. Berrodin, "Labor Contract Analysis for Michigan Municipalities," *Michigan Municipal League Info. Bulletin No. 117* (April, 1970).

away in prior negotiations. Understandably, the union refused. When labor pioneer Samuel Gompers was asked what American labor really wanted, he is said to have responded, "More." That is what negotiations are all about.

Plans for negotiation must be carefully worked out in advance, making every effort to anticipate the positions the other side will take. As Mr. Edwards stated, the negotiators should be willing to discuss virtually anything that the other party introduces at the table. Refusing to discuss an issue at the outset is poor tactics. Discussion does not preclude taking a firm position on the items included in the final agreement. As a rule, you make more mileage in negotiations by letting the other side explore a proposal and talk it to death. Cutting them off before they even have a chance to make their proposal creates more resentment and hostility.

Always allow the other side to save face. The employer, especially, needs to understand that the employee bargaining agency is in part a political organization. It has to justify its actions to the membership. Thus, when it appears that the bargaining representatives are ready to drop proposals, allow them to do so without actually saying that they are abandoning a position. For example, suppose you inquire how many issues are still undecided and they list five items, but your list shows fifteen items still open. Don't ask about the other ten. Grant them silence and avoid any questions which would place them in a position of public embarrassment.

Keep your options open. Too often negotiators for employers announce that a position is final and find they must renege on it later. Make no such statement until you are absolutely sure it is the end of the road.

Above all else, honor every commitment made at the bargaining table. If you cannot make a definite commitment because you need the prior approval of your board, say so clearly. Nothing destroys credibility and effectiveness at the bargaining table more effectively than reneging on a commitment.

Theodore Sachs*

My perspective differs from Mr. Clark's because I have represented teachers and others on the union side of the table.

Bargaining unit composition is one of several issues of practical

* Rothe, Marston, Mazey, Sachs, O'Connell, Nunn & Freid, P.C., Detroit, Michigan.

importance already settled before the collective bargaining process begins. The view that unit determination is a nonadversary proceeding is a legal fiction. The composition of the bargaining unit may very well determine whether there is going to be any organization at all or whether there will be an effective distribution of power on both sides.

If the certified unit is excessively large, the union may have trouble wielding sufficient power to influence the bargaining relationship. The rule Mr. Howlett alluded to—that of accepting the largest practicable unit consistent with the various interests involved—is not followed by the National Labor Relations Board (NLRB) or by many of the states. Instead, an alternative test is commonly applied, referring to "an" as opposed to "the" appropriate bargaining unit, in the effort to maximize employee self-organization. From labor's point of view that is what these acts are all about. We believe that unit determination should facilitate what is usually declared to be the statutory purpose, namely, effective organization among employees having a community of interest.

On that basis, various agencies and courts have suggested that a proposed bargaining unit should always be considered an appropriate unit where no alternate is proposed by another labor organization. This view makes sense to me, despite the fact that the unit may be inconvenient from the employer's viewpoint and that it may not be the optimum bargaining unit in size or makeup. I am not disturbed by the prospect of what has been labeled excessive fragmentation. If fragmentation is so obviously excessive that the arrangement is unworkable, then it should not be done. In many instances, however, divisions less than the whole may well be compatible with the best expression of the employees' community of interest.

I take issue with Mr. Clark's suggestion that some reservation of management rights should be written into state law and assured, especially in the formative stages of public sector bargaining. I think this kind of limiting statutory provision should never be made. Nor should such provisions be issued by administrative agencies, as the NLRB has done. It is especially crippling to include such provisions at the outset of a bargaining relationship because this precludes agreement on matters which may be of mutual and legitimate concern. If there is to be any management rights limitation, it should be strictly a matter for bargaining between the parties and should be expressed in negotiated contracts. The strained distinctions between mandatory, permissive, and prohibited subjects should not carry over into the higher education field. Here I agree with Mr. Clark. These restrictions tend to evaporate at the bargaining table. The parties do talk, and should be talking, about matters of common concern. Moreover, administrative rules which impose these artificial distinctions on the bargaining process are no less damaging than similar statutory provisions. Every effort should be made to afford the parties flexibility in bargaining. Neither the clients nor the lawyers know what such artificial definitions mean. They cannot live with them and should not be expected to.

Why has further litigation not ensued after the North Dearborn Heights determination by trial examiner, to which Mr. Howlett alluded? The answer is not merely that teachers want more and are interested in money but that both parties are prepared to deal with these subjects instead of running for legal cover to avoid talking about them. If they cannot reach agreement, they simply do not reach agreement. So be it, but at least they attempt to resolve problems of mutual and significant consequence.

Some ten years ago, before Michigan's Public Employment Relations Act was passed, a local school district in the Detroit area had perhaps the granddaddy of school strikes and of school collective bargaining contracts. The collective bargaining contract, achieved after a strike of several days' duration, ran six or seven paragraphs. Most of the issues people now insist teachers should not be talking about were the gut issues in that dispute. Disagreement over these issues had provoked the conflict in the first place. I would make the point that imposing restrictions on the ability of parties to solve their problems will provoke precisely those confrontations we wish to forestall.

As Mr. Clark said, the private sector model is likely to be used in the public sector as well. The legal framework is similar. Most of the professionals who get involved in public sector bargaining will have gotten their experience in the private sector. For better or worse, their biases and proclivities go with them.

Although not necessarily for the same reasons, I also agree with Mr. Clark's observations on bargaining technique. His suggestion that the other side must be allowed to save face is especially good, and it cuts both ways. Public bodies are political institutions, with political axes to grind and constituencies to serve, and they must be permitted to reach their conclusions gracefully.

The conclusions Mr. Clark derives from the Municipal League Survey do not impress me the same way. The lack of strike clauses in public contracts is not particularly upsetting, since the Michigan statute prohibits strikes anyway. What more would a contract clause add?

The absence of a management rights clause in such contracts does not seem very significant, either. Some of Michigan's most able practitioners on the management side are undeterred by the absence of such clauses. They represent their clients effectively and negotiate what seems to be appropriate and necessary under the circumstances. Conversely, those negotiators who have been most hardnosed in exacting the pound of flesh, putting in the legalese and the clauses which are difficult to live with, later reap the harvest of strike. Those are the communities in which the pressures build.

In all these areas of bargaining it can only be in the mutual interest of both parties to deal in good faith, because they need that kind of relationship in order to work responsibly together in the future.

J. David Kerr*

The Michigan Constitution states that the boards of universities —notably Michigan State, Wayne State, and The University of Michigan—have the power to supervise their respective institutions and control the expenditure of their funds. Those words are not empty promises.

Before 1850 the Michigan legislature attempted to order The University of Michigan to establish certain departments, particularly a department of homeopathic medicine. The 1850 constitution was adopted to prevent the legislature from meddling in university affairs. The best interests of the university and the faculty require such autonomy. The recent legislative mandate[5] that faculty members must teach a specified number of hours as a condition for

---

* University Counsel, Central Michigan University, Mt. Pleasant.
5. Mich. Pub. Act No. 122, §19 (Sept. 29, 1971). This provision was ruled unconstitutional by Judge Marvin J. Salmon in Regents of The University of Michigan v. State, No. 7659-C (Ingham County Cir. Ct., Dec. 6, 1971).

continuing state appropriations to the university emphasized the danger. If the universities cannot retain their autonomy, the legislature will set the terms and conditions of employment for faculty and staff. The matter of bargainable issues is also a question of constitutional autonomy. The National Labor Relations Board is now beginning to exact damage penalties in addition to issuing orders to bargain in unfair labor practice suits. This indicates that the issue is more than just about talking together—it is about superintending the control of bargaining agencies over administrations and vice versa.

Collective bargaining is a process, not an adversary proceeding. The federal act, according to its preamble, purports to serve industrial peace. Among other things, the Michigan act purports to protect employees and prevent strikes. To my mind, however, neither act has been particularly successful in promoting industrial peace.

How might the situation be improved? More thinking is needed about how the collective bargaining process can be improved rather than how each side can get more out of the other. First, the union has to be regarded guilty of unfair labor practices if it does not deal fairly—e.g., if it does not place all its demands on the table or if it says it will work for contract ratification and does not. Both are very common experiences in Michigan negotiations.

Second, unions should be required to report their receipts and expenditures, including the amounts they spend on political activities. Public bodies must make their budgets and expenditures regularly available to the public. It is important to require the same of unions, especially if they lobby for their interests or campaign for the people who will be ratifying their contracts.

Third, sanctions should be attached to no-strike laws. These sanctions should be geared both toward strikes that result from bargaining and strikes that occur after an agreement is reached. The American Federation of Service and Maintenance Employees is always threatening to strike whenever it fails to get what it wants, even after an agreement has been made. In such instances, a union should be decertified for at least a year and be required to petition again. To strike after an agreement has been reached is against the public interest.

We should consider having separate boards for different groups of public employees. The state of Washington, for example, has separate boards for K-12 systems, junior colleges, and senior colleges. The supporting argument for this method is the greater expertise to be found in each area. After all, what kind of service is a mediator going to give a university if his whole experience has been with police and firefighter cases?

I believe bargaining agents, now elected for indefinite periods, should stand for reelection periodically, at least every five years. Other people ought to be able to get on the ballot. A counterargument to periodic reelection asserts that the unions will stir up a lot of trouble before each election in order to emphasize the good job they are doing. Nevertheless, I believe the advantage of periodic reelection outweighs the perils.

We should also consider legislation limiting the stricter requirement of bargaining in good faith to issues of wages and fringe benefits. Employers should be required only to meet and confer on all other areas, not to reach agreement. Certainly provision should be made for talking about other things than wages and fringe benefits. But I do not think they should always be required to agree, as might be the case where an unfair labor practice suit is brought before the employment relations board and the board says, "No, you've got to compromise, at least." My proposal would reduce the threat of outside control over elected or appointed governing boards while giving people ample opportunity to meet and confer.

William F. McHugh*

There is a tremendous need to train people who are going to be involved in the collective bargaining process. The opportunity for creative accomplishment in resolving disputes and working out problems is immense. Michigan probably leads the country, with the possible exception of New York, in human resources and educational institutions able to train such people. The state enjoys a level of sophistication relatively absent elsewhere. Schools of education, law, business, and public administration, and schools with modest industrial and labor relations programs have not yet demonstrated a feeling of responsibility in this area. The time has

* Formerly Special Counsel, Employment Relations, State University of New York; presently Associate Professor of Law, American University Law School, Washington, D.C.

come for them to introduce their students to the overall industrial labor relations picture and train them in the techniques of conflict resolution, notably mediation, arbitration, and factfinding.

Generally, a broad scope of subjects should be covered in collective bargaining with faculty. This is entirely consistent with the traditional relationship between faculty and institutions of higher education. The administration should not give away the shop. But unionization will undoubtedly become a major force, in time covering a broad range of subjects. The sooner we recognize this the better. I wholeheartedly agree, therefore, that it is a serious mistake to impose statutory restrictions on the scope of negotiations.

I favor large, comprehensive units which can accommodate a certain amount of coalition bargaining with subordinate units in borderline situations, such as the law and medical faculties. If bargaining agents are truly oriented to academic life, as I think they will be, they will recognize the need to permit mini-bargaining within the context of the master negotiations. Tandem sessions could be arranged and provisions made for the peculiar problems of certain schools or faculties.

Moreover, a larger unit insures a more secure, sophisticated, and powerful bargaining agent. Thus, the potential for responsible leadership from the bargaining agent is greater, especially in the avoidance of endless internal squabbles between employee organizations. In general, it does not seem that larger units diminish opportunities of the competing bargaining agents to organize. In some cases a particular organization might do better with a smaller unit. But we seem to be beyond the point, at least in the public sector, where insisting on the larger unit could defeat collective bargaining. At the State University of New York there are some fifteen thousand professionals in one statewide unit and we succeeded in negotiating a contract.[6]

The faculty senate is the certified bargaining agent at Nassau Community College in New York. The faculty senate in the State University of New York system could probably have qualified but chose not to enter the race. Several issues should be considered in deciding whether to support the senate as a bargaining agent.

---

6. No other state system has a huge unit configuration like this. The state teachers college system in New Jersey and the City University of New York both have comprehensive contracts, but with like institutions. Hawaii might become a second during the 1971-72 academic year.

First, does the senate have sufficient money and staff to make the bargaining process work the way it should? Can it afford to retain an attorney and a business agent? Does it have access to computers and research resources essential for bargaining in the larger institutions? Second, does the unit configuration correspond to the composition of the senate? Where called for, will the senate broaden its constituency to include professional support staff? Can it compete with other agencies in the election if it does not do so? Third, to what extent is the senate dominated by management? Will its inclusion of management members present difficulties before the state employment relations board? Presumably, when the senate is functioning in its bargaining capacity the management members could be excluded from participation. But this is not a very neat arrangement, and the continuing composition of the organization would still present difficulties. Finally, I think having an active academic senate and a bargaining agent cooperatively related is of great educational and political value. The senate tends to act as a balance wheel. An issue the agent does not want to handle on political grounds can be dispatched with greater authority by the senate, and at times vice versa. The senate can also act as a tempering factor in relations between the bargaining agent and the administration.

Appendixes

APPENDIX A

Public Employee State Laws

Virtually all of the state laws granting collective bargaining rights to public employees have been passed since 1959, the date of Wisconsin's comprehensive act. Indeed, most of these laws have been enacted since 1965, with a substantial increase in legislative activity occurring since 1969.[1] This summary includes statutes applicable to public employees generally, in the states or their subdivisions, and to employees in the public schools or in higher education. Omitted are the several statutes covering police and firefighters and those applicable to such categories as nurses (Montana), public transit or utilities employees (Louisiana and Ohio, respectively), and nonprofessional private sector employees.

As of January 1, 1972, statutes of the kind included in our survey appear not to have existed in the following twenty-one states: Alabama, Arizona, Arkansas, Colorado, Georgia, Illinois, Iowa, Indiana, Kentucky, Louisiana, Mississippi, New Mexico, North Carolina, Ohio, South Carolina, Tennessee, Texas, Utah, Virginia, West Virginia, and Wyoming.

Comprehensive legislation has been enacted in about half of the twenty-nine states with laws summarized here. "Comprehensive" means different things to different writers. We have used the term to refer to any law securing collective bargaining rights to public employees at the state level or within its subdivisions. A

---

1. The following looseleaf services report all statutes and amendments in the field:

   (1) *Government Employee Relations Report* (weekly). Bureau of National Affairs, Inc., 1231 24th St. N.W., Washington, D.C. 20037.

   (2) *Labor Law Reports*. Commerce Clearing House, 425 13th St., N.W., Washington, D.C. 20004.

   (3) *Labor Relations Reporter, State Labor Laws* (Binders 4 and 4A). Bureau of National Affairs, Inc., 1231 24th St. N.W., Washington, D.C. 20037.

fully comprehensive set of statutes would cover virtually all public and private employees with the exception of categories such as elected officials and uniformed state police, and would provide for unit and agent determination, unfair practice complaints, grievances, and dispute resolution.

A more detailed comparative study is not available, but some recent publications contain useful material. Joel Seidman examined comprehensive laws in sixteen states for their positions on bargaining rights and obligations, scope of bargaining, prohibited practices, right to strike, and impasse resolution.[2] Frederick R. Livingston and Andrea S. Christensen pointed out inconsistencies between the statutes and proposed federal legislation to achieve greater uniformity.[3] Russell A. Smith's analysis of state and local advisory reports on public employment legislation headed a 1969 symposium on "Labor Relations in the Public Sector."[4] An extensive comparison of federal and state laws by Tracy H. Ferguson appeared in 1968.[5] A survey of laws in thirty-nine states was done by Richard S. Rubin in 1968.[6] A brief comparison of statutory provisions was done by Arvid Anderson in 1969.[7] In 1970, Jay W. Waks made a survey of laws in twenty-nine states.[8] Where relevant, the statutes referred to in these studies are included here, with additions and amendments to January 1, 1972.

To indicate the variety of concepts used, each statute is summarized under the eleven items listed below, if they appear in the law.

(1) Public employees covered
(2) Explicit provisions for higher education
(3) Administering agency, if any
(4) The bargaining obligation

2. J. Seidman, "State Legislation on Collective Bargaining by Public Employees," 22 Lab. L.J. 13 (Jan. 1971).
3. F. R. Livingston and A. S. Christensen, "State and Federal Regulation of Collective Negotiations in Higher Education," 1971 Wis. L. Rev. 91.
4. R. A. Smith, 67 Mich. L. Rev. 891 (Mar. 1969). See also Chapter 2.
5. T. H. Ferguson, "Collective Bargaining in Universities and Colleges," 19 Lab. L.J. 778 (Dec. 1968).
6. R. S. Rubin, A Summary of State Collective Bargaining Law in Public Employment (Ithaca: New York State School of Industrial and Labor Relations, Cornell University, 1968).
7. A. Anderson, "Public Employee Bargaining," 1 Urban Lawyer 312 (Fall 1969).
8. Jay W. Waks, "Impact of the Agency Shop on Labor Relations in the Public Sector," 55 Cornell L. Rev. 547 (Apr. 1970).

(5) The scope of negotiations
(6) Unit determination and the bargaining agency
(7) Principal rights and prohibition
(8) Collection of dues and fees
(9) Impasse procedures
(10) Grievance procedures
(11) Other notable features

Alabama

Ala. Code tit. 55, §§317(1)—317(4) [Supp. 1967].

A general statutory prohibition against public employee labor unions or organizations does not apply to teachers in public schools, trade schools, and institutions of higher learning; to municipal and county employees; and to certain employees of the state docks board. The penalty for union membership of nonexempt public employees is forfeiture of all rights resulting from public employment. There appears to be no specific legislation protecting or regulating the right of the exempt groups to organize and bargain collectively.

Alaska

Alaska Stat. §§23.40.010—23.40.040, added by ch. 108, L. 1959; as amended by ch. 231, L. 1968.

(1) Employees of the state or its political subdivisions are covered.

(4) The state and its subdivisions may contract with a labor organization but are not required to by the statute. No further statutory requirements are made.

Alaska Stat. §§14.20.550—14.20.610, added by ch. 18, L. 1970; as amended by ch. 43, L. 1971.

(1) This statute grants public school teachers the right to bargain collectively.

(4), (5) School boards, including the state Board of Education, "shall negotiate . . . in good faith on matters pertaining to their employment and the fulfillment of their professional duties." Administrative personnel may negotiate independently, if they so choose, by secret ballot.

(6) The employer must recognize a bargaining agency chosen by

the majority of employees in a school district as the exclusive representative of all except superintendents. The board must hold an election to determine a bargaining agency if 25 percent of the employee group request it. The size of the negotiating unit is limited to five representatives each. Although negotiators may agree to meet in executive session, final agreements must be made at a public school board meeting.

(7) The legal responsibilities and powers of the school board, including its right to make final policy decisions, are reserved to the board.

California

Cal. Gov't Code §§3500—3510, added by Stats 1961, ch. 1964; as amended by H.B. 1107 (1971).

(1) The provisions cover all employees of public agencies except elected officials and the governor's appointees. Public agencies are all governmental subdivisions and instrumentalities, except public school districts, now covered by the Winton Act of 1965.

(3) The governing body may adopt rules to administer the provisions. In the absence of local procedures, disputes may be submitted to the Department of Conciliation of the Department of Industrial Relations.

(4), (5) There is a mutual obligation to "meet and confer in good faith" on all "matters relating to employment conditions and employer-employee relations" except "the merits, necessity, or organization of any service or activity provided by law or executive order." Agreements are not binding until approved by the governing body.

(6) A formally recognized employee organization has the right of exclusive representation. Professional employees have the right to a separate unit. The governing body may limit or prohibit the right of organization of certain positions or classes of positions primarily concerned with enforcement of state or local law.

(7) Organization and noninterference rights are accorded employees. The public agency may adopt rules and regulations regarding employment relations pursuant to the statute.

(9) Mediation may be agreed to by the parties, or the dispute may be submitted to the Department of Conciliation.

Cal. Gov't Code §§3525—3536, added by Stats 1971, ch. 254, effective December 1, 1971.

(1) These provisions were added to cover employees of the state, meaning such state agencies, boards, commissions, administrative officers, or other representatives as may be designated by law. The governor's appointees and elected officials are excluded.

(3) The state may adopt rules to administer the provisions.

(4), (5) The state is required to meet and confer on request and shall consider all matters relating to employment conditions and employer-employee relations, including, but not limited to, wages, hours, and other terms and conditions of employment.

(6) Professional employees have the right to a separate unit. The state may limit or prohibit the right of designated classes of employees to organize.

(7) The right of organization and of representation are accorded employees, except for the statutory restriction noted in (6) above.

Cal. Educ. Code §§13080—13088, added by Stats 1965, ch. 2041; as amended by Stats 1970, ch. 1412, ch. 1413.

(1) The Winton Act of 1965 removed public school employees from the general category of public agency employees and specifically provided for collective bargaining of public school employee organizations.

(3) The public school employer (i.e., each employer as defined in §13081) is required to adopt reasonable rules and regulations for the administration of employer-employee relations under the act. Certain required and recommended rules and provisions are enumerated.

(4), (5) The employer "shall meet and confer with representatives of certificated and classified employee organizations upon request" on employment conditions and employer-employee relations, including, but not limited to, wages, hours, and other terms and conditions of employment. An employee organization has standing to sue the employer. There is also an obligation to meet and confer with representatives of certificated employees on procedures relating to educational objectives, course content, textbooks, and related matters within the employer's discretion. The term "meet and confer" is defined as a mutual obligation to exchange information freely and to make and consider recommendations under orderly procedures in a conscientious effort to reach agreement.

(6) Employees have the right to choose their own organization, but if more than one organization represents certificated employees, provision is made for one certificated employee council

of five to nine members chosen proportionately to meet with the employer. Each organization may appoint a number of council members proportionate to the ratio its membership bears to the total number of certificated employees.

(7) The statute prohibits employer appointment of classified employee representatives. Interference with the individual employees' rights by the employer or the employee organization is prohibited. The public school employer makes the final decision as to those matters specified for negotiation under §13085.

(9) A procedure for the "resolution of persistent disagreements" is to be worked out by the parties. If no procedure can be agreed upon, one party may request a committee of three to make nonbinding recommendations.

(11) The Winton Act asserts that its provisions are intended to "strengthen" such matters as tenure, merit, and civil service. Moreover, the 1970 amendment to §13080 added the following paragraph:

It is the further intention of the Legislature that nothing contained in this article shall be construed to restrict, limit, or prohibit the full exercise of the functions of any academic senate or faculty council established by a school district in a community college to represent the faculty in making recommendations to the administration and governing board of such school district with respect to district policies on academic and professional matters.

The 1970 amendment to the act also required that all initial wage proposals of the employee organizations must be presented to the employer at a public meeting and made a matter of public record.

Connecticut

Conn. Gen. Stat. Rev. §§10—153a-f, added by 1961, P.A. 562; as amended by 1969, P.A. 811.

(1) Public school 'teachers and certified administrators below the rank of assistant superintendent (unless employed directly by the board) are covered by the statute.

(4), (5) The statute imposes a mutual "duty to negotiate" and to "meet" and "confer in good faith" on salaries and other conditions of employment, but the obligation "shall not compel either party" to agree to a proposal or make a concession.

(6) Teachers and certified administrators are to be placed in separate units, and the statute provides who may be included in each unit. A majority of the employees in either unit may, by petition for recognition, designate any organization of certified professional employees as exclusive representative. Extensive provisions cover the selection of representatives.

(7) The right to organize free of interference from the employer is assured. Strikes are prohibited and injunction is the statutory remedy for enforcement.

(9) A governor-appointed arbitration panel is available for advisory mediation and nonbinding arbitration of disputes. The costs are divided equally between the parties. The secretary of the state Board of Education has the power to require use of arbitration services and may make nonbinding recommendations.

Delaware

Del. Code Ann. tit. 19, §§1301—1312, added by 55 Del. Laws, ch. 126, 1965; as amended by 57 Del. Laws, ch. 669, 1970.

(1) This comprehensive law covers all public employees of the state and its agencies, counties and their agencies, and those municipalities which elect by legislative action of their governing bodies to come within the act. Public employees do not include elected officials, the governor's appointees, and certified professional employees of the public schools.

(3) The Department of Labor is the administering agency.

(4), (5) The parties have a mutual obligation to "bargain collectively," i.e., to meet and confer and negotiate in good faith, and to execute a written agreement with respect to employment relations. They are not compelled to agree or concede, however.

(6) Determination of the employee unit and exclusive representation are provided for.

(7) Organization rights are accorded. Strikes are prohibited. There is no unfair practices provision.

(8) Dues are deducted upon written authorization of the employee.

(9) Disputes on all matters except wages and salaries may be submitted by either party to the Department of Labor or, upon

agreement of both parties, to arbitration pursuant to the statutory procedure of tit. 19, ch. 1.

Del. Code Ann. tit. 14, §§4001—4013, added by 57 Del. Laws, ch. 298, 1969.

(1) The law covers certificated nonadministrative public school employees and excludes supervisory or staff personnel. It was enacted because certified professional employees of public school systems were prohibited from organizing under Delaware's general law covering public employees (Del. Code Ann. tit. 19, §§1301—1312).

(3) The district school boards are directed to administer the statutory requirements as to petitions, elections, and other matters, with right of approval by the state Board of Education.

(4), (5) The statute imposes on both parties a "duty to negotiate in good faith with respect to salaries, employee benefits, and working conditions" and to "meet at reasonable times and confer in good faith" on those matters.

(6) A majority of the employees choose the exclusive representative, which is certified for a minimum of two years following recognition or election.

(7) Employees have the right to organize free of employer interference. Tactics (e.g., strikes) which circumvent the teachers' contract are unlawful. If the exclusive representative violates the provisions, certification is revoked and ineligibility of two years is imposed. Violation by any employee organization results in a one-year suspension of dues collection. Strikes are prohibited, and individual strikers get unexcused absences.

(8) The employer is required to deduct dues upon written request of the individual employee.

(9) Factfinding and nonbinding arbitration procedures are set out, with costs divided equally.

(11) Other statutory provisions in title 14 take precedence over this chapter (40) if agreements pursuant to this chapter are in conflict with any other chapter.

District of Columbia

District Commissioner's Order #70-229, June 19, 1970, established a Board of Labor Relations to protect collective bargaining rights under the National Labor Relations Act and to resolve disputes involving public service employees. The National Labor Relations Board is said to have plenary jurisdiction over unfair labor practices and matters of representation in the District and exercises that jurisdiction without regard to the regular jurisdictional criteria.

Florida

Fla. Stat. §839.221, added by Laws 1959, ch. 59–223.

All public employees of the state or any of its political subdivisions have the right to organize or to join or continue to belong to organizations free of interference or coercion. They have the right to present proposals on salaries and other conditions of employment through representatives they choose. But striking or asserting the right to strike against a public employer, or knowingly belonging to an organization that asserts the right to strike, is prohibited. One who does so cannot be hired or retained in public employment.

Two 1971 Florida statutes established the right of public school teachers in two counties (Hillsborough and Pinellas) to organize and negotiate. Although the laws were passed within the same week, they are not identical. (Hillsborough, L. 1971, ch. 71-686, effective July 3, 1971; Pinellas, L. 1971, ch. 71-875, effective June 27, 1971.)

(1) Teachers are defined the same in both statutes.

(4) Hillsborough requires the board to meet and confer in good faith within ten days after request; Pinellas states that the parties "may begin" negotiating in good faith within ten days.

(5) Hillsborough defines the scope of negotiations in more detail, but both have a broad range of negotiable matters.

(6) Selection of representatives in both is by a majority of the unit.

(7) Both bestow rights to organize, to negotiate, and to have recognition of the bargaining agent. Both prohibit strikes, but Pinellas defines strike extensively.

(8) Hillsborough has a dues collection provision.

(9) Hillsborough provides for arbitration by a board of three, with selection of one by each side and a third by those two. If

the third one is not agreed upon, either party may request the American Arbitration Association to name a third. In either case, the third serves as chairman. Decision by arbitration is advisory only, with fees borne equally.

Georgia

In 1968, Georgia enacted a statute (Ga. L. 1968, No. 967) granting the right of organization and collective bargaining to all public employees of Chatham County and the City of Savannah. Any statute or provision in conflict with the act was said to be repealed by the act. The Georgia Supreme Court ruled the statute unconstitutional on the grounds that a 1962 law (Ga. Code Ann. §§39-309, 39-310) gave municipalities the authority to control employment matters of their employees. *Local 574, International Association of Firefighters, AFL-CIO v. Floyd,* 72 LRRM 2504 (1969).

Hawaii

Session Laws of Hawaii, P.A. 171, L. 1970, as amended by P.A. 212, L. 1971. See 4 Labor Relations Reporter SLL 21:224.

(1), (2) All public employees in Hawaii are covered by the act except elected and appointed officials or other top-level personnel, individuals concerned with confidential employee-employer relations, part-time and temporary workers, and the Hawaii national guard. Section 6(a) of the act lists thirteen appropriate bargaining units for all employees throughout the state in those categories. Faculty of the University of Hawaii and the community college system constitute one unit, and personnel other than faculty make up another unit.

(3) The act creates the Hawaii Public Employment Relations Board as the agency to administer the act. The board has three full-time paid members appointed by the governor—one representative of labor, one of management, and one of the public.

(4), (5) Collective bargaining is defined as a mutual obligation to "meet at reasonable times, to confer and negotiate in good faith" concerning wages, hours, and other terms and conditions of employment, with neither party under compulsion to agree or concede. The statute excludes certain matters from the bargaining process: classification; retirement benefits; salary ranges; and the statutory incremental, and longevity steps. The unit principle controls, and the principle of equal pay for equal work prevails. Managerial rights are listed in detail and are reserved to the employer.

(6) The statute directs that all state employees in any of the thirteen categories enumerated constitute an appropriate bargaining unit. There is statutory provision for the option to be in specific units such as registered nurses, firemen, or policemen, or to vote to belong to the larger categories for nonsupervisory white collar or blue collar, or supervisory white collar or blue collar employees. Specific guidelines to determine the employee negotiating unit are included in §6(b) of the act. Section 8(c) covers employee participation in the actual bargaining process.

(7) The statute asserts organization rights and the right to exclusive representation. Section 12 of the act permits strikes under certain circumstances, while prohibiting strikes in others. Striking is unlawful for an employee not in an appropriate unit with a certified exclusive representative or in a unit subject to binding arbitration. An employee in an appropriate unit, not prohibited for the above reasons, may strike if (1) the statutory requirements with respect to resolution of disputes have been complied with in good faith; (2) proceedings to prevent prohibited practices have been exhausted; (3) it is sixty days after the factfinding board has made public its recommendations; and (4) the representative has given ten-day notice of intent to strike. Other provisions of section 12 direct the board to act to avoid strikes endangering public health or safety [§12(c)], detail the procedure for declaring a strike illegal, and authorize injunctive proceedings for enforcement. Section 13 lists eight unfair practices prohibited to a public employer or its representative and five practices prohibited to a public employee or his representative. Penalties are stated. Section 14 provides that a controversy concerning prohibited practices may be submitted to the board.

(8) Section 4 authorizes payroll deductions for union dues and for service fees in the case of nonunion employees.

(9), (10) Section 11 provides that an agreement may include a grievance procedure or an impasse procedure culminating in binding arbitration. If this is not done, disputes or impasses may be submitted to the board for a binding decision. The board may determine independently that an impasse exists and assist in its resolution by following the statutory procedures of mediation, factfinding, and arbitration. Costs for mediation and factfinding are borne by the board; all other costs are borne by the parties involved.

(11) Any person who, by violence or other means, willfully prevents any officials or any of their agents or employees from carrying out their duties under the act shall be fined $500, imprisoned up to a year, or both.

Section 10(b) provides that all cost items agreed upon are subject to legislative appropriation by the appropriate body and upon submission must be accepted or rejected as a whole.

Idaho

Idaho has no general labor relations act, but a number of statutes declare support for the organizational rights of employees for the purpose of achieving voluntary agreement. (§44-701 of the 1933 Anti-Injunction Act; §§44-103, 44-107, and 44-107A of the 1949 act establishing the Department of Labor.)

Municipalities have the power to enter into collective bargaining agreements if they wish and if no local ordinance forbids it. (Attorney General Opinion, March 18, 1959.)

L. 1971, H.B. 209. See 4 Labor Relations Reporter SLL 22:223.

(1) The act covers certificated employees of a school district, but superintendents, supervisors, or principals may be excluded if the negotiation agreement so specifies.

(4), (5) The two parties are to meet and confer in good faith to reach an agreement on matters specified in a negotiation agreement previously made between the parties.

(6) The majority of the employees designate an exclusive representative. Negotiators for employees must be members of the representative organization and professional employees of the local school district.

(7) Organization rights are provided. Section 6 of the act states that the lawful powers, duties, and responsibilities of the legislature, state board of education, and local boards are not affected by the act.

(9) Appointment of mediators is authorized, with procedure and compensation to be determined by the parties. If mediation fails, the parties may agree to advisory factfinding, with provision for appointment of factfinders by the state superintendent of public instruction in the event the parties cannot agree.

Indiana

The General Assembly retains the power to enter into bargaining agreements with exclusive representatives until such power is granted to state agencies. (Attorney General's Opinion, August 8, 1969.) State supervisory or professional employees are advised not to join associations primarily composed of their subordinate employees, though they may do so. (Attorney General's Opinion No. 25, June 6, 1968.) An earlier opinion states that, unless otherwise forbidden by statute, state and local public officials may consult with employee representatives on wages, hours, and working conditions. (Attorney General's Opinion No. 22, October 6, 1966.)

Kansas

S.B. 333, L. 1971, effective March 1, 1972. See 4 Labor Relations Reporter SLL 26:231.

(1) The act covers all public employees of any public agency except supervisory employees, professional employees of school districts (covered by H.B. 1647), elected and management officials, and confidential employees. A "public agency" is defined as the state and its agencies and every governmental subdivision, including special districts, boards, and other similar units. Any public employer other than the state and its agencies may elect, by majority vote of its governing body, to bring itself and its employees under the act. This binds both employer and employee by the provisions of the act until rescission by a majority vote of the governing body. The vote to rescind cannot take effect until the end of the next complete budget year following the vote.

(3) The public employment relations board created by the act is the administering agency.

(4), (5) The act imposes a mutual obligation to meet and confer in good faith in order to freely exchange information, opinions, and proposals to try to reach agreement on grievances and conditions of employment, subject to federal and state laws and ordinances; rights of employees and employers as defined in this act; and the authority of civil service commissions and personnel boards or their agencies. A contract is limited to three years.

(6) The act provides for unit determination and exclusive representation. Specific guidelines for unit delineation are set out in §7 of the act.

(7) Organization and noninterference rights are specified. Pro-

hibited practices are enumerated as to both employer and the employee organization. Strikes and lockouts are prohibited, and injunctive relief is authorized.

(9) Procedures for dispute resolution may be included in memoranda of agreement. If there are no such procedures, or they fail, the board may appoint mediators, and, if mediation fails, a fact-finding board. If that fails, every governing body, except the state and its agencies, holds a hearing and takes action. The final hearing procedure is inapplicable to the state and its agencies.

(10) Grievance procedures are provided for.

H.B. 1647, effective March 23, 1970. See 4 Labor Relations Reporter SLL 26:228.

(1), (2) The law covers both certificated professional personnel and administrative personnel employed by a board of education or by a community junior college board of trustees. Administrative employees must be in a separate unit.

(3) The state board of education decides questions of representation.

(4), (5) Professional negotiation is defined as meeting, conferring, consulting, and discussing in good faith to reach agreement concerning terms and conditions of professional service.

(6) Representatives are exclusive for all members of each unit (teaching or administrative).

(7) Organization rights are covered. The act states that nothing in the act is to be construed to authorize a strike. Managerial rights imposed by law are reserved, but boards are required to grant recognition and negotiate.

(9), (10) An agreement may include procedures for final and binding arbitration of disputes. Where such procedures are provided, an aggrieved party may seek a summary court order directing arbitration.

Maine

Me. Rev. Stat. Ann. tit. 26, §§961—972, added by 1969, ch. 424; as amended by 1970, ch. 578.

(1) The act covers employees of "any officer, board, commission, council, committee or other persons or body acting on behalf of any municipality or town or any subdivision thereof, or of any school, water, sewer or other district." The following are excluded:

elected or appointed people, top-level or confidential administrative people, superintendents and assistant superintendents of school systems, employees of less than six months, and temporary employees.

(3) The commissioner of the Department of Labor and Industry administers the act and the Maine Board of Arbitration and Conciliation may be used for factfinding.

(4), (5) The statute imposes a mutual obligation "to confer and negotiate in good faith" with respect to wages, hours, working conditions, and contract grievance arbitration. Neither party is compelled to agree to concede. Public employers of teachers cannot negotiate about educational policies. Civil service matters lie outside the scope of bargaining. However, an agreement may contain provisions for arbitration of grievances regarding changes in employee status, and these shall control in the event of conflict with municipal civil service or personnel board policy.

(6) The exclusive bargaining agent is chosen by the majority of the bargaining unit. A unit may include professionals and nonprofessionals only if a majority of the professionals vote for inclusion. Principals and other supervisory employees may be included in school units. The employer may voluntarily recognize the bargaining agent or petition the commissioner for an election. There is a right of appeal to the Public Employees Labor Relations Appeal Board from rulings of the commissioner on determination of unit or agent.

(7) The statute protects the employees' right to organize free from employer interference or blacklisting. Employee strikes and blacklisting are prohibited. Injunction is the court remedy of parties aggrieved by violation of the statute.

(9) Provisions are made for mediation, factfinding, and arbitration, which is binding in areas other than salaries, pensions, and insurance.

Maryland

Md. Ann. Code, art. 77, §160, added by 1968, ch. 483; as amended by 1971, ch. 427.

(1) The statute covers all certificated public school employees except superintendents and negotiators for the employer.

(3) The State Board of Education conducts elections for exclusive representation.

(4), (5) The employer "shall meet and negotiate" (i.e., "confer in good faith") with the employee representative upon the latter's request with regard to "salaries, wages, hours, and other working conditions." This is subject to final determination by the employer and subject, further, to higher level determination of fiscal matters. (Baltimore also has a 1968 regulation mandating negotiation in good faith with municipal employees.)

(6) The statute provides specific requirements for exclusive representation.

(7) The right to organize free of interference is guaranteed. The penalty for striking, which is prohibited, is revocation of exclusive representative designation and a two-year ineligibility and suspension of payroll deductions for one year. The law is subject to other provisions of the code and rules of tenure.

(8) Collection of dues is not specifically provided for, but it may be assumed from the above provision for suspension of collection upon violation of the no-strike provision.

(9) The State Board of Education mediates an impasse in negotiations, as provided by §160(i). The parties may include in their agreement a provision for binding arbitration.

Massachusetts

Mass. Gen. Laws Ann. ch. 149, §§178B—N, as amended by 1970, 292, 340, 445 and 463.

(1) The law is applicable to all employees of the state or any political subdivision thereof except elected or appointed personnel and executive officers of municipalities and those state employees who would have a conflict of interest between their official duties and employee organization activity. Sections 178 B—F are applicable to all employees of the state and its subdivisions. Sections 178 G—N cover municipal employees. Section 178G specifically includes professional employees at the municipal level. The provisions are similar, except where indicated below.

(3) The Labor Relations Commission administers the law.

(4), (5) The statute imposes a mutual obligation to "meet" and "confer in good faith" with respect to conditions of employment. Neither party can be compelled to agree or concede. Contract periods are limited to three years.

(6) Appropriate collective bargaining units are to be based on a

community of interest. If agreement on the unit cannot be reached, the Labor Relations Commission resolves the dispute. Professionals and nonprofessionals may join in a unit only if a majority of the professionals vote for inclusion. Exclusive representation is achieved either by consent or by election supervised by the commission.

(7) Rights of organization are assured. Strikes are prohibited, as is interference on both sides.

(8) Collection of agency service fees from municipal employees is authorized.

(9) At the state level, requests for factfinding are made to the director of personnel and standardization. At the municipal level, petitions for factfinding are directed to the board of conciliation and arbitration. Costs are to be divided equally.

(10) At the state level, unfair practices on either side may be taken to the commission, which may issue findings of fact and recommendations. At the municipal level, the commission may issue cease and desist orders and take other affirmative actions relative to such unfair practices. The use of other arbitration tribunals regarding disputes over interpretations or applications of agreements is also permitted. Municipal employee grievances are brought to the commission, which can order reinstatement of a discharged employee.

(11) At the municipal level, where there is conflict between the agreement and any law, ordinance, or by-law, the latter prevail, except for regulations made by the chief of police or the fire department. Funds for implementation are also subject to appropriation by the local legislative body except in certain school situations.

Michigan

Mich. Comp. Laws Ann. §§423.201—423.216, *as amended by P.A. 1965, No. 379.*

(1) Michigan has a comprehensive law covering public employees.

(3) The administering agency is the Michigan Employment Relations Commission, which is invested with broad powers in areas where statutory specifications are lacking.

(4), (5) The statute imposes a mutual obligation to "bargain collectively" over "wages, hours, and other terms and conditions of employment," defined as meeting at reasonable times and conferring in good faith.

(6) The commission decides the appropriate unit and conducts elections for exclusive representation.

(7) Strikes and employer consent to strikes are prohibited, and the prohibited conduct is elaborately described. The right to organize without interference is affirmed. Interference, discrimination, and other unfair labor practices by the employer are remediable by the labor mediation board. There is no similar list of unfair practices by employees.

(10) Grievances are submitted to the labor mediation board.

Minnesota

S.B.4, L. 1971, effective July 1, 1972, repealing the previous public employee law and the teachers law of 1967. See 4A Labor Relations Reporter SLL 33:248c.

(1) The public employment labor relations act of 1971 is comprehensive and applies to all public employees of the state, its political subdivisions, and any agency or instrumentality of either. Excluded are only those employees such as elected officials and part-time employees enumerated in §3 of the act. Specific statutory procedures cover all facets of employer-employee relations.

(2) The University of Minnesota and all state and junior colleges are explicitly named as public employers [§3(4)].

(3) A two-layer administrative procedure is established, using the director of the bureau of mediation services and the public employment relations board created by the act.

(4), (5) The statute distinguishes between a mutual obligation to "meet and negotiate" in good faith on terms and conditions of employment, excluding educational policies of school districts, and a "meet and confer" obligation to exchange views and concerns [§3(15), (16), (18)]. Policy consultations with professional employees are encouraged, and provision is made for per diem compensation for consultants selected in the manner provided by the statute (§13). The scope of discussion includes all matters not specified as subjects for negotiation in §3.

Several types of bargaining obligations of employees are thus provided for in the act, and certain restrictions are placed on the scope of negotiation required. There is an obligation (a) to meet and negotiate with the exclusive representative on grievance procedures and the terms and conditions of employment; (b) to meet and confer with professional employees on policy and all matters relating to their employment; and (c) to meet and confer with supervisory and confidential employees and with principals and assistant principals, or their representatives, on the terms and conditions of their employment. There is no obligation to negotiate as to matters of inherent managerial policy or the educational policies of a school district with a teachers' representative.

(6) There is provision for unit determination, formal and informal recognition, exclusive representation for bargaining purposes, and negotiation procedures. Informal recognition is granted any employee organization which has the right to meet and confer.

(7) Organization and noninterference rights are asserted. Strike is defined in §3(12) and prohibited by §4. Violation of the section is punishable by termination of employment, and there is a procedure for a hearing on removal. Organizations in violation lose status as exclusive representatives and are ineligible for two years.

(8) Provision is made for dues check-off.

(9) An elaborate procedure for impasse resolution, including binding arbitration, is set out in §9. District courts have jurisdiction to enjoin or restrain threatened violations of the act, appoint hearing referees, and hear and decide appeals from arbitration decisions made pursuant to the statutory grievance procedure.

(10) All contracts must include a grievance procedure providing compulsory binding arbitration for grievances. If such a procedure cannot be agreed upon, the parties are subject to the grievance procedure promulgated by the director of mediation services pursuant to the authority given him in §11(5)(i). Every employee has the right to independent review of any grievance arising out of his employment.

Missouri

Mo. Ann. Stat. §§105.500—105.530, as amended by Laws 1967, p. 192.

(1) Employees of any public body are covered by the statute, except police, deputy sheriffs, state highway patrolmen, the national guard, and all teachers of public schools, colleges, and universities.

(3) The state board of mediation resolves issues concerning bargaining units and representative status, with appeal to the circuit court authorized.

(4), (5) The public employer is obliged to "meet, confer, and discuss" proposals of the exclusive representative with regard to salaries and other conditions of employment. There is no mandate to adopt or execute an agreement.

(6) The appropriate unit is one which establishes a "community of interest." An exclusive representative is designated by a majority vote.

(7) The law is not to "be construed as granting a right to . . . strike."

Montana

H.B. 455, L. 1971, effective July 1, 1971. See 4A Labor Relations Reporter SLL 36:213.

(1) The Professional Negotiations Act for teachers covers certified public school employees in classes designated by §3 of the act and certificated principals in class 3 who elect to be covered.

(3) The public school boards administer the act.

(4), (5) The act imposes a mutual obligation "to meet and confer" on matters relating directly to the employer-teacher relationship (i.e., salary, hours, and other terms of employment) and to bargain for agreement. Excluded from bargaining are matters of curricula, operation policy, and the selection of teachers and other school faculties. Agreements must be ratified by a majority of the employee unit and a majority of the board if the latter used a professional negotiator.

(6) An appropriate unit means all of the teachers employed by a district. Principals may elect to be included or to be in a separate unit. Any teacher organization which has a majority of the teachers as members shall be recognized as the exclusive representative. There is provision for election in other cases.

(7) Organization and noninterference rights are provided. Prohibited unfair practices of both employer and employees are enumerated. Strikes, boycotts, and picketing are listed as unfair practices. Judicial review is authorized. Penalties for violation of the no-strike provision are imposed.

(9) Advisory mediation by a panel selected as the statute directs is available.

Nebraska

Neb. Rev. Stat. §§79-1287—79-1295 (Laws 1967, ch. 518).

(1) The Nebraska Teachers Professional Negotiation Act covers certificated employees in the public school districts.

(3) District boards of education adopt rules to administer negotiations.

(4), (5) The statute requires only that the board meet or confer with an organization recognized by a majority of the board members. The employee representative makes a written request to meet and confer, specifying the areas to be discussed. The board has thirty days to accept or reject.

(9) If the parties cannot agree, a three-member factfinding board is chosen (one chosen by each party and the third chosen by the two selected members) to make advisory recommendations. The state Department of Education helps secure this service.

Nevada

Laws 1969, ch. 650, as amended by A.B. 178, Laws 1971, ch. 340. See 4A Labor Relations Reporter SLL 38:226.

(1) The Local Government Employee-Management Relations Act covers local government employees of any political subdivision or any public or quasi-public corporation, including school districts and special districts and nurses employed by the state.

(3) The Local Government Employee-Management Relations Board administers the act. The board is created by the act and its three members are appointed by the governor.

(4), (5) The statute imposes a mutual obligation to negotiate in good faith concerning wages, hours, and conditions of employment, subject to the reservations of management rights enumerated in §§10-12.

(6) The employer determines the appropriate bargaining unit following the statutory guidelines in §12. Appeals from decisions may be taken to the local government employee-management relations board. The board's decision is binding, subject to judicial review.

(7) The employees have organization and noninterference rights. Strikes are illegal, and an application to the employer for recognition of an organization must contain a pledge not to strike. Management rights are reserved.

(9) Upon failure to reach agreement by negotiation, the dispute

may be submitted to factfinding or arbitration as provided in §15. If the parties do not agree that the results shall be binding, the governor may so order.

(10) The Local Government Employee-Management Relations Board hears complaints of aggrieved parties. The judicial remedy for enforcement of a board order is an injunction.

New Hampshire

N.H. Rev. Stat. Ann. §§*98-C:1—98-C:7, added by 1969, 290:1; as amended by 1970, 41:1.*

(1), (2) The act covers classified state employees and nonacademic employees (except department heads and executive officers) of the University of New Hampshire, including Keene State College, Plymouth State College, and the Merrimack Valley Branch.

(3) For all except the nonacademic university and state college employees, a three-man commission administers the act. The members are the chairman of the state personnel commission, the commission of labor, and the secretary of state. For higher education employees, the commission is the university vice president-treasurer, a person chosen by the nonacademic employees, and a third member chosen by the two.

(4) The chief executive officer of a unit or his representative is required to meet with the employee representative upon request and to "bargain in good faith" in order to reach agreement.

(5) The contract may be for five years and may include, but is not limited to, grievance procedures, procedures for conferring about personnel policies, mediation or factfinding procedures, and arbitration (which may be binding unless it is incompatible with existing law or requires appropriation of additional funds).

(6) The commission determines the appropriate unit of not less than ten employees, and for nonacademic employees of not less than the entire campus of any one division.

(7) Organization and noninterference rights are assured. Every agreement must contain a no-strike clause which survives the agreement and is in effect until a new agreement is negotiated; individual and organization penalties are imposed for striking. The state retains the prerogatives of management listed in §98-C:7.

(8) Provision is made for dues collection if individually authorized.

(10) The agreement may contain grievance procedures.

N.H. Rev. Stat. Ann. §31:3.

This section provides that towns may enter into collective bargaining contracts with employee unions.

New Jersey

N.J. Rev. Stat. Ann. §§34:13A-1—34:13A-11, as amended by L. 1968, ch. 303.

(1) The Employer-Employee Relations Act covers public and private employees in the public sector excluding elected officials, administrators, members of boards and commissions, and the superintendent or other chief administrator of a school district.

(3) The act creates a division of private employment dispute settlement and a division of public employment relations as administering agencies. A public employment relations commission is within the latter division.

(4), (5) The parties in the public sector shall meet at reasonable times and "negotiate in good faith" as to grievances and terms and conditions of employment. Rules governing working conditions must be negotiated with the public employer representative before they are established.

(6) The division decides the appropriate public employer unit under the statutory guidelines: a unit cannot include supervisors and employees except under stated circumstances; professionals and nonprofessionals, as well as craft and noncraft employees, may be in one unit only if a majority of the professionals or the craft employees vote for inclusion.

(7) Organization and noninterference rights are assured. The act asserts that nothing in it shall be construed to interfere with the right of private employees to strike. No unfair practices provision is included.

(9) The commission is authorized to effect voluntary resolution of an impasse.

(10) Public employers must negotiate written policies on grievance procedures and they may provide for binding arbitration.

New York

N.Y. Civ. Serv. Law, as amended by L. 1971, ch. 503.

(1) The act covers public employees, excluding appointees, the militia, and managerial or confidential employees.

(2) Included as a public employer is any governmental entity operating a public school, college, or university.

(3) The public employment relations board administers the act.

(4), (5) The statute imposes a mutual obligation to "negotiate collectively in good faith" concerning "salaries, wages, hours and other terms and conditions of employment." Some contract provisions become binding only with legislative approval.

(6) Elaborate procedures are set forth to determine representation status, including the power of local governments to establish their own procedures. In disputes the public employment relations board defines the appropriate unit.

(7) Employees have organization and noninterference rights. Strikes and the cause, investigation, encouragement, or confirmation of strikes are prohibited. Strikers are subject to one year of probation and to deduction of twice their daily pay for each day they are out. An organization forfeits rights and is subject to a fine payable from dues deduction if available no other way. Before certification, any right to strike or assist with a strike must be disclaimed.

(8) The act provides for dues deductions.

(9) A procedure for resolution of disputes in which an impasse is deemed to exist (no agreement twenty days before the end of the employer's fiscal year) includes voluntary arbitration. Legislative bodies may act as a final resort in disputes.

(11) Injunctive relief is available through the supreme court. Special provision is made for local government procedures, especially in New York City.

North Carolina

N.C. Gen. Stat. §§95-85—95-88 (1959).

These provisions prohibit public employees from becoming members of unions for purposes of collective bargaining, declares contracts between government units and labor unions to be illegal, and declares any violation to be a misdemeanor. The prohibition on union membership and the misdemeanor provision were invalidated and the no-contract provision was upheld by a special three-judge U.S. District Court in *Atkins v. City of Charlotte,* 70 LRRM 2732.

North Dakota

N.D. Cent. Code §§15-38.1-02—15-38.1-15, added by S.L. 1969, ch. 172.

(1) Public school teachers and administrators are covered by the act.

(3) The act creates an education factfinding commission. Local school boards also administer the act.

(4), (5) There is a mutual obligation to "meet at reasonable times" and "negotiate in good faith" as to "terms and conditions of employment and employer-employee relations," the formulation of an agreement (which may include binding arbitration), and interpretation of any existing agreement.

(6) School boards accept or reject employee determination of an appropriate unit and employees, upon acceptance, select a representative organization. There is provision for elections. Administrators and teachers use separate units.

(7) Organization rights are assured. Strikes are prohibited and the penalty is loss of wages. Powers of boards are reserved.

(9) An impasse is defined, and mediation and factfinding for resolving it are set forth in the act.

Oklahoma

H.B. 1325, L. 1971. See 4A Labor Relations Reporter SLL 46:230.

(1) Certified public school teachers and nonprofessional school employees are covered.

(3) Local school boards administer the act.

(4), (5) The statute imposes a mutual obligation to "negotiate in good faith on items affecting the performance of professional services."

(6) The exclusive representative is chosen by the majority of the unit. Teachers and nonprofessionals must have separate units.

(7) Strikes are prohibited and penalties are imposed for violation.

(9) The statute provides for a three-member factfinding committee to resolve impasses.

Oregon

L. 1963, ch. 647, as amended by S.B. 55, L. 1969, effective July 1, 1969. See 4A Labor Relations Reporter SLL 47:234a.

(1) The law covers the state and any of its agencies and institutions and includes any political subdivision that requests the aid of the public employee relations board in settling a dispute with a labor organization.

(3) The public employee relations board administers the act.

(4), (5) The statute imposes a mutual obligation to meet and confer in good faith with respect to employment relations, including, but not limited to, matters of direct or indirect monetary benefits, hours, vacation, sick leave, grievance procedures, and other conditions of employment.

(6) Provision is made for exclusive representation by organizations certified by the public employee relations board. Any board or commission which, pursuant to state law, administers a civil service system is required to establish rules for the designation of the bargaining unit and election of the representative.

(7) Organization and noninterference rights are provided.

(9) Mediation, factfinding, and voluntary arbitration are provided in the statute. The attorney general has ruled that binding arbitration clauses are valid in public employee contracts. (Attorney General's Opinion No. 6571, November 1, 1968.)

Ore. Rev. Stat. §§342.450—342.470, as amended by L. 1971, ch. 755, effective September 9, 1971.

(1) Teachers and administrators of public schools are covered by the law.

(3) The district school board is the administering agency.

(4), (5) The law imposes a mutual obligation "to confer, consult and discuss in good faith," in a free exchange of information, opinions, and proposals, to try to reach agreement on "salaries and related economic policies" affecting professional services, grievance procedures, and compensation for additional duties.

(6) Specific procedures for unit determination and exclusive representation include election based on 40 percent certified enrollment in an organization or 30 percent on a petition (plus 10 percent for each additional organization).

(7) Organization rights are stated.

(9) There is a directed timetable for negotiations in relation to a mandated budget calendar. Mediation is required if agreement is not reached sixty days before the fixed date for delivery of

the budget message. Factfinding is required if agreement is lacking ten days after appointment of the mediator. The factfinder must report in writing within fifteen days. Consultation is permitted throughout the mediation-factfinding period.

L. 1971, ch. 582 has similar provisions for nonteaching, classified school personnel.

Pennsylvania

Penna. Stat. Ann. tit. 43, §1101.101—1101.2301, added by Act No. 195, effective July 23, 1970.

(1) The comprehensive public employee relations act covers employees of the state and its political subdivisions and "any nonprofit organization or institution and any charitable, religious, scientific, literary, recreational, health, educational or welfare institution receiving grants or appropriations from local, state or federal governments" if not covered by the private sector state act or the National Labor Relations Act.

(3) The state labor relations board is the administering agency.

(4), (5) The law imposes a mutual obligation to "meet" and "confer in good faith" regarding "wages, hours, and other terms and conditions of employment." There is also a requirement only to "meet and discuss" policy matters that affect the above. Public employers are not required to bargain with units of first level supervisors, but only to "meet and discuss" with them.

(6) There are provisions for exclusive representation and for unit determination, the latter to be made in accordance with the specific statutory criteria (e.g., professionals must agree by majority vote to inclusion with nonprofessionals in a unit and first level supervisors must have their own unit).

(7) Strikes and refusal to cross a picket line by guards at prison or mental hospitals and by personnel essential to the functioning of the courts are prohibited. Others may strike or refuse to cross a picket line only after the statutory impasse procedures have been exhausted, and this action will not be prohibited unless or until it creates "a clear and present danger or threat to the health, safety or welfare of the public." Unfair labor practices on both sides are listed with detailed procedures for prevention and for court response to their occurrence during the bargaining process.

(8) Dues check-off and maintenance of membership are proper subjects for bargaining.

(9) Impasse resolution is keyed to a schedule of deadlines for mediation and factfinding related to the fixed budget submission date (the state pays half the cost of factfinding). Voluntary binding arbitration is also permitted, and it is a required final step for guards in prisons and mental hospitals and personnel essential to the functioning of the courts. Agreements or arbitration decisions requiring legislative action are effective only if such legislation is enacted.

(10) Arbitration of grievances is mandatory and the grievance procedure is a proper subject of bargaining.

Rhode Island

R.I. Gen. Laws Ann. §§36-11-1—36-11-6, as amended by P.L. 1970, ch. 116.

(1) The law covers state employees, including employees and members of state police below the rank of lieutenant. The provisions of the state labor relations act are applicable to state employees, but the right to strike is denied.

(3) The state labor relations board is the administering agency.

(4), (5) The statute imposes an obligation on the employer to "negotiate" on such "matters pertaining to wages, hours and working conditions" as are within the officials' budgetary control. Exclusive procedures under a merit system statute or rule must be followed.

(6) Provisions are made in the state labor relations act for determination of the unit and for exclusive representation.

(7) Organization and noninterference rights are accorded but strikes are prohibited. The state labor relations act provision as to unfair practices of employees is applicable.

(9), (10) State officials have the duty "to exert every reasonable effort" to resolve disputes. Supervisors at all levels have the responsibility to act promptly on grievances.

R.I. Gen. Laws Ann. §§28-9.4-1—28-9.4-19, as reenacted by P.L. 1970, ch. 9.

(1) The Municipal Employees' Arbitration Act covers municipal employees except elected and administrative officials, board and commission members, certified teachers, policemen, firefighters,

supervisors, and part-time employees. Teachers, firemen, and policemen are covered by other statutes.

(3) The state labor relations board is the administering agency.

(4), (5) The employer is obligated "to meet and confer in good
faith" concerning "hours, salary, working conditions and all other
terms and conditions of employment."

(6) Explicit provisions are made for determination of the unit
and the exclusive agent. Written notice must be given regarding
money matters at least 120 days before the last day on which
funds can be appropriated to cover the first year of the contract
period.

(7) Organization rights are accorded. Strikes are illegal.

(9), (10) Unresolved issues may be brought to mediation and
conciliation on request of either party, or if that fails, to final
and binding arbitration as provided by the statute. Arbitration fees
are borne equally. The services of the state director of labor and
his conciliators are available for both disputes and grievances.

*R.I. Gen. Laws Ann. §§28-9.3-1—28-9.3-16, as enacted by P.L. 1966,
ch. 146.*

(1) Certified teachers are covered by the act. Superintendents,
assistant superintendents, principals, and assistant principals are
excluded.

(3) The state labor relations board supervises elections for representatives.

(4), (5) The statute imposes an obligation on the employer to
"meet and confer in good faith" on "hours, salary, working conditions and all other terms and conditions of professional employment."

(6) Provisions for exclusive representation are included. The unit
is the certified teachers employed by each school committee.

(7) The right to organize and to bargain collectively is stated.
The act asserts that its provisions are not to be construed to
accord the right to strike.

(9) Unresolved issues may be submitted to mediation or arbitration. The statute sets time periods for both procedures. The decision of the arbitrators must be made public and is binding on all
matters except money. Appeal lies from the decision only on
grounds of fraud or illegality. Fees for mediation and arbitration
are borne equally.

South Dakota

S.D. Comp. Laws Ann. §§3-18-1—3-18-16, added by L. 1970, ch. 3-18.

(1) All public employees are covered by the law, including appointed officials.

(3) The commissioner of the labor division of the state industrial commission administers the act upon approval by resolution of the governing body. Rules and regulations pursuant to the act have been adopted.

(4), (5) The parties meet and negotiate with respect to grievance procedures and conditions of employment.

(6) Exclusive representation is provided. If the appropriate representation unit cannot be agreed upon, the labor commissioner defines it.

(7) The right to organize and to submit grievances is asserted. Strikes, supervisor consent to strikes, and inciting to strike are prohibited, with heavy individual and organizational penalties imposed. Employers are authorized to seek injunctive relief in case of a strike.

(9) In case of an impasse, a party may request the labor commissioner to intervene or agree to any other procedure.

(10) "Grievance" is defined in §3-18-1.1. Each governing officer or board is required to enact a grievance procedure. If this is not done, the labor commissioner may be requested to act.

Texas

The attorney general has ruled that public employees have the right to present grievances concerning wages, hours, or working conditions through a labor union that does not claim the right to strike or to bargain collectively. [Attorney General's Opinion No. M-77, May 18, 1967]. Article 5154c, L. 1947, forbids collective bargaining contracts by public employers and employees and prohibits strikes by such employees.

Vermont

Vt. Stat. Ann. tit. 3, §§901–1007, added by ch. 27, L. 1969.

(1), (2) Employees of the state and of state colleges are covered. (Public school teachers and administrators are covered by 1969, ch. 127, noted below.)

(3) The administering agency is the state employee labor relations board created by the act.

(4), (5) The act imposes a mutual obligation to "meet" and "confer in good faith" with respect to all matters relating to the relationship between the employer and employees except matters controlled by statute. The contract period is limited to three years.

(6) The board determines the appropriate unit under detailed statutory criteria included with the express purpose of avoiding over-fragmentation. Exclusive representation is provided for.

(7) Organization and noninterference rights are stated. Management rights are reserved. Strikes and recognition of picket lines are prohibited. The kinds of conduct which constitute unfair labor practices are enumerated as to both employers and employees, with specific procedures for their "prevention."

(9) A factfinding panel may be authorized by the board if negotiations are deadlocked. The parties may agree to be bound by panel recommendations not in conflict with any statutes or rules.

(10) The board hears grievances of state employees in accordance with procedural rules it is required to promulgate. All other eligible persons may appeal to the board. Statutory grievance procedures are set out for personnel exempt or excluded from coverage by the act. Judicial review is provided.

Vt. Stat. tit. 16, §§1981–2010, added by 1969, No. 57.

(1) Public school teachers and administrators, except superintendents and assistant superintendents, are covered by the act.

(4), (5) The representatives shall "meet" and "negotiate in good faith" on matters of salary, related economic conditions of employment, procedures for complaints and grievances relating to employment, and any matters mutually agreed upon and not forbidden by statute.

(6) Provision is made for exclusive representation and unit determination. Teachers and administrators must have separate units. The superintendent, assistant superintendent, and principal cannot serve as negotiating agents for the teachers' organization.

(7) Organization and noninterference rights are stated. All decisions of the school board on disputed matters are final if made in compliance with the act.

(9) There is provision for mediation and factfinding with the

costs to be borne equally. The factfinding report is advisory only and is to be made public. Injunction may be sought only upon a showing that there is a clear and present danger to the school program. (Municipal employees with certain excluded designations are granted the right to bargain by Vt. Stat. §§1701—1710.)

Washington

Wash. Rev. Code §§41.56.010—41.56.900, added by L. 1967, ch. 108; as amended by L. 1971, ch. 19.

(1) The act covers employees of any county and municipal corporation or political subdivision of the state except marine, public utility, and port authority employees, and teachers, all of whom are covered by other statutes. Appointed, elected, and administrative employees are excluded.

(3) The Department of Labor and Industries administers the act.

(4), (5) The act imposes a mutual obligation to meet, confer, and negotiate in good faith and to execute a written agreement with respect to grievance procedures and personnel matters, including wages, hours, and working conditions. Matters delegated to civil service commissions and personnel boards are excluded.

(6) There is provision for exclusive representation; general guidelines are included for determination of an appropriate unit.

(7) Organization and noninterference rights are stated. Strikes are prohibited. Unfair labor practices of both sides are enumerated and a departmental procedure for handling complaints is set out.

(8) The agreement may provide for dues check-off.

(9) Mediation utilizing the state mediation service of the Department of Labor and Industries, is authorized by the act.

(11) The act creates a committee to study the operation of the act looking toward improvement of relationships.

L. 1971, H.B. 739, effective August 9, 1971. See 4A Labor Law Reporter SLL 58:242e.

(1), (2) The act applies to academic employees in community college districts described as any teacher, counselor, librarian, or department head, division head, or administrator employed by any community college district, excepting the chief administrative officer of each district.

(3) District boards of trustees and the director of the state system of community colleges administer.

(4), (5), (6) The employee organization chosen by secret ballot of the majority has the right, after using established administrative channels, to meet, confer, and negotiate with the board of trustees of the district or a committee thereof to "communicate the considered professional judgment of the academic staff prior to the final adoption by the board of proposed community college district policies relating to, but not limited to, curriculum, textbook selection, in-service training, student teaching programs, personnel, hiring and assignment practices, leaves of absence, salaries and salary schedules and noninstructional duties."

(9) Dispute resolution is by a committee appointed by the director of the state system of community colleges.

L. 1971, ch. 19, §10, effective April 2, 1971. See 4A Labor Relations Reporter SLL 58:242.

The provision directs the higher education personnel board to adopt rules and regulations to govern employer-employee relations. Among the procedures directed to be covered are the following: determination of appropriate bargaining units within an institution, listing specific criteria to be considered; exclusive representation; grievance procedures; collective negotiations on all matters within the discretion of the institution or board; payroll deductions of organization dues; and revision of employee classification plans and salary schedules. Employees have no right to strike.

The rules are required to provide for administration by local boards, subject to audit and review by the state higher education personnel board.

Wash. Rev. Code §§28.72.010—28.72.090, added by 1965, ch. 143.

(1) The act covers all certificated employees of school districts except the chief administrative officer.

(3) The local boards administer the act.

(4), (5), (6) Representatives of an organization chosen by secret ballot of the majority of the employees have the right, after using established administrative channels, to "meet, confer and negotiate with the board of directors of the school district or a committee thereof to communicate the considered professional judgment of the certificated staff prior to the final adoption by the board of proposed school policies relating to, but not limited to, curriculum, textbook selection, in-service training, student teaching programs, personnel, hiring and assignment practices, leaves of absence, salaries and salary schedules and noninstructional duties."

(7) Employees have organization and nondiscrimination rights.

(9) Disputes may be taken to an advisory committee appointed by the state superintendent of public instruction. Final decisions are made by the boards.

Wisconsin

Wis. Stat. Ann. §§111.80–111.94, added by L. 1965, ch. 612, effective January 1, 1967; as amended by L. 1969, ch. 276.

(1) The comprehensive act covers employees of the state, including professional employees.

(3) The Employment Relations Commission of the Department of Administration administers the act and adopts rules pursuant to the act.

(4), (5) There is a mutual obligation to bargain collectively on terms and conditions of employment. The statute (§111.91) enumerates the bargainable subjects:

(1) Matters subject to collective bargaining are the following conditions of employment for which the appointing officer has discretionary authority:

(a) Grievance procedures;

(b) Application of seniority rights as affecting the matters contained herein;

(c) Work schedules relating to assigned hours and days of the week and shift assignments;

(d) Scheduling of vacations and other time off;

(e) Use of sick leave;

(f) Application and interpretation of established work rules;

(g) Health and safety practices;

(h) Intradepartmental transfers; and

(i) Such other matters consistent with this section and the statutes, rules and regulations of the state and its various agencies.

(2) Nothing herein shall require the employer to bargain in re-

lation to statutory and rule provided prerogatives of promotion, layoff, position classification, compensation and fringe benefits, examinations, discipline, merit salary determination policy and other actions provided for by law and rules governing civil service.

(6) The commission determines the appropriate unit and may, but is not required to, allow employees to determine whether they wish to be a separate unit. There are statutory criteria for inclusion of professional employees and for separate craft units. Exclusive representation is provided.

(7) Organization and noninterference rights are asserted. Management rights are reserved. Strikes are prohibited and an enumeration of other practices prohibited as to both employers and employees is found in §111.84.

(8) There is provision for collection of dues.

(9) Arbitration is provided through the commission and may be binding by agreement of the parties. Procedures to obtain mediation and factfinding are set out in the act.

Wis. Stat. Ann. §111.70, enacted by L. 1961, ch. 663; as amended by L. 1969, ch. 276.

This act, with provisions substantially similar to the state employee act, covers municipal employees except policemen, sheriff's deputies, and county traffic officers.

Two Model State Acts

Two model comprehensive state labor-management relations acts were prepared by the U.S. Advisory Commission on Intergovernmental Relations in 1970, the second one revised in 1971. Although the commission favored the "meet and confer" approach of the first bill,* it drafted the second "collective negotiations" bill recognizing that " . . . some States may well wish to consider other language." Both documents call for the establishment of a public employee relations agency to administer provisions for unit determination, recognition, election and certification of representatives, dues check-off, prohibited practices, and dispute settlement. All brackets and footnotes were present in the revised draft. These model bills are included not as recommendations but as the most cohesive available attempts to handle current problems, apart from the state statutes themselves.

STATE PUBLIC LABOR—MANAGEMENT RELATIONS ACT

Suggested Legislation[1]

[Title should conform to State requirements. The following is a suggestion: "An Act to Establish a Framework of Public Employer-

---

* In its report *Labor-Management Policies for State and Local Government* (ACIR Report A-35, Sept. 1969). The following texts are taken, with permission, from *New Proposals for 1972: ACIR Legislative Program* (Washington, D.C.: Advisory Commission on Intergovernmental Relations, Aug. 1971), pp. 75-98.

1. The following statute incorporates a "meet and confer in good faith" approach to labor-management relations in the State and local public service. A draft embodying a "collective negotiations" approach appears on page 17. On balance, the Advisory Commission on Intergovernmental Relations tends to favor the meet and confer in good faith approach, but recognizes that different States will take varying positions regarding sections of this draft legislation; hence, the inclusion of alternate language.

Employee Relations by Providing Uniform and Orderly Methods for Dealings Between Employees and Organizations Thereof and Employing Public Agencies and for Related Purposes."]

(Be it enacted, etc.)

Section 1. Findings and Purpose. The legislature hereby finds and declares that:

(1) the people of this State have a fundamental interest in the development of harmonious and cooperative relationships between government and its employees;

(2) recognition by public employers of the right of public employees to organize and full acceptance of the principle and procedure of full communication between public employers and public employee organizations can alleviate various forms of strife and unrest;

(3) the State has a basic obligation to protect the public by attempting to assure the orderly and uninterrupted operations and functions of government;

(4) the status of public employees neither is, nor can be, completely comparable to that of private employees, in fact or law, because of inherent differences in the employment relationship arising out of the unique fact that the public employer was established by and run for the benefit of all the people and its authority derives not from contract nor the profit motive inherent in the principle of free private enterprise, but from the constitution, statutes, municipal charters, and civil service rules and regulations; and

(5) this difference between public and private employment is further reflected in the constraints that bar any abdication or bargaining away by public employers of their continuing legislative discretion and in the fact that State constitutional provisions as to contract, property, and due process do not have the same force with respect to the public employer-employee relationship.

It is the purpose of this act to obligate public agencies, public employees, and their representatives to enter into discussions with affirmative willingness to resolve grievances and disputes relating to wages, hours, and other terms and conditions of employment, acting within the framework of laws and charter provisions. It is also the purpose of this act to promote the improvement of employer-employee relations within the various public agencies of the State and its political subdivisions by providing a uniform basis for recognizing the right of public employees to join organizations of their own choice, or to refrain from joining, and be represented by such organizations in their employment relations and dealings with public agencies.

Section 2. Definitions. As used in this act:

(1) "Public employee" means any person employed by any public agency excepting those persons classed as legislative, judicial, or supervisory public employees; elected and top management appointive officials; and certain categories of confidential employees including those who have responsibility for administering the public labor-management relations law as a part of their official duties.

(2) "Supervisory employee" means any individual having authority, in the interest of the employer, (i) to hire, transfer, suspend, lay off, recall, promote, discharge, assign, reward, or discipline other employees, or (ii) responsibly to direct them, or (iii) to adjust their grievances, or (iv) effectively to recommend such action, if in connection with the foregoing the exercise of such authority is not of a merely routine or clerical nature, but requires the use of independent judgment.

(3) "Confidential employee" means one whose unrestricted access to confidential personnel files or information concerning the administrative operations of a public agency, or whose functional responsibilities or knowledge in connection with the issues involved in the meet and confer in good faith process, would make his membership in the same organization as rank-and-file employees incompatible with his official duties.

(4) "Public agency" or "public employer" means the State of [   ] and every governmental subdivision; school and non-school special district; public and quasi-public corporation; public agency; town, city, county, city and county, and municipal corporation; and authority, board, or commission, whether incorporated or not and whether chartered or not.

(5) "Governing body" means the legislative body of the public employer or the body possessing legislative powers. In the case of independent school districts, it means the board of education, board of trustees, or sole trustee, as the case may be.

(6) "Representative of the public employer" and "designated

representative" means the chief executive officer of the public employer or his designee, except where the governing body provides otherwise.

(7) "Employee organization" means any organization which includes employees of a public agency and which has as one of its primary purposes representing such employees in discussions with that public agency over grievances and wages, hours, and other terms and conditions of employment.

(8) "Recognized employee organization" means an employee organization which has been formally acknowledged by the public agency or certified as representing a majority of the nonsupervisory employees of an appropriate unit.

(9) "Agency" means the Public Employee Relations Agency established pursuant to this act.

(10) "Meet and confer in good faith" means the process whereby the chief executive of a public agency, or such representatives as it may designate, and representatives of recognized employee organizations have the mutual obligation personally to meet and confer in order to exchange freely information, opinions, and proposals, to endeavor to reach agreement on matters within the scope of discussions, and to seek by every possible means to implement agreements reached.

(11) "Memorandum of agreement" means a written memorandum of understanding arrived at by the representatives of the public agency and a recognized employee organization, which may be presented to the governing body or its statutory representative and to the membership of such organization for appropriate action.

(12) "Mediation" means effort by an impartial third party to assist in reconciling a dispute regarding wages, hours, and other terms and conditions of employment between representatives of the public agency and the recognized employee organization through interpretation, suggestion, and advice.

(13) "Fact-finding" means investigation of such a dispute by an individual, panel, or board with the fact-finder submitting a report to the parties describing the issues involved. The report may contain recommendations for settlement and may be made public.

(14) "Advisory arbitration" means interpretation of the terms of an existing or a new memorandum of agreement or investigation of disputes by an impartial third party whose decision is not binding upon the parties.

(15) "Voluntary arbitration" means a procedure wherein both parties jointly agree to submit their dispute over the interpretation of the terms of an existing agreement or over a new memorandum of agreement to an impartial third party whose decision may be final and binding or advisory and non-binding, depending on the nature of the initial agreement.

(16) "Strike" means the failure by concerted action with others to report for duty, the wilful absence from one's position, the stoppage of work, or the abstinence in whole or in part from the full, faithful, and proper performance of the duties of employment, or in any manner interfering with the operation of any public agency, for the purpose of inducing, influencing, or coercing a change in the conditions or compensation or the rights, privileges, or obligations of employment.

Section 3. Public Employee Relations Agency.

(a) There is hereby created [in the State department of] a board, to be known as the [Public Employee Relations Agency], which shall consist of [5] members appointed by the Governor, by and with the advice and consent of the Senate from persons representative of the public. Not more than [3] members of the Agency shall be members of the same political party. Each member shall be appointed for a term of [6] years, except that [2] shall be appointed for a term to expire [2] years following the effective date of this act, [2] for a term that shall expire [4] years following the effective date of this act, and [1] for a term that shall expire [6] years following the effective date of this act. A member appointed to fill a vacancy shall be appointed for the unexpired term of the member whom he is to succeed.

(b) Members shall hold no other public office or public employment in the State or its political subdivisions. [The chairman shall give his full time to his duties.]

(c) Members of the Agency other than the chairman, when performing the duties of the Agency, shall be compensated at the rate of [one hundred dollars a day], together with an allowance of actual and necessary expenses incurred in the discharge of their responsibilities hereunder. The chairman shall receive an annual salary to be fixed [by the Governor] within the amount available therefor by appropriation, in addition to an allowance for expenses actually and necessarily incurred by him in the performance of his duties.

(d) The Agency may appoint an executive director and such other persons, including but not limited to mediators, members of fact-finding boards, and representatives of employee organizations and public employers to serve as technical advisers to such fact-finding boards, as it may from time to time deem necessary for the performance of its functions. The Agency shall prescribe their duties, fix their compensation, and provide for reimbursement of their expenses within the amounts made available therefor by appropriation.

(e) In addition to the authority provided in other sections, the Agency may:

(1) Make studies and analyses of, and act as a clearing-house of information relating to, conditions of employment of public employees throughout the State.

(2) Provide technical assistance and training programs to assist public employers in their dealings with employee organizations.

(3) Request from any public agency such assistance, services, and data as will enable the Agency properly to carry out its functions and powers.

(4) Establish procedures for the prevention of improper public employer and employee organization practices as provided in Section 13 of this act, provided that in the case of a claimed violation of paragraph (5) of subdivision (b) or paragraph (4) of subdivision (c) of such section, procedures shall provide only for an entering of an order directing the public agency or employee organization to meet and confer in good faith. The pendency of proceedings under this paragraph shall not be used as the basis to delay or interfere with determination of representation status pursuant to Section 7 of this act or with meeting and conferring. The Agency shall exercise exclusive nondelegable jurisdiction of the power granted to it by this paragraph.

(5) Establish, after consulting with representatives of employee organizations and of public agencies, panels of qualified persons broadly representative of the public, to be available to serve as mediators, members of fact-finding boards, or arbitrators.

(6) Hold such hearings and make such inquiries, as it deems necessary, to carry out properly its functions and powers.

(7) For the purpose of such hearings and inquiries, administer oaths and affirmations, examine witnesses and documents, take testimony and receive evidence, compel attendance of witnesses

and the production of documents by the issuance of subpoenas, and delegate such powers to any member of the Agency or any person appointed by the Agency for the performance of its functions. Such subpoenas shall be regulated and enforced [under the civil practice law and rules].

(8) Make, amend, and rescind, from time to time, such rules and regulations, including but not limited to those governing its internal organization and conduct of its affairs, and exercise such other powers, as may be appropriate to effectuate the purposes and provisions of this act.

Section 4. Public Employee Rights. Public employees shall have the right to form, join, and participate in the activities of employee organizations of their own choosing for the purpose of meeting and conferring with public employers or their designated representatives with respect to grievances and wages, hours, and other terms and conditions of employment. Public employees also shall have the right to refuse or fail to join or participate in the activities of employee organizations.

Section 5. Supervisory Employees. Supervisory employees may form, join, and participate in the activities of employee organizations, provided such organizations do not include non-supervisory employees. A public agency shall not extend formal recognition to a supervisory organization for the purpose of meeting and conferring with respect to grievances and conditions of employment, but may consult or otherwise communicate with such an organization on appropriate matters. The public employer shall determine whether an individual is to be considered a supervisory or confidential employee for meet and confer purposes, subject to appeal to the Agency.

Section 6. Public Employer Rights. Nothing in this act is intended to circumscribe or modify the existing right of a public agency to:

(1) direct the work of its employees;

(2) hire, promote, assign, transfer, and retain employees in positions within the public agency;

(3) demote, suspend, or discharge employees for proper cause;

(4) maintain the efficiency of governmental operations;

(5) relieve employees from duties because of lack of work or for other legitimate reasons;

(6) take actions as may be necessary to carry out the mission of the agency in emergencies; and

(7) determine the methods, means, and personnel by which operations are to be carried on.

Section 7. Recognition of Employee Organizations.

(a) Public employers shall recognize certain employee organizations for the purpose of representing their members in dealings with such employers. Employee organizations may establish reasonable provisions for an individual's admission to or dismissal from membership.

(b) Where a public employer has recognized an employee organization or where such organization has been certified by the Agency as representing a majority of the employees in an appropriate unit, or recognized formally, pursuant to the provisions of this act, the public employer shall meet and confer in good faith with such employee organization in the determination of the terms and conditions of employment of their public employees as provided in this act, and the administration of grievances arising thereunder, and may enter into a memorandum of agreement with such employee organization.

(c) When a representational question stemming from the designation of an appropriate unit is raised by a public agency, employee organization, or employees, the Public Employee Relations Agency, established pursuant to this act, shall, at the request of any of the parties, investigate such question and, after a hearing, rule on the definition of the appropriate unit. In defining the unit, the Agency shall take into consideration, along with other relevant factors, the principles of efficient administration of government, the existence of a community of interest among employees, the history and extent of employee organization, geographical location, the provisions of Section 5 of this act, and the recommendations of the parties involved.

(d) Following investigation of a question concerning whether an employee organization represents a majority of the employees in an appropriate unit, the Public Employee Relations Agency, at the request of any of the parties, shall examine such question and certify to the parties in writing the name of the representative that has been designated. The filing of a petition for the investigation or certification of a majority representative by any of the parties shall constitute a question within the meaning of this section. In any such investigation, the Agency may provide for an appropriate hearing, may determine voting eligibility, and may take a secret ballot of employees in the appropriate unit involved to ascertain such representative for the purpose of formal recognition. If the Agency has certified a formally recognized majority representative in an appropriate unit, as provided in this section, it shall not be required to consider the matter again for a period of one year. The Agency may promulgate such rules and regulations as may be appropriate to carry out the provisions of subsections (c) and (d) of this section.

Section 8. Rights Accompanying Formal Recognition.

(a) A public employer shall extend to an employee organization certified or recognized formally, pursuant to this act, the right to represent the employees of the appropriate unit involved in meet and confer proceedings and in the settlement of grievances and the right to unchallenged representation status, consistent with Section 7(d), during the 12 months following the date of certification or formal recognition.

(b) A public employer may extend to such an organization the right to membership dues deduction, upon presentation of dues deduction authorization cards signed by individual employees.

(c) A reasonable number of representatives of formally recognized employee organizations may be given time off without loss of compensation during normal working hours to meet and confer with public employers on matters falling within the scope of discussions.

Section 9. Procedures for Determining the Recognition Status of Local Employee Organizations.

(a) Every public agency, other than the State and its authorities acting through its governing body, may establish procedures, not inconsistent with the provisions of Sections 7 and 8 of this act and after consultation with interested employee organizations and employer representatives, to resolve disputes concerning the recognition status of employee organizations composed of employees of such agency.

(b) In the absence of such procedures, these disputes shall be submitted to the Public Employee Relations Agency in accordance with Section 7 of this act.

Section 10. Scope of a Memorandum of Agreement. The scope of a memorandum of agreement may extend to all matters relating to employment conditions and employer-employee relations, including, but not limited to, wages, hours, and other terms and conditions of employment except, however, that the scope of a memorandum of agreement shall not include proposals relating to (i) any subject preempted by Federal or State law or by municipal charter, (ii) public employee rights defined in Section 4 of this act, (iii) public employer rights defined in Section 6 of this act, or (iv) the authority and power of any civil service commission, personnel board, personnel agency, or its agents established by constitutional provision, statute, charter, or special act to set and administer standards dealing with the impartial recruitment of candidates, to conduct and grade merit examinations, and to rate candidates in the order of their relative excellence from which appointments or promotions may be made to positions in the competitive division of the classified service of the public employer served by such civil service commission or personnel board. A memorandum of agreement may contain a grievance procedure culminating in advisory arbitration of unresolved grievances and disputed interpretations of such agreement.

Section 11. Implementation of a Memorandum of Agreement. If agreement is reached by the representative of the public employer and the recognized employee organization, they shall jointly prepare a memorandum of understanding and, within [14] days, present it to the governing body for determination. After receiving a report from the chief financial officer of the public agency as to the effect the terms of such memorandum will have upon the agency, the governing body, as soon as practicable, shall consider the memorandum and take appropriate action. If a settlement is reached with an employee organization, the governing body or the representative of the public employer shall implement the settlement in the form of a law, ordinance, resolution, executive order, rule, or regulation, as the case may be. If the governing body or the designated representative rejects a proposed memorandum, the matter shall be returned to the parties for further deliberation.

Section 12. Resolution of Disputes Arising in the Course of Discussions.

(a) Public employers may include in memoranda of agreement concluded with formally recognized or certified employee organizations a provision setting forth the procedures to be invoked in the event of disputes which reach an impasse in the course of meet and confer proceedings. For purposes of this section, an impasse shall be deemed to exist if the parties fail to achieve agreement at least [60] days prior to the budget submission date of the public employer. In the absence or upon the failure of dispute resolution procedures contained in agreements, resulting in an impasse, either party may request the assistance of the Public Employee Relations Agency or the Agency may render such assistance on its own motion, as provided in subdivision (b) of this section.

(b) On the request of either party, or upon the Agency's own motion, if it determines an impasse exists in meet and confer proceedings between a public employer and a formally recognized or certified employee organization, the Agency shall aid the parties in effecting a voluntary resolution of the dispute, and appoint a mediator or mediators, representative of the public, from a list of qualified persons maintained by the Agency.

(c) If the impasse persists [10] days after the mediator(s) has been appointed, the Agency shall appoint a fact-finding board of not more than [3] members, each representative of the public, from a list of qualified persons maintained by the Agency. The fact-finding board shall conduct a hearing, may administer oaths, and may request the Agency to issue subpoenas.

It shall make written findings of facts and recommendations for resolution of the dispute and, not later than [20] days from the day of appointment, shall serve such findings on the public employer and the recognized employee organization. If the dispute continues [10] days after the report is submitted to the parties, the report may be made public by the Agency.

(d) If the parties have not resolved the impasse by the end of a [40] day period commencing with the date of appointment of the fact-finding board, (i) the representative of the public employer involved shall submit to the governing body or its duly authorized committee(s) a copy of the findings of fact and recommendations of the fact-finding board, together with his recommendations for settling the dispute; (ii) the employee organization may submit to the governing body or its duly authorized committee(s) its recommendations for settling the dispute; (iii) the governing body or such committee(s) shall forthwith conduct a hearing at which the parties shall be required to explain their positions with respect to the board; and (iv) thereafter, the governing body shall take such action as it deems to be in the public interest, including the interest of the public employees involved.

(e) Meet and confer proceedings and mediation, fact-finding, and arbitration meetings and investigations shall not be subject to the provisions of [insert State "right to know" law].

(f) The costs for mediation services provided by the Agency shall be borne by the Agency. All other costs, including that of fact-finding services, shall be borne equally by the parties to a dispute.

Section 13. Prohibited Practices; Evidence of Bad Faith.

(a) Commission of a prohibited practice, as defined in this section, among other actions, shall constitute evidence of bad faith in meet and confer proceedings.

(b) It shall be a prohibited practice for a public employer or its designated representative wilfully to:

(1) Interfere, restrain, or coerce public employees in the exercise of rights granted in Section 4 of this act;

(2) Dominate, interfere, or assist in the formation, existence, or administration of any employee organization;

(3) Encourage or discourage membership in any employee organization, agency, committee, association, or representation plan by discrimination in hiring, tenure, or other terms or conditions of employment;

(4) Discharge or discriminate against an employee because he has filed any affidavit, petition, or complaint or given any information or testimony under this act, or because he has formed, joined, or chosen to be represented by any employee organization;

(5) Refuse to meet and confer with representatives of recognized employee organizations as required in Section 7 of this act;

(6) Deny the rights accompanying certification or formal recognition granted in Section 8 of this act;

(7) Blacklist any employee organization or its members for the purpose of denying them employment because of their organizational activities; or

(8) Avoid mediation and fact-finding endeavors as provided in Section 12 of this act.

(c) It shall be a prohibited practice for public employees or employee organizations wilfully to:

(1) Interfere with, restrain, or coerce public employees in the exercise of rights granted in Section 4 of this act;

(2) Interfere with, restrain, or coerce a public employer with respect to rights protected in Section 6 of this act or with respect to selecting a representative for the purposes of meeting and conferring;

(3) Refuse to meet and confer with a public employer as required in Section 7 of this act;

(4) Avoid mediation and fact-finding efforts as provided in Section 12 of this act; or

(5) Engage in a strike.

(d) In applying this section, fundamental distinctions between private and public employment shall be recognized, and no body of Federal or State law applicable, wholly or in part to the private employment, shall be regarded as binding or controlling precedent.

Section 14. Violations of Prohibited Practices.

(a) Any controversy concerning prohibited practices may be submitted to the Agency. Proceedings against the party alleged to have committed a prohibited practice shall be commenced by service upon it by the Agency of a written notice, together with a copy of the charges. The accused party shall have [7] days within which to serve a written answer to such charges. The Agency's hearing shall be held promptly thereafter and at such hearing, the parties shall be permitted to be represented by counsel and to summon witnesses in their behalf. Compliance with the technical rules of evidence shall not be required. The Agency may use its rule-making power, as provided in Section 3, to make any other procedural rules it deems necessary to carry on this function.*

(b) The Agency shall state its findings of facts upon all the testimony and shall either dismiss the complaint or determine that a prohibited practice has been or is being committed. If the Agency finds that the party accused has committed or is committing a prohibited practice, the Agency shall petition the [court of appropriate jurisdiction] to punish such violation, and shall file in the [court] the record in the proceedings. Any person aggrieved by a final order of the Agency granting or denying in whole or in part the relief sought may obtain a review of such order in the [court of appropriate jurisdiction] by filing a complaint praying that the order of the Agency be modified or set aside, with copy of the complaint filed on the Agency, and thereupon the aggrieved party shall file in the [court] the record in the proceedings, certified by the Agency. Findings of the Agency as to the facts shall be conclusive unless it is made to appear to the satisfaction of the [court of appropriate jurisdiction] that the findings of fact were not supported by substantial evidence.

---

* Where a State has adopted an administrative procedures act, this section should be made to conform to it.

Section 15. Internal Conduct of Public Employee Organizations.

(a) Every employee organization which has or seeks recognition as a representative of public employees of this state and of its political subdivisions shall file with the Public Employee Relations Agency a registration report, signed by its president or other appropriate officer, within [90] days after the effective date of this act. Such report shall be in a form prescribed by the Agency and shall be accompanied by [two] copies of the employee organization's constitution and bylaws. A filing by a national or international employee organization of its constitution and bylaws shall be accepted in lieu of a filing of such documents by each subordinate organization. All changes or amendments to such constitutions and bylaws shall be promptly reported to the Agency.

(b) Every employee organization shall file with the Agency an annual report and an amended report whenever changes are made. Such reports shall be in a form prescribed by the Agency, and shall provide the following information:

(1) The names and addresses of the organization, any parent organization or organizations with which it is affiliated, the principal officers, and all representatives;

(2) The name and address of its local agent for service of process;

(3) A general description of the public employees or groups of employees the organization represents or seeks to represent;

(4) The amounts of the initiation fee and monthly dues members must pay;

(5) A pledge, in a form prescribed by the Agency, that the organization will conform to the laws of the State and that it will accept members without regard to age, race, sex, religion, or national origin; and

(6) A financial report and audit.

(c) The constitution or bylaws of every employee organization shall provide that:

(1) Accurate accounts of all income and expenses shall be kept, an annual financial report and audit shall be prepared, such accounts shall be open for inspection by any member of the organization, and loans to officers and agents shall be made only on terms and conditions available to all members.

(2) Business or financial interests of its officers and agents, their spouses, minor children, parents, or otherwise, that conflict with the fiduciary obligation of such persons to the organization shall be prohibited.

(3) Every official or employee of an employee organization who handles funds or other property of the organization, or trust in which an organization is interested, or a subsidiary organization, shall be bonded. The amount, scope, and form of the bond shall be determined by the Agency.

(d) The governing rules of every employee organization shall provide for: periodic elections by secret ballot subject to recognized safeguards concerning the equal right of all members to nominate, seek office, and vote in such elections; the right of individual members to participate in the affairs of the organization; fair and equal treatment of its members; the right of any member to sue the organization; and fair and equitable procedures in disciplinary actions.

(e) The Agency shall prescribe such rules and regulations as may be necessary to govern the establishment and reporting of trusteeships over employee organizations. Establishment of such trusteeships shall be permitted only if the constitution or bylaws of the organization set forth reasonable procedures.

(f) An employee organization that has not registered or filed an annual report, or that has failed to comply with other provisions of this act, shall not be recognized for the purpose of meeting and conferring with any public employer regarding the terms and conditions of work of its members. Recognized employee organizations failing to comply with this act may have such recognition revoked by the Agency. All proceedings under this subsection shall be conducted in accordance with [the State administrative procedure act]. Prohibitions shall be enforced by injunction upon the petition of the Agency to [court of appropriate jurisdiction]. Complaints of violation of this act shall be filed with the Agency.

Section 16. Local Public Agency Options.

This act, except for Sections 2, 3(e)(3), 4, 5, 6, 7, 8, 13, 14, and 15, shall be inapplicable to any public employer, other than the State and its authorities, which, acting through its governing body, has adopted by local law, ordinance, or resolution its own provisions and procedures which have been submitted to the Agency by such public employer and as to which there is in effect a determination by the Agency that such provisions and procedures and the continuing implementation thereof do not derogate the rights granted under this act.

Section 17. Separability. [Insert separability clause.]

Section 18. Effective Date. [Insert effective date.]

STATE PUBLIC LABOR—MANAGEMENT RELATIONS ACT

(Collective Negotiations)

[*Title should conform to State requirements. The following is a suggestion: "An Act to Establish a Framework of Public Employer-Employee Relations by Providing Uniform and Orderly Methods for Collective Negotiations Between Employees and Organizations Thereof and Employing Public Agencies and for Related Purposes."*

(Be it enacted, etc.)

Section 1. Findings and Purpose. The legislature hereby finds and declares that:

(1) the people of this State have a fundamental interest in the development of harmonious and cooperative relationships between government and its employees;

(2) recognition by public employers of the right of public employees to organize and full acceptance of the principle and procedure of collective negotiations between public employers and public employee organizations can alleviate various forms of strife and unrest. Experience in the private and public sectors of our economy has proved that unresolved disputes in the public service are injurious to the public, the governmental agencies, and public employees;

(3) experience in private and public employment has also proved that protection by law of the right of employees to organize and negotiate collectively safeguards employees and the public from injury, impairment and interruptions of necessary services, and removes certain recognized sources of strife and unrest, by encouraging practices fundamental to the peaceful adjustment of disputes arising out of differences as to wages, hours, and other working conditions, and by establishing greater equality of bargaining power between public employers and public employees; and

(4) the State has a basic obligation to protect the public by attempting to assure the orderly and uninterrupted operations and functions of government.

It is the purpose of this act to obligate public agencies, public employees, and their representatives to enter into collective negotiations with affirmative willingness to resolve grievances and disputes relating to wages, hours, and other terms and conditions of employment. It is also the purpose of this act to promote the improvement of employer-employee relations within the various public agencies of the State and its political subdivisions by providing a uniform basis for recognizing the right of public employees to join organizations of their own choice, or to refrain from joining, and be represented by such organizations in their employment relations and dealings with public agencies.

Section 2. Definitions. As used in this act:

(1) "Public employee" means any person employed by any public agency excepting those persons classed as legislative, judicial, or supervisory public employees; elected and top management appointive officials; and certain categories of confidential employees including those who have responsibility for administering the public labor-management relations law as a part of their official duties.

(2) "Supervisory employee" means any individual having authority, in the interest of the employer, (i) to hire, transfer, suspend, lay off, recall, promote, discharge, assign, reward, or discipline other employees, or (ii) responsibly to direct them, or (iii) to adjust their grievances, or (iv) effectively to recommend such action, if in connection with the foregoing the exercise of such authority is not of a merely routine or clerical nature, but requires the use of independent judgment.

(3) "Confidential employee" means one whose unrestricted access to confidential personnel files or information concerning the administrative operations of a public agency or whose functional responsibilities or knowledge in connection with the issues involved in the collective negotiations process, would make his membership in the same organization as rank-and-file employees incompatible with his official duties.

(4) "Public agency" or "public employer" means the State of [   ] and every governmental subdivision; school and nonschool special district; public and quasi-public corporation; public agency; town, city, county, city and county, and municipal corporation; and authority, board, or commission, whether incorporated or not and whether chartered or not.

(5) "Governing body" means the legislative body of the public employer or the body possessing legislative powers. In the case of independent school districts, it means the board of education, board of trustees, or sole trustee, as the case may be.

(6) "Representative of the public employer" and "designated representative" means the chief executive officer of the public employer or his designee, except where the governing body provides otherwise.

(7) "Employee organization" means any organization which includes employees of a public agency and which has as one of its primary purposes representing such employees in collective negotiations with that public agency over grievances and wages, hours, and other terms and conditions of employment.

(8) "Recognized employee organization" or "exclusive representative" means an employee organization which has been formally acknowledged by the public agency or certified as representing a majority of the non-supervisory employees of an appropriate unit.

(9) "Agency" means the Public Employee Relations Agency established pursuant to this act.

(10) "Collective negotiations" means performance of the mutual obligation of the employer through its chief executive officer or designated representative and the recognized employee organization to meet at reasonable times and negotiate in good faith with respect to wages, hours, and other conditions of employment, or the negotiation of an agreement, or any question arising thereunder, and the execution of a written contract incorporating any agreement reached if requested by either party, but such obligations does not compel either party to agree to a proposal or require the making of a concession.

(11) "Agreement" means a written contract between an employer and an employee organization, usually for a definite term, defining the conditions of employment, including wages, hours, vacations, holidays, and overtime payments, and the procedures to be followed in settling disputes or handling issues that arise during the term of the contract.

(12) "Mediation" means effort by an impartial third party to assist in reconciling a dispute regarding wages, hours, and other terms and conditions of employment between representatives of the public agency and the recognized employee organization through interpretation, suggestion, and advice.

(13) "Fact-finding" means investigation of such a dispute by an individual, panel, or board with the fact-finder submitting a report to the parties describing the issues involved. The report may contain recommendations for settlement and may be made public.

(14) "Binding arbitration" means interpretation of the terms of an existing or a new agreement by an impartial third party whose decision shall be final and binding.

(15) "Voluntary arbitration" means a procedure wherein both parties jointly agree to submit their dispute over the interpretation of the terms of an existing agreement or over a new agreement to an impartial third party whose decision may be final and binding or advisory and non-binding, depending on the nature of the initial agreement.

(16) "Strike" means the failure by concerted action with others to report for duty, the wilful absence from one's position, the stoppages of work, or the abstinence in whole or in part from the full, faithful, and proper performance of the duties of employment, or in any manner interfering with the operation of any public agency, for the purpose of inducing, influencing, or coercing a change in the conditions or compensation or the rights, privileges, or obligations of employment.

Section 3. Public Employee Relations Agency. [(a) There is hereby created [in the State department of   ] a board, to be known as the [Public Employee Relations Agency], which shall consist of [5] members appointed by the Governor, by and with the advice and consent of the Senate from persons representative of the public. Not more than [3] members of the Agency shall be members of the same political party. Each member shall be appointed for a term of [6] years, except that [2] shall be appointed for a term to expire [two] years following the effective date of this act, [2] for a term that shall expire [4] years following the effective date of this act, and [1] for a term that shall expire [6] years following the effective date of this act. A member appointed to fill a vacancy shall be appointed for the unexpired term of the member whom he is to succeed.]

[(a) There is hereby created the Public Employee Relations Agency, which shall be composed of [5] members. The Governor shall appoint two members who shall serve at his pleasure.

A State Labor Committee also may be created and its membership shall be open to any labor organization which represents employees as defined in the act. The Committee shall adopt reasonable rules for the purpose of designating and removing labor members of the Agency. The first meeting of the Committee shall be convened by a representative of the labor organization having the largest number of members who are employees as defined in the act. This representative shall serve as acting chairman of the State Labor Committee until a permanent chairman is selected in accordance with the rules adopted by the Committee.

The State Labor Committee, in accordance with its rules, shall appoint [2] members of the Public Employee Relations Agency, who shall serve at the pleasure of the Committee. If the Committee fails to appoint such members within [28] days following the naming of the Governor's appointees, the Governor shall appoint [2] additional members representative of employee organizations who shall serve at his pleasure. The fifth member of the Agency shall be elected and designated chairman by the unanimous vote of the other [4] members, after which he shall be appointed by the Governor. If a chairman has not been elected within [10] days following the appointment of the other [4] members, the Governor shall designate the chairman. The chairman shall serve for [3] years, commencing from the date of his appointment. Vacancies in the office of any member shall be filled in the same manner as herein provided for appointment. [3] members, consisting of the chairman, at least one member appointed by the Governor and at least one member appointed by the Committee shall at all times constitute a quorum of the Agency.]

(b) Members shall hold no other public office or public employment in the State or its political subdivisions. [The chairman shall give his full time to his duties.]

(c) Members of the Agency other than the chairman shall, when performing the duties of the Agency, shall be compensated at the rate of [one hundred dollars a day], together with an allowance of actual and necessary expenses incurred in the discharge of their responsibilities hereunder. The chairman shall receive an annual salary to be fixed [by the Governor] within the amount available therefor by appropriation, in addition to an allowance for expenses actually and necessarily incurred by him in the performance of his duties.

(d) The Agency may appoint an executive director and such other persons, including but not limited to mediators, members of fact-finding boards, and representatives of employee organizations and public employers to serve as technical advisers to such fact-finding boards, as it may from time to time deem necessary for the performance of its functions. The agency shall prescribe their duties, fix their compensation, and provide for reimbursement of their expenses within the amounts made available therefor by appropriation.

(e) In addition to the authority provided in other sections, the Agency may:

(1) Make studies and analyses of, and act as a clearing-house of information relating to, conditions of employment of public employees throughout the State.

(2) Provide technical assistance and training programs to assist public employers in their dealings with employee organizations.

(3) Request from any public agency such assistance, services, and data as will enable the Agency properly to carry out its functions and powers.

(4) Establish procedures for the prevention of improper public employer and employee organization practices as provided in Section 13 of this act, provided that in the case of a claimed violation of paragraph (5) of subdivision (b) or paragraph (4) of subdivision (c) of such section, procedures shall provide only for an entering of an order directing the public agency or employee organization to negotiate collectively. The pendency of proceedings under this paragraph shall not be used as the basis to delay or interfere with determination of representation status pursuant to Section 7 of this act or with negotiating collectively. The Agency shall exercise exclusive nondelegable jurisdiction of the power granted to it by this paragraph.

(5) Establish, after consulting with representatives of employee organizations and of public agencies, panels of qualified persons, broadly representative of the public, to be available to serve as mediators, arbitrators, members of fact-finding boards, or arbitrators.

(6) Hold such hearings and make such inquiries, as it deems necessary, to carry out properly, its functions and powers;

(7) For the purpose of such hearings and inquiries, administer oaths and affirmations, examine witnesses and documents, take testimony and receive evidence, compel attendance of witnesses and the production of documents by the issuance of subpoenas, and delegate such powers to any member of the Agency or any person appointed by the Agency for the performance of its functions. Such subpoenas shall be regulated and enforced [under the civil practice law and rules].

(8) Make, amend, and rescind, from time to time, such rules and regulations, including but not limited to those governing its internal organization and conduct of its affairs, and exercise such other powers, as may be appropriate to effectuate the purposes and provisions of this act.

Section 4. Public Employee Rights. Public employees shall have the right of self-organization, and may form, join, or assist any employee organization, to negotiate collectively through representatives of their own choosing on questions of grievances and wages, hours, and other terms and conditions of employment and to engage in other concerted activities for the purpose of collective negotiations or other mutual aid or protection, free from interference, restraint or coercion. Public employees also shall have the right to refuse to join employee organizations.

Section 5. Supervisory Employees. Supervisory employees may form, join, and participate in the activities of employee organizations, provided such organizations do not include non-supervisory employees. A public agency shall not extend exclusive recognition to a supervisory organization for the purpose of negotiating collectively with respect to grievances and conditions of employment, but may consult or otherwise communicate with such an organization on appropriate matters. The public employer shall determine whether an individual is to be considered a supervisory or confidential employee for collective negotiations purposes, subject to appeal to the Agency.

[*Section 6. Public Employer Rights.* Nothing in this act is intended to circumscribe or modify the existing right of a public agency to:

(1) direct the work of its employees;

(2) hire, promote, assign, transfer, and retain employees in positions within the public agency;

(3) demote, suspend, or discharge employees for proper cause;

(4) maintain the efficiency of governmental operations;

(5) relieve employees from duties because of lack of work or for other legitimate reasons;

(6) take actions as may be necessary to carry out the mission of the agency in emergencies; and

(7) determine the methods, means, and personnel by which operations are to be carried on.]

Section 7. Recognition of Employee Organizations. (a) Public employers shall recognize certain employee organizations for the purpose of representing their members in collective negotiations with such employers. Employee organizations may establish reasonable provisions for an individual's admission to or dismissal from membership.

(b) Where a public employer has recognized an employee organization or where such organization has been certified by the Agency as representing a majority of the employees in an appropriate unit, or recognized exclusively, pursuant to the provisions of this act, the public employer shall negotiate collectively with such employee organization in the determination of the terms and conditions of employment, and the administration of grievances arising thereunder, of their public employees as provided in this act, and may enter into an agreement with such employee organization.

(c) When a question concerning the representation of employees stemming from the designation of an appropriate unit is raised by a public agency, employee organization, or employees, the Public Employee Relations Agency, established pursuant to this act, shall, at the request of any of the parties, investigate such question and, after a hearing, rule on the definition of the appropriate unit. In defining the unit, the Agency shall take into consideration, along with other relevant factors, the principles of efficient administration of government, the existence of a community of interest among employees, the history and extent of employee organization, geographical location, the provisions of Section 5 of this act, and the recommendations of the parties involved.

(d) Following investigation of a question concerning whether an employee organization represents a majority of the employees in an appropriate unit, the Public Employee Relations Agency at the request of any of the parties, shall examine such questions and certify to the parties in writing the name of the representative that has been designated. The filing of a petition for the investigation or certification of majority representative by any of the parties shall constitute a question within the meaning of this section. In any such investigation, the Agency may provide for an appropriate hearing, may determine voting eligibility, and may take a secret ballot of employees in the appropriate unit involved to ascertain such representative for the purpose of exclusive recognition. If the Agency has certified an exclusively recognized majority representative in an appropriate unit, as provided in this section, it shall not be required to consider the matter again for a period of one year. The Agency may promulgate such rules and regulations as may be appropriate to carry out the provisions of subsections (c) and (d) of this section.

Section 8. Rights Accompanying Exclusive Recognition. (a) A public employer shall extend to an employee organization certified or recognized exclusively, pursuant to this act, the right to represent the employees of the appropriate unit involved in collective negotiations proceedings and in the settlement of grievances and the right to unchallenged representation status, consistent with Section 7(d), during the 12 months following the date of certification or exclusive recognition.

(b) A public employer shall extend to such an organization the right to membership dues deduction, upon presentation of dues deduction authorization cards signed by individual employees, provided that all employee organizations may have the right to membership dues deduction until the formally recognized representative has been determined. Public employees who are not members of the exclusively recognized employee organization may be required to pay fees to such organization for its representational services, provided that such fees shall not exceed the amount of regular membership dues.

(c) A reasonable number of representatives of exclusively recognized organizations shall be given time off without loss of compensation during normal working hours to bargain collectively with public employers on matters falling within the scope of negotiations.

Section 9. Procedures for Determining the Recognition Status of Local Employee Organizations. (a) Every public agency, other than the State and its authorities, acting through its governing body, may establish procedures, not inconsistent with the provisions of Sections 7 and 8 of this act and after consultation with interested employee organizations and employer representatives, to resolve disputes concerning the recognition status of employee organizations composed of employees of such agency.

(b) In the absence of such procedures, these disputes shall be submitted to the Public Employee Relations Agency in accordance with Section 7 of this act.

Section 10. Scope of an Agreement. The scope of an agreement may extend to all matters relating to employment conditions and employer-employee relations, including, but not limited to, wages, hours, and other terms and conditions of employment. An agreement may contain a grievance procedure culminating in final and binding arbitration of unresolved grievances and disputed interpretations of such agreement. Where there is a conflict between any agreement reached by a public employer and a recognized employee organization and approved in accordance with the provisions of this act on matters appropriate to collective negotiations, as defined in this act, and any rule or regulation adopted by the public employer or its agent such as a personnel board or civil service commission, the terms of such agreement shall prevail. [Subject to approval by the governing body,] where there is a conflict between any agreement reached by a public employer and a recognized employee organization and approved in accordance with the provisions of this act on matters appropriate to collective negotiations, as defined in this act, and any charter, special act, ordinance, any general statute directly relating to hours of work of policemen or firemen, or any general statute providing for the method of covering or removing employees from coverage under the [   ] employees retirement system, the terms of such agreement shall prevail. Nothing herein shall diminish the authority and power of any civil service commission, personnel board, personnel agency or its agents established by constitutional provision, statute, charter, or special act to conduct and grade merit examinations and to rate candidates in the order of their relative excellence from which appointments or promotions may be made to positions in the competitive division of the classified service of the public employer served by such civil service commission or personnel board.

Section 11. Implementation of an Agreement. (a) Any agreement reached by the public employer and the exclusive representative shall be reduced to writing and executed by both parties.

(b) The agreement shall be valid and enforced under its terms when entered into in accordance with the provisions of this act. No publication thereof shall be required to make it effective.

(c) A request for funds necessary to implement the written agreement and for approval of any other matter requiring the approval of the governing body, shall be submitted by the representative of the public employer to the governing body within [14] days of the date on which such agreement is executed. Matters requiring the approval of the governing body shall be submitted by the representative of the public employer within [14] days of the date the body convenes if it is not in session at the time the agreement is executed. Failure by the representative of the public employer to submit such request to the governing body within the appropriate period shall be a refusal to negotiate in good faith, in violation of Section 13(b)(5) of this act. The request shall be considered approved if the governing body fails to vote to approve or reject the request within [30] days of the end of the period for submission to the body. The representative of the public employer may implement provisions of the agreement not requiring action by the governing body, to be effective and operative in accordance with the terms of the agreement. If the governing body rejects the provisions submitted to it by the designated representative, either party may reopen all or part of the remainder of the agreement.

Section 12. Resolution of Disputes Arising in the Course of Negotiations. (a) Public employers may include in agreements concluded with exclusively recognized or certified employee organizations a provision setting forth the procedures to be invoked in the event of disputes which reach an impasse in the course of negotiating proceedings. For purposes of this section, an impasse shall be deemed to exist if the parties fail to achieve agreement at least [60] days prior to the budget submission. In the absence or upon the failure of dispute resolution procedures contained in agreements resulting in an impasse, either party may request the assistance of the Public Employee Relations Agency or the Agency may render such assistance on its own motion, as provided in subdivision (b) of this section.

(b) On the request of either party, or upon the Agency's own motion, in the event it determines an impasse exists in negotiating proceedings between a public employer and an exclusively recognized or certified employee organization, the Agency shall aid the parties in effecting a voluntary resolution of the dispute, and appoint a mediator or mediators, representative of the public, from a list of qualified persons maintained by the Agency.

(c) If the impasse persists [10] days after the mediator(s) has been appointed, the Agency shall appoint a fact-finding board of not more than [3] members, each representative of the public, from a list of qualified persons maintained by the Agency. The fact-finding board shall conduct a hearing, may administer oaths, and may request the Agency to issue subpoenas. It shall make written findings of facts and recommendations for resolution of the dispute and, no later than [20] days from the day of appointment, shall serve such findings on the public employer and the recognized employee organization. If the dispute continues [10] days after the report is submitted to the parties, the report shall be made public by the Agency.

(d) If an impasse persists after the findings of fact and recommendations are made public by the fact-finding board, the Agency shall have the power to take whatever steps it deems appropriate to resolve the dispute, including (i) the making of recommendations after giving due consideration to the findings of fact and recommendations of the fact-finding board, but no other such board shall be appointed, and (ii) upon request of the parties, assisting in providing for voluntary arbitration.

(e) In the event that the parties have not resolved their impasse by the end of a [50] day period commencing with the date of appointment of the fact-finding board (i) the representative of the public employer involved shall submit to the governing body or its duly authorized committee(s) a copy of the findings of fact and recommendations of the fact-finding board, together with his recommendations for settling the dispute; (ii) the employee organization may submit to such governing body or its duly authorized committee(s) recommendations for settling the dispute; (iii) the governing body or such committee(s) shall forthwith conduct a hearing at which the parties shall be required to explain their positions with respect to the board; and (iv) thereafter, the governing body shall take such action as it deems to be in the public interest, including the interest of the public employees involved.

(f) Collective negotiations proceedings and mediation, fact-finding, and arbitration meetings and investigations shall not be subject to the provisions of [insert State "right to know" law].

(g) The costs for mediation services provided by the Agency shall be borne by the Agency. All other costs, including those of fact-finding and arbitrating services, shall be borne equally by the parties to a dispute.

Section 13. Prohibited Practices; Evidence of Bad Faith. (a)

Commission of a prohibited practice, as defined in this section, among other actions, shall constitute evidence of bad faith in collective negotiations proceedings.

(b) It shall be a prohibited practice for a public employer or its designated representative wilfully to:

(1) Interfere, restrain, or coerce public employees in the exercise of rights granted in Section 4 of this act;

(2) Dominate, interfere, or assist in the formation, existence, or administration of any employee organization;

(3) Encourage or discourage membership in any employee organization, agency, committee, association, or representation plan by discrimination in hiring, tenure, or other terms or conditions of employment.

(4) Discharge or discriminate against an employee because he has filed any affidavit, petition, or complaint or given any information or testimony under this act, or because he has formed, joined, or chosen to be represented by any employee organization;

(5) Refuse to negotiate collectively with representatives of recognized employee organizations as required in Section 7 of this act;

(6) Deny the rights accompanying certification or exclusive recognition granted in Section 8 of this act;

(7) Blacklist any employee organization or its members for the purpose of denying them employment because of their organizational activities;

(8) Avoid in mediation, fact-finding, and arbitration endeavors as provided in Section 12 of this act;

(9) Institute or attempt to institute a lockout; or

(10) Deal directly with employees on matters falling within the scope of negotiations circumventing the exclusive representative.

(c) It shall be a prohibited practice for public employees or employee organizations wilfully to:

(1) Interfere with, restrain, or coerce public employees in the exercise of rights granted in Section 4 of this act;

(2) Interfere with, restrain, or coerce a public employer with respect to rights protected in Section 6 of this act or with respect to selecting a representative for the purposes of negotiating collectively;

(3) Refuse to bargain collectively with a public employer as required in Section 7 of this act;

(4) Avoid in mediation, fact-finding, and arbitration efforts as provided in Section 12 of this act; or

(5) Engage in a strike.

Section 14. Violations of Prohibited Practices. (a) Any controversy concerning prohibited practices may be submitted to the Agency. Proceedings against the party alleged to have committed a prohibited practice shall be commenced by service upon it by the Agency of a written notice, together with a copy of the charges. The accused party shall have [7] days within which to serve a written answer to such charges. The Agency's hearing will be held promptly thereafter and at such hearing, the parties shall be permitted to be represented by counsel and to summon witnesses in their behalf. Compliance with the technical rules of evidence shall not be required. The Agency may use its rule-making power, as provided in Section 3, to make any other procedural rules it deems necessary to carry on this function.*

(b) The Agency shall state its findings of facts upon all the testimony and shall either dismiss the complaint or determine that a prohibited practice has been or is being committed. If the Agency finds that the party accused has committed or is committing a prohibited practice, the Agency shall petition the [court of appropriate jurisdiction] to punish such violation, and shall file in the [court] the record in the proceedings. Any person aggrieved by a final order of the Agency granting or denying in whole or in part the relief sought may obtain a review on such order in the [court of appropriate jurisdiction] by filing in the [court] a complaint praying that the order of the Agency be modified or set aside, with copy of the complaint filed on the Agency, and thereupon the aggrieved party shall file in the [court] the record in the proceedings, certified by the Agency. Findings of the Agency as to the facts shall be conclusive unless it is made to appear to the satisfaction of the [court of appropriate jurisdiction] that the findings of fact were not supported by substantial evidence.

Section 15. Internal Conduct of Public Employee Organizations. (a) Every employee organization which has or seeks recognition as a representative of public employees of this state and of its political subdivisions shall file with the Public Employee Relations

---

* Where a State has adopted an administrative procedures act, this section should be made to conform to it.

Agency a registration report, signed by its president or other appropriate officer, within [90] days after the effective date of this act. Such report shall be in a form prescribed by the Agency and shall be accompanied by [two] copies of the employee organization's constitution and bylaws. A filing by a national or international employee organization of its constitution and bylaws shall be accepted in lieu of a filing of such documents by each subordinate organization. All changes or amendments to such constitutions and bylaws shall be promptly reported to the Agency.

(b) Every employee organization shall file with the Agency an annual report and an amended report whenever changes are made. Such reports shall be in a form prescribed by the Agency, and shall provide information on the following:

(1) The names and addresses of the organization, any parent organization or organizations with which it is affiliated, the principal officers, and all representatives;

(2) The name and address of its local agent for service of process;

(3) A general description of the public employees or groups of employees the organization represents or seeks to represent;

(4) The amounts of the initiation fee and monthly dues members must pay;

(5) A pledge, in a form prescribed by the Agency, that the organization will conform to the laws of the State and that it will accept members without regard to age, race, sex, religion, or national origin; and

(6) A financial report and audit.

(c) The constitution or bylaws of every employee organization shall provide that:

(1) Accurate accounts of all income and expenses shall be kept, and annual financial report and audit shall be prepared, such accounts shall be open for inspection by any member of the organization, and loans to officers and agents shall be made only on terms and conditions available to all members.

(2) Business or financial interests of its officers and agents, their spouses, minor children, parents, or otherwise, that conflict with the fiduciary obligation of such persons to the organization shall be prohibited.

(3) Every official or employee of an employee organization who

handles funds or other property of the organization, or trust in which an organization is interested, or a subsidiary organization, shall be bonded. The amount, scope, and form of the bond shall be determined by the Agency.

(d) The governing rules of every employee organization shall provide for: periodic elections by secret ballot subject to recognized safeguards concerning the equal right of all members to nominate, seek office, and vote in such elections; the right of individual members to participate in the affairs of the organization; and fair and equitable procedures in disciplinary actions.

(e) The Agency shall prescribe such rules and regulations as may be necessary to govern the establishment and reporting of trusteeships over employee organizations. Establishment of such trusteeships shall be permitted only if the constitution or bylaws of the organization set forth reasonable procedures.

(f) An employee organization that has not registered or filed an annual report, or that has failed to comply with other provisions of this act, shall not be recognized for the purpose of negotiating with any public employer regarding the terms and conditions of work of its members. Recognized employee organizations failing to comply with this act may have such recognition revoked by the Agency. All proceedings under this subsection shall be conducted in accordance with [the State administrative procedure act]. Prohibitions shall be enforced by injunction upon the petition of the Agency to [court of appropriate jurisdiction]. Complaints of violation of this act shall be filed with the Agency.

Section 16. Local Public Agency Options. This act, except for Sections 2, 3(e)(3), 4, 5, 6, 7, 8, 13, 14, and 15, shall be inapplicable to any public employer, other than the State and its authorities, which, acting through its governing body, has adopted by local law, ordinance, or resolution its own provisions and procedures which have been submitted to the Agency by such public employer and as to which there is in effect a determination by the Agency that such provisions and procedures and the continuing implementation thereof are substantially equivalent to the rights granted under this act.

Section 17. Separability. [Insert separability clause.]

Section 18. Effective Date. [Insert effective date.]

Executive Order No. 11491:
Labor-Management Relations
in the Federal Service

President Richard Nixon's Executive Order No. 11491, which drew from the first such order (No. 10988) by John F. Kennedy in 1962, was issued on October 29, 1969.[1] It established the Federal Labor Relations Council to administer and interpret the order, decide major policy issues, prescribe regulations, and make recommendations to the president. It also established the Federal Service Impasses Panel as an agency within the council and provided that the Assistant Secretary of Labor-Management Relations have authority to decide on appropriate unit issues, supervise elections, determine eligibility for national consultation rights, act on violations of the order through cease and desist judgments and affirmative action judgments, and in certain cases to rule on unfair labor practice complaints. The following excerpts indicate some of the major features.

Policy—Section 1

... (a) Each employee of the executive branch of the Federal Government has the right, freely and without fear of penalty or reprisal, to form, join, and assist a labor organization or to refrain from any such activity, and each employee shall be protected in the exercise of this right. Except as otherwise expressly provided in this Order, the right to assist a labor organization extends to participation in the management of the organization and acting for the organization in the capacity of an organization representative, including presentation of its views to officials of the executive

---

1. Exec. Order No. 11491, 3 C.F.R. 191 (1969 Comp.); Exec. Order No. 10988, 3 C.F.R. 521 (1959-1963 Comp.).

branch, the Congress, or other appropriate authority. The head of each agency shall take the action required to assure that employees in the agency are apprised of their rights under this section and that no interference, restraint, coercion, or discrimination is practiced within his agency to encourage or discourage membership in a labor organization.

(b) Paragraph (a) of this section does not authorize participation in the management of a labor organization or acting as a representative of such an organization by a supervisor, except as provided in section 24 of this Order, or by an employee when the participation or activity would result in a conflict or apparent conflict of interest or otherwise be incompatible with law or with the official duties of the employee. . . .[2]

Labor Organization—Section 2(e)

. . . "Labor organization" means a lawful organization of any kind in which employees participate and which exists for the purpose, in whole or in part, of dealing with agencies concerning grievances, personnel policies and practices, or other matters affecting the working conditions of their employees; but does not include an organization which—

(1) consists of management officials or supervisors, except as provided in section 24 of this Order;

(2) asserts the right to strike against the Government of the United States or any agency thereof, or to assist or participate in such a strike, or imposes a duty or obligation to conduct, assist or participate in such a strike;

(3) advocates the overthrow of the constitutional form of government in the United States; or

(4) discriminates with regard to the terms or conditions of membership because of race, color, creed, sex, age, or national origin . . .[3]

Application—Section 3

. . . (a) This Order applies to all employees and agencies in the

---

2. With slight editorial changes, this subsection is identical with the 1962 Executive Order.
3. The 1962 Executive Order used the term "employee organization." The explicit exclusion of management officials or supervisors was added in 1969, as were the prohibitions against discrimination by sex or age. Later sections in the 1962 order dealt with the separation of managers and supervisors. The remainder is identical in meaning.

executive branch, except as provided in paragraphs (b), (c) and (d) of this section.

(b) This Order (except section 22) does not apply to—

(1) the Federal Bureau of Investigation;

(2) the Central Intelligence Agency;

(3) any other agency, or office, bureau, or entity within an agency, which has as a primary function intelligence, investigative, or security work, when the head of the agency determines, in his sole judgment, that the Order cannot be applied in a manner consistent with national security requirements and considerations; or

(4) any office, bureau or entity within an agency which has as a primary function investigation or audit of the conduct or work of officials or employees of the agency for the purpose of ensuring honesty and integrity in the discharge of their official duties, when the head of the agency determines, in his sole judgment, that the Order cannot be applied in a manner consistent with the internal security of the agency.

(c) The head of an agency may, in his sole judgment, suspend any provision of this Order (except section 22) with respect to any agency installation or activity located outside the United States, when he determines that this is necessary in the national interest, subject to the conditions he prescribes.

(d) Employees engaged in administering a labor-management relations law or this Order shall not be represented by a labor organization which also represents other groups of employees under the law or this Order, or which is affiliated directly or indirectly with an organization which represents such a group of employees. . . .[4]

Recognition—Section 7

. . . (a) An agency shall accord exclusive recognition or national consultation rights at the request of a labor organization which meets the requirements for the recognition or consultation rights under this Order.

(b) A labor organization seeking recognition shall submit to the agency a roster of its officers and representatives, a copy of its constitution and by-laws, and a statement of its objectives.

(c) When recognition of a labor organization has been accorded,

---

4. This section adds 3(b)(4) and 3(d) to the 1962 order.

the recognition continues as long as the organization continues to meet the requirements of this Order applicable to that recognition, except that this section does not require an election to determine whether an organization should become, or continue to be recognized as, exclusive representative of the employees in any unit or subdivision thereof within 12 months after a prior valid election with respect to such unit.

(d) Recognition, in whatever form accorded, does not—

(1) preclude an employee, regardless of whether he is a member of a labor organization, from bringing matters of personal concern to the attention of appropriate officials under applicable law, rule, regulation, or established agency policy; or from choosing his own representative in a grievance or appellate action;

(2) preclude or restrict consultations and dealings between an agency and a veterans organization with respect to matters of particular interest to employees with veterans preference; or

(3) preclude an agency from consulting or dealing with a religious, social, fraternal, or other lawful association, not qualified as a labor organization, with respect to matters or policies which involve individual members of the association or are of particular applicability to it or its members. Consultations and dealings under subparagraph (3) of this paragraph shall be so limited that they do not assume the character of formal consultation on matters of general employee-management policy, except as provided in paragraph (e) of this section, or extend to areas where recognition of the interests of one employee group may result in discrimination against or injury to the interests of other employees.

(e) An agency shall establish a system for intra-management communication and consultation with its supervisors or associations of supervisors. These communications and consultations shall have as their purposes the improvement of agency operations, the improvement of working conditions of supervisors, the exchange of information, the improvement of managerial effectiveness, and the establishment of policies that best serve the public interest in accomplishing the mission of the agency. . . .

Formal and informal recognition, included in Sections 7(f) and 8 of the 1962 order, are replaced by national consultation rights. Thus, only exclusive recognition remains. Informal recognition permitted an employee organization to present its views on matters of concern. Formal recognition was previously accorded organiza-

tions having at least ten percent of the unit membership, where exclusive representation was not present. In neither case were the government agencies required to respond. In Section 9 of the 1969 order, national consultation rights are accorded qualified organizations representing a substantial number of employees of a given agency. Section 10 states how exclusive recognition is attained.

Agreements—Sections 11 and 12

Sec. 11. *Negotation of agreements.* (a) An agency and a labor organization that has been accorded exclusive recognition, through appropriate representatives, shall meet at reasonable times and confer in good faith with respect to personnel policies and practices and matters affecting working conditions, so far as may be appropriate under applicable laws and regulations, including policies set forth in the Federal Personnel Manual, published agency policies and regulations, a national or other controlling agreement at a higher level in the agency, and this Order. They may negotiate an agreement, or any question arising thereunder; determine appropriate techniques, consistent with section 17 of this Order, to assist in such negotiation; and execute a written agreement or memorandum of understanding.

(b) In prescribing regulations relating to personnel policies and practices and working conditions, an agency shall have due regard for the obligation imposed by paragraph (a) of this section. However, the obligation to meet and confer does not include matters with respect to the mission of an agency; its budget; its organization; the number of employees; and the numbers, types, and grades of positions or employees assigned to an organizational unit, work project or tour of duty; the technology of performing its work; or its internal security practices. This does not preclude the parties from negotiating agreements providing appropriate arrangements for employees adversely affected by the impact of realignment of work forces or technological change.

(c) If, in connection with negotiations, an issue develops as to whether a proposal is contrary to law, regulation, controlling agreement, or this Order and therefore not negotiable, it shall be resolved as follows:

(1) An issue which involves interpretation of a controlling agreement at a higher agency level is resolved under the procedures of the controlling agreement, or, if none, under agency regulations;

(2) An issue other than as described in subparagraph (1) of this paragraph which arises at a local level may be referred by either party to the head of the agency for determination;

(3) An agency head's determination as to the interpretation of the agency's regulations with respect to a proposal is final;

(4) A labor organization may appeal to the Council for a decision when—

(i) it disagrees with an agency head's determination that a proposal would violate applicable law, regulation of appropriate authority outside the agency, or this Order, or

(ii) it believes that an agency's regulations, as interpreted by the agency head, violate applicable law, regulation of appropriate authority outside the agency, or this Order.

Sec. 12. *Basic provisions of agreements.* Each agreement between an agency and a labor organization is subject to the following requirements—

(a) in the administration of all matters covered by the agreement, officials and employees are governed by existing or future laws and the regulations of appropriate authorities, including policies set forth in the Federal Personnel Manual; by published agency policies and regulations in existence at the time the agreement was approved; and by subsequently published agency policies and regulations required by law or by the regulations of appropriate authorities, or authorized by the terms of a controlling agreement at a higher agency level;

(b) management officials of the agency retain the right, in accordance with applicable laws and regulations—

(1) to direct employees of the agency;

(2) to hire, promote, transfer, assign, and retain employees in positions within the agency, and to suspend, demote, discharge, or take other disciplinary action against employees;

(3) to relieve employees from duties because of lack of work or for other legitimate reasons;

(4) to maintain the efficiency of the Government operations entrusted to them;

(5) to determine the methods, means, and personnel by which such operations are to be conducted; and

(6) to take whatever actions may be necessary to carry out the mission of the agency in situations of emergency; and

(c) nothing in the agreement shall require an employee to be-

come or to remain a member of a labor organization, or to pay
money to the organization except pursuant to a voluntary, written
authorization by a member for the payment of dues through payroll deductions.

The requirements of this section shall be expressly stated in the
initial or basic agreement and apply to all supplemental, implementing, subsidiary, or informal agreements between the agency
and the organization . . .[5]

*The subsequent sections concern grievance procedures, Sections
13 and 14; approval of agreements, Section 15; negotiation disputes and impasses, Sections 16 and 17; standards of conduct for
labor organizations, Section 18; unfair labor practices by management, Section 19; use of official time, Section 20; allotment of
dues, Section 21; adverse action appeals, Section 22; agency implementation, Section 23; savings clauses regarding actions taken under the 1962 order, Section 24; guidance, training, review and information services, Section 25; and effective date, Section 26.*

---

5. The meet and confer language in Section 11(a) is the same as that in
the 1962 order (Section 6(a)) except that the term "in good faith" is
added.

The Cornell Case

183 NLRB 41
United States of America
Before the National Labor Relations Board

Cornell University, Employer
and
Association of Cornell Employees — Libraries
}
Case 3-RC-4768

Cornell University, Employer and Petitioner
and
Staff Association of the Metropolitan District Office, School of Industrial and Labor Relations, Cornell University
}
Case 3-RM-440

Cornell University, Employer and Petitioner
and
Association of Cornell Employees—Libraries
}
Case 3-RM-441

Cornell University, Employer and Petitioner
and
Civil Service Employees Association, Inc.
}
Case 3-RM-442

Syracuse University, Employer and Petitioner
and
Service Employees International Union, Local 200, AFL-CIO
}
Case 3-RM-433

Decision

Upon petitions duly filed under Section 9(c) of the National Labor Relations Act, as amended, a consolidated hearing was held before John W. Irving, Hearing Officer of the National Labor Relations Board.

Following the hearing and pursuant to Section 102.67 of the National Labor Relations Board Rules and Regulations and Statements of Procedure, Series 8, as amended, by direction of the Regional Director for Region 3, the case was transferred to the Board for decision. Briefs were filed by the Employers, the Association of Cornell Employees—Libraries, Civil Service Employees Association, and Service Employees International Union, AFL-CIO, in behalf of Service Employees International Union, Local 200, AFL-CIO.[1] The Hearing Officer's rulings made at the hearing are free from prejudicial error and are hereby affirmed.

On the entire record in this case, the Board finds:

1. Cornell University and Syracuse University, the employers herein, have filed representation petitions seeking elections to determine the bargaining representatives of certain of their non-academic employees. Association of Cornell Employees—Libraries (herein called ACE) has also filed a petition seeking to represent a group of library employees.

The threshhold question is whether the Board has or should assert jurisdiction over nonprofit colleges and universities in view of the 1951 decision in the *Columbia University* case.[2] In that case, the Board decided that it would not effectuate the policies of the Act "to assert its jurisdiction over a nonprofit, educational institution where the activities involved are noncommercial in nature and

---

1. With the Board's consent the following parties submitted *amici curiae* briefs supporting the Board's assertion of jurisdiction: AFL-CIO, Boston University, Colgate University, Dowling College, Fordham University, Hamilton College, Lasell Junior College, Maria Regina College, New York University, Rochester Institute of Technology, St. John Fisher College, University of Rochester, Wheaton College, Yale University, NAACP Legal Defense and Educational Fund, Inc.

Parties opposing Board assertion of jurisdiction: Association of Independent California Colleges and Universities, Association of Private Colleges and Universities of Georgia, Baylor University, California Institute of Technology, California State Colleges, Federation of Independent Illinois Colleges, New York State Labor Relations Board, Oregon Independent Colleges Association, Southern Methodist University, Texas Christian University, University of Miami, University of the Pacific. Also the National Association of State Labor Relations Agencies passed a resolution in October 1969, requesting the Board to continue its exemption for private colleges and universities.

2. Trustees of Columbia University, 97 NLRB 424.

intimately connected with charitable and educational activities of the institution."[3]

All the petitioners urge the Board to overrule the *Columbia University* case. Syracuse and Cornell argue that the operations and activities of educational institutions as a class, and of Cornell and Syracuse in particular, have an overwhelming impact and effect on interstate commerce, that the operations of universities and colleges have increasingly become matters of Federal interest, and that this interest coupled with the failure of the States adequately to recognize and legislate for labor relations affecting these institutions and their employees now justifies the Board in asserting jurisdiction. In support of their contention as to the impact of the operations of Syracuse and Cornell, as well as of educational institutions as a class, upon interstate commerce, the Employers have presented extensive documentation of financial activities which are set forth hereinafter.

Syracuse University

Syracuse University is the largest employer in the city of Syracuse, New York. It has about 3,500 academic and nonacademic employees. The current student population is 21,000, of whom 4,000-5,000 are from out-of-State, and 900 from out-of-country. In addition to facilities in New York State, Syracuse has facilities in South America, Holland, Italy, and France.

The purchasing department of the University makes annual purchases approximating $8,000,000, of which more than $5,000,000 originate outside the State of New York. In addition, the University Book Store and Food Service annually make out-of-State purchases valued at more than $2,000,000. The University operates a theatre which annually makes out-of-State purchases valued at about $300,000. The University realizes $500,000 annually from the sale of tickets for football games, and $250,000 from the sale of television and radio rights.

Syracuse has an annual operating budget of $66,000,000. It has an investment portfolio valued at $36,000,000, which includes stockholdings in industrial firms, banks, and utilities. It also is the sole stockholder in a country club whose employees are represented by

---

3. *Id.* at 427.

a Union certified by the NLRB. Further, it has real estate investments outside New York State valued at $750,000.

Finally, Syracuse is a party to numerous sponsored research contracts with such Federal agencies as the Department of Defense, National Aeronautics and Space Administration, Institute of Health, and Department of Labor and such private sponsors as the Ford and Carnegie foundations. The annual value of these research contracts is in excess of $13,000,000.

Cornell University

Cornell University is the largest employer in Tompkins County, New York. It has more than 8,000 employees in New York State, of whom 2,700 are academic and 5,700 nonacademic. Cornell presently has an enrolled student body exceeding 14,000. Fifty percent of these students are from outside the State of New York. There are also in excess of 1,100 students from 87 foreign countries enrolled at the University.

The University has offices in Ohio, Massachusetts, Illinois, Florida, and Pennsylvania, and operates an observatory in Puerto Rico.

During 1968-69, the University's publishing department purchased goods valued at $16,400,000. Of this sum, $10,750,000 represented purchases of items manufactured outside the State of New York. During the same period, Cornell University Press made purchases of almost $1,000,000, of which more than half represented direct or indirect purchases of out-of-State manufactured products. During this same year, the Press made sales valued at $942,000 to purchasers outside the State. Cornell also owns a radio station, a CBS affiliate, which in 1968-1969 received $296,000 from local and regional advertising, and $38,000 from national advertising.

Cornell's annual expenditures amount to $142,300,000. Its current assets are valued at $282,500,000. Included is an investment portfolio of over $250,000,000 which consists, *inter alia,* of investments in industrial concerns, banks, insurance companies, and public utilities.

During 1968-69, Cornell had research contracts amounting to $26,600,000 sponsored by various agencies of the Federal Government, including National Science Foundation, Public Health Service, Atomic Energy Commission, Department of Defense, and National Aeronautics and Space Administration. In addition, the University received $6,000,000 for research projects sponsored by such foundations as Ford, Carnegie, and Rockefeller.

Discussion

Section 2(2) of the Act defines an "employer" as follows:
... any persons acting as an agent of an employer, directly, or indirectly, but shall not include the United States or any wholly owned Government corporation, or any Federal Reserve Bank, or any State or political subdivision thereof, or any corporation or association operating a hospital, if no part of the net earnings inures to the benefit of any private shareholder or individual. . . .

Although Section 2(2) specifically excludes nonprofit hospitals from the Act's coverage, it contains no such exclusion of private, nonprofit educational institutions. In the *Columbia University* case, the Board reviewed the then recently enacted Taft-Hartley amendments to the National Labor Relations Act and concluded that

... the activities of Columbia University affect commerce sufficiently to satisfy the requirements of the statute and the standards established by the Board for the normal exercise of its jurisdiction . . .[4]

However, the Board, as a discretionary matter, declined to assert such jurisdiction because of statements in the House Conference Report[5] which seemed to indicate approval of what the Report believed to have been the Board's pre-1947 practice of declining in the exercise of its discretion to assert jurisdiction over certain nonprofit organizations.[6] The Board concluded:

Under all the circumstances, we do not believe that it would effectuate the policies of the Act for the Board to assert its jurisdiction over a nonprofit, educational institution where the activities involved are noncommercial in nature and intimately connected with the charitable purposes and educational activities of the institution.

It should be noted that, although the House Conference Report referred to the Board's pre-1947 practice with respect to exercising jurisdiction over nonprofit employers, the 1947 amendments themselves placed no curb on the Board's discretionary jurisdiction except as to nonprofit hospitals. The Report did not say that,

4. *Id.* at 425.
5. House Report No. 510, 80th Cong. 1st Sess., p. 32.
6. See discussion in Columbia University, *supra* at 426-427.

because the Board had decided before 1947 it would not effectuate the policies of the Act to assert jurisdiction over certain employers, it must continue to refuse to assert such jurisdiction indefinitely in the future despite change of circumstances. This hardly seems inadvertent. Congress was well aware that the Board's discretionary standards for asserting jurisdiction were not fixed, but had been changed from time to time. The very fact that Congress rejected the 1947 House proposals for the specific exemption from the Act of broad classes of charitable or nonprofit organizations seems to indicate that Congress was content to leave to the Board's informed discretion in the future as it had in the past, whether and when to assert jurisdiction over nonprofit organizations whose operations had a substantial impact upon interstate commerce.

We adhere to the view that the Board has statutory jurisdiction over nonprofit educational institutions whose operations affect commerce. But we shall no longer decline to assert jurisdiction over such institutions as a class.

In the intervening two decades since *Columbia University* was decided, the Board has declined to assert jurisdiction over nonprofit universities if the activity involved was noncommercial and intimately connected with the school's educational purpose.[7] However, an analysis of the cases reveals that the dividing line separating purely commercial from noncommercial activity has not been easily defined.[8]

---

7. See, e.g., Leland Stanford Junior University, 152 NLRB 704; University of Miami, 146 NLRB 1148. The courts have not directly passed on the validity of the Board's interpretation of Section 2(2) and its legislative history. However, this question is referred to in Office Employees v. N.L.R.B., 353 U.S. 313, where the Supreme Court reversed the Board's refusal to assert jurisdiction over nonprofit labor unions as a class. Although the Court quoted language from the 1947 Conference Report with apparent approval, it nevertheless stated that "the Board has never recognized such a blanket rule of exclusion over all nonprofit employers. It has declined jurisdiction on an *ad hoc* basis over religious, educational, and eleemosynary employers. . . ." (*Id.* at 318.) See also Hotel Employees Local 255 v. N.L.R.B., 358 U.S. 99, where the Supreme Court ruled that it was not permissible for the Board to decline jurisdiction over an industry which substantially affects commerce.

8. *Compare* Woods Hole Oceanographic Institution, 143 NLRB 568, MIT (Lincoln Laboratory), 110 NLRB 1611, *and* California Institute of Technology, 102 NLRB 1402 (jurisdiction asserted) *with* Armour Research Foundation of Illinois Institute of Technology, 107 NLRB 1052 (jurisdiction declined).

Those who urge adherence to the *Columbia University* doctrine,[9] contend that the legislative history of the Taft-Hartley amendments establishes that Congress intended to exempt nonprofit educational institutions from the coverage of the Act. They further argue that Congress ratified its earlier position by amending the Act in 1959 without commenting on or altering the 1947 Conference Report relative to exclusion.

It is true that the legislative history of the 1959 Landrum-Griffin Act is completely silent on the matter of nonprofit employers. We are not persuaded, however, that congressional silence may be construed as indicating continued congressional approval of either the 1947 legislative history or Board reliance on it. The fact remains that Section 2(2) contains no express exemption for nonprofit employers. More to the point is that in 1959 Congress enacted Section 14(c) which for the first time both authorized and set limits on the Board's discretionary refusal to exercise jurisdiction.

Two years before the enactment of Section 14(c), the Supreme Court ruled in *Guss v. Utah Labor Relations Board*[10] that the States were powerless to entertain cases which fell within the NLRB's statutory jurisdiction, even though the Board had declined to assert such jurisdiction. Thus, a "no man's land" was created where employers and employees were denied a Federal forum for the resolution of labor disputes and yet were unable to turn to the States for alternative relief.[11] Ample evidence in the legislative history reveals that Section 14(c) was the congressional response designed to eliminate the "no-man's land."[12] Toward this end, 14(c)(1) states that the Board in its discretion may "decline to assert jurisdiction over any labor dispute involving any class or category of employers, where, in the opinion of the Board, the effect of such labor dispute on commerce is not sufficiently substantial to warrant the exercise of its jurisdiction. . . ." Conversely, it impliedly confirms the Board's authority to expand its jurisdiction to any class of employers whose operations substantially af-

---

9. E.g., *amici curiae* briefs of Association of Independent California Colleges and Universities, and New York State Labor Relations Board.
10. 353 U.S. 1 (1957).
11. *Legislative History of the Labor Management Reporting and Disclosure Act of 1959*, at 422 (cited hereinafter as *LH*).
12. *Id.* at 1150, 1084, 1582.

fect commerce. Section 14(c)(2) further attempts to narrow the "no-man's land" gap by empowering the States to exercise jurisdiction when the Board declines to so assert.

While the language of Section 14(c) does not compel the Board to assert jurisdiction, it does manifest a congressional policy favoring such assertion where the Board finds that the operations of a class of employers exercise a substantial effect on commerce.

In light of these statutory guidelines, Syracuse and Cornell have called upon the Board to reexamine the soundness of the *Columbia University* doctrine as it applies to colleges and universities today.[13] Petitioners introduced extensive evidence at the hearing to document their claim that educational institutions as a class have not only a substantial, but massive impact on interstate commerce. After carefully examining all the evidence submitted, we are compelled to conclude that whatever guidance the 1947 Conference Report provided to the situation which existed in 1951 when *Columbia University* was decided, the underlying considerations no longer obtain two decades later.

No claim is made that education is not still the primary goal of such institutions. Indeed, more than two million students are enrolled in colleges today, almost double the number attending in 1951.[14] Yet to carry out its educative functions, the university has become involved in a host of activities which are commercial in character.

Thus, the approximately 1,450 private 4- and 2-year colleges and universities in the United States have on their payrolls some 247,000 full-time professionals and 263,000 full- and part-time nonprofessional employees.[15] Operating budgets of private educational facili-

---

13. In the past it has been the nonprofit employer who has opposed Board assertion of jurisdiction. In this regard, see Lovelace Foundation, 165 NLRB 743; Leland Stanford Junior University, 152 NLRB 704; MIT., 152 NLRB 598; University of Miami Institute of Marine Science, Division, 146 NLRB 1448. Crotty Brothers, N.Y. Inc., 146 NLRB 755; *Cf.* Woods Hole Oceanographic Institution, 143 NLRB 568.

14. *Projections of Educational Statistics to 1975-76*, National Center for Education Statistics, 1966, p. 11. Nearly one million students left their States of origin to pursue their education, *Digest of Education Statistics*, U.S. Dept. of Health, Education and Welfare, p. 71. Another 110,000 are from foreign countries. *A Fact Book of Higher Education, American Council on Education*, 3d issue, p. 8170.

15. "Numbers and Characteristics of Employees in Institutions of Higher Education", *Higher Education*, National Center for Educational Statistics, 1966.

ties were an estimated $6 billion in 1969, an increase of $300 million over the previous fiscal year.[16] Income is derived not only from the traditional sources such as tuition and gifts, but from the purely commercial avenues of securities investments and real estate holdings. Revenues of private institutions of higher education for fiscal year 1966-67 totaled over $6 billion.[17] More than $1.5 billion of that sum came from Government appropriations.[18] Private colleges and universities also realized a commercial profit of $70,678,000 from furnishing housing and food services.[19]

Expenditures to operate and maintain these academic communities necessarily include purchases of food, furniture, office equipment, supplies, utilities, and the like, much of which is obtained through the channels of interstate commerce. Merely to house its students the average private college budgeted $323,000 for fiscal 1969, and allotted another $360,000 for food services.[20] Further, the expanding nature of higher education is reflected in the amount of new construction being planned. In 1969, over 1,000 institutions planned some 3,000 separate building projects with a total estimated value of $4.35 billion, one-half billion dollars more than was appropriated the preceding year.[21]

Another phenomenon clearly distinguishing the current situation from the one which existed in 1951 is the expanded role of the Federal Government in higher education. In the last 12 years alone, three legislative acts have been passed which authorize allocations of millions of dollars of Federal aid for education.[22] Total Federal funds for private and public education in 1969 amounted to $5 billion.[23] This figure, moreover, does not include moneys expended for student loans, sponsored research, or Government-approved construction.

16. *College and University Business,* October 1968, McGraw-Hill.
17. "Financial Statistics of Institutions of Higher Education: Current Funds Revenues and Expenditures," *Higher Education,* National Center for Educational Statistics, 1966.
18. *Id.* at p. 14.
19. *Id.* at pp. 14-15.
20. *College and University Business,* September 1968, 52-59.
21. *College and University Business,* January 1969, pp. 37-40.
22. National Defense Education Act of 1958; Higher Education Act of 1963; International Education Act of 1966. *American Universities and Colleges,* American Council on Education, pp. 22-26.
23. *Digest of Educational Statistics,* p. 107, U.S. Department of Health, Education and Welfare.

Increased Federal financial involvement in education is paralleled by an expanding congressional recognition that employees in the nonprofit sector are entitled to the same benefits which Federal statutes provide to employees in the profitmaking sphere.[24] Of particular pertinence here is the amendment of the Fair Labor Standards Act in 1966 extending coverage to nonprofit private universities and hospitals. In 1968, the Supreme Court upheld the constitutionality of the amendments, holding that such institutions are engaged in commerce.[25] In support of this conclusion, the Court stated, *inter alia:* "It is clear that labor conditions in schools and hospitals can affect commerce. . . . Strikes and work stoppages involving employees of schools and hospitals, events which unfortunately are not infrequent, obviously interrupt and burden this flow of goods across state lines."[26]

Given the congressional amendments to the FLSA and the Supreme Court decision upholding them, it is no longer sufficient to say that merely because employees are in a nonprofit sector of the economy, the operations of their employers do not substantially affect interstate commerce.

However, those who oppose Board jurisdiction contend that many private colleges, unlike Cornell and Syracuse, have remained relatively small and local in character and labor disputes involving their employees do not burden interstate commerce.[27] They also allege that private colleges represent a declining proportion of higher educational institutions in the United States. Therefore, if the National Labor Relations Board were to take jurisdiction, it would be over only a fractional segment of the field. A more logical approach, they submit, is to have all such institutions subject to State control, thereby avoiding the conflict and instability that allegedly would result were both Federal and local agencies

---

24. E.g., the Social Security Law has been amended to permit educational institutions to elect coverage for their employees (Sec. 210a, Social Security Act, 42 USC 40). In November 1969, the House of Representatives approved a bill which would extend unemployment insurance to educational institutions (H.R. 14705).
25. Maryland v. Wirtz, 392 U.S. 183.
26. *Id.* at 194, 195.
27. We note, for example, that among the 51 member institutions of the Association of Independent California Colleges and Universities, 37 reported annual operating expenditures of over $1 million. Five institutions did not report. Appendixes A and B, *amicus curiae* brief of Independent California Colleges and Universities.

to function within a single State. We find no merit in these arguments.

It may be true that Cornell and Syracuse count among the largest of the private universities in the country. Nevertheless, within this class of employers, there are a number which, although smaller than these two universities, are sufficiently large so that their activities have a substantial impact on commerce.

It may also be true that, in certain respects, public colleges and universities tend to be larger than their private counterparts. Thus, only 29 percent of the student population is enrolled in private colleges and universities.[28] Further, the rate of growth in terms of numbers of public institutions is more rapid than the growth rate for private schools.[29]

This does not diminish the fact that 2,102,000 students are currently enrolled in private colleges, an increase of 21½ percent in the past 5 years.[30] Moreover, there are still 489 more private colleges in this country than public ones.[31] Although the private sector has not grown to the same extent as has the public on a sheer percentage basis, it has grown substantially.[32]

In any event, we note that in all cases where the Board applies a size criterion, expressed in dollar volume, in its assertion of jurisdiction, a portion of the industry is relegated to the State or other control. While complete uniformity in the application of Federal or State controls might be desirable in theory, in practice the resulting remission to State control of those enterprises falling below the Board's own jurisdictional standard has not in the past resulted in substantial instability or uncertainty in the application of the law.

The evidence clearly establishes that universities are enlarging both their facilities and their economic activities to meet the needs of mounting numbers of students. Greatly increased expenditures by the Federal Government also testify to an expanding national interest in higher education. Keeping pace with these developments

---

28. A Fact Book on Higher Education, American Council on Education, Washington, D.C. Issue No. 1, 1969, p. 9009.
29. Id.
30. "Opening Fall Enrollment in Higher Education," Higher Education, National Center for Education Statistics, 1968, p. 5.
31. A Fact Book on Higher Education, supra note 27, Issue No. 3, p. 8117.
32. Id. Private institutions have increased in number from 1,218 in 1951 to 1,489 in 1968.

is the surge of organizational activity taking place among employees on college campuses. With or without Federal regulation, union organization is already a fait accompli at many universities.[33] Indeed, labor disputes have already erupted at a number of universities.[34] As advancing waves of organization swell among both nonprofessional and academic employees, it is unreasonable to assume that such disputes will not continue to occur in the future.

As noted previously, Section 14(c) was enacted primarily to provide forums to resolve labor disputes for those employers and employees who were denied Federal relief. Congress was aware that by 1959 only 12 States had any labor relations law.[35] Presumably, Congress then expected that the other States would establish agencies to fill the void. If so, these expectations have been disappointed. To date, a total of 15 States have enacted labor-management legislation.[36] In only eight of these States has the legislation been written or interpreted so as to expressly cover employees of private educational institutions.[37] Moreover, even in those eight, the laws may be inadequate. For example, New York for years has had an equivalent of the Wagner Act, yet it contains no remedies for unfair labor practices which may be committed by unions. To put it another way, there are 35 states without labor codes under which matters such as union organization, collective bargaining, and labor disputes may be determined.

Consequently, we are convinced that assertion of jurisdiction is required over those private colleges and universities whose operations have a substantial effect on commerce to insure the orderly, effective and uniform application of the national labor policy.

---

33. See Tracy Ferguson, "Collective Bargaining in Universities and Colleges," 19 Lab. Law J. 778, 791-804.
34. E.g., at Duke University, over 600 students and faculty members demonstrated to back demands that the wages of nonacademic employees be raised. New York Times, July 8, 1968. Also during the 1968 student demonstrations at Columbia University, a student group was quoted as saying: "the cafeteria workers on campus who are almost entirely Negro or Puerto Rican—they still aren't allowed to organize. Some of them have been working here for 10 years. . . ." New Yorker, May 4, 1968, at p. 43.
35. LH 422.
36. Colorado, Connecticut, Hawaii, Kansas, Massachusetts, Michigan, Minnesota, New York, North Dakota, Oregon, Pennsylvania, Rhode Island, Utah, Vermont, and Wisconsin. Tracy Ferguson, "Collective Bargaining in Universities and Colleges," 19 Lab. Law J. 778, 786-789.
37. The eight states are: Colorado, Connecticut, Hawaii, Massachusetts, Michigan, Minnesota, New York, and Wisconsin.

In view of all the foregoing considerations, we can no longer adhere to the position set forth in the *Columbia University* decision. Accordingly, that case is overruled. Charged with providing peaceful and orderly procedures to resolve labor controversy, we conclude that we can best effectuate the policies of the Act by asserting jurisdiction over nonprofit, private educational institutions where we find it to be appropriate.

At this time, the Board is not prepared to establish jurisdictional standards for nonprofit colleges and universities as a class for the instant proceedings do not give us a sufficient basis for selecting an appropriate measure by which to determine whether the policies of the Act will be effectuated by the exercise of jurisdiction in a particular case. Therefore, we leave the development of an appropriate jurisdictional standard for subsequent adjudication.

Whatever dollar-volume standard we ultimately adopt for asserting jurisdiction over educational institutions can best be left to determination in future situations involving institutions which are far nearer the appropriate dividing line. In view of the foregoing facts disclosing the substantial involvement in operations in commerce and affecting commerce by Cornell and Syracuse Universities, there is no question that Cornell and Syracuse are engaged in commerce within the meaning of the Act. Accordingly, we find that it will effectuate the policies of the Act to assert jurisdiction herein.

2. The labor organizations involved claim to represent certain employees of the employers.

3. Service Employees International Union, Local 200, AFL-CIO, was elected collective-bargaining representative for a unit of full-time and regular part-time service and maintenance employees at Syracuse University in an election conducted under the direction of the New York State Labor Relations Board.[38]

At the hearing in the instant proceeding, the University and

---

38. As described in the RM petition the unit includes:
    All full-time and regular part-time hourly paid service and mainte-nance employees, including those in the following departments: cus-todial; steam station; mailing, telephone and warehouse; electric; plumbers and steam fitting; machine shop and garage and tin shop; carpenters, painters and masons; laborers and grounds; night opera-tions; dormitory maintenance. Additionally, the hourly paid noncleri-cal employees in the purchasing department working at the Ainsley Drive warehouse, and the stockroom clerk in the book store depart-ment at the . . . warehouse and the book store truck drivers. . . .

Local 200 virtually stipulated to the appropriateness of the above unit and were engaged at that time in collective bargaining. Both parties have urged the Board to honor the State certification of the Local in the event jurisdiction is asserted.

It is well established that the Board will recognize the validity of State-conducted elections and certifications where that election procedure was free of irregularities and reflected the true desires of the employees.[39] Since neither party contends that the State-conducted election was attended by any irregularities, we shall accord the same effect to the results of the State election as we would attach to a determination of representatives based upon an election conducted by the Board. Accordingly, there is no question concerning representation of Syracuse University employees at this time. We shall, therefore, dismiss Syracuse University's petition.

4. A question affecting commerce does exist concerning the representation of certain employees of Cornell University within the meaning of Section 9(c)(1) and Section 2(6) and (7) of the Act.

Cornell has filed a petition seeking an election in a unit of all the University's nonacademic, nonsupervisory employees throughout the State of New York. Civil Service Employees Association agrees that a statewide unit is appropriate. Association of Cornell Employees—Libraries (ACE) requests a separate unit for approximately 270 nonprofessional, nonsupervisory employees of the Cornell libraries on the Ithaca campus. Staff Association of the Metropolitan District Office, School of Industrial Relations, Cornell University, United Federation of College Teachers, Local 1460 (UFCT), contends that a unit composed of 17 professionals and 20 nonprofessionals in the district office of the New York State School of Industrial Relations located in New York City is appropriate.

ACE Unit

In terms of the University's organizational structure, the libraries constitute a separate administrative unit. As such, this unit has established its own work rules and administers its own budget. There are 13 separate libraries on the Ithaca campus, with two-

39. See Western Meat Packers, Inc., 148 NLRB 444; enforcement denied on grounds unrelated to general rule. N.L.R.B. v. Western Meat Packers, Inc., 380 F. 2d 804 (C.A. 10); West Indian Co. Ltd., 129 NLRB 1203; Olin-Mathieson Chemical Corp., 115 NLRB 1501; T-H Products, 113 NLRB 1246.

thirds of all proposed unit employees located in the main library. The ratio between library employees and others housed in the same building varies from 3 to 80 percent, depending on the size of the particular library.

There was conflicting testimony as to whether the nonprofessional employees' work in the libraries is distinct. On the other hand, there were assertions that, although much library work today is done by nonprofessionals, it is of semi-professional character requiring a certain amount of training. Thus, new library employees now receive an 8- to 10-hour orientation as well as on-the-job training. Forty percent of the jobs allegedly require a college background. There are 9 job titles identifying positions which exist solely within the library system; 17 other classifications are used campuswide. However, while the 9 job titles may be singular, apparently the job content is not. For example, "library assistants," "library searchers," and "proofreaders" perform duties comparable to many university clericals, research aides, and proofreaders throughout the campus.

With respect to employee interchange, 12 library positions were filled by employees transferring from other campus jobs during the 1967 academic year. During this time, 46 promotions and 11 transfers in the library system were of library employees. Over 60 percent of new hires were recruited from off-campus.

ACE, formed as a labor organization approximately 2½ years ago, has a constitution and a dues-paying membership and holds regular meetings. It has never been officially recognized by the University nor entered into collective-bargaining negotiations, but has represented library employees at a number of meetings held with University administrators and has handled numerous unit-wide grievances as well as those of individual employees.

UFCT Unit

Because it is located some 280 miles from Ithaca, the New York City extension office of the Industrial and Labor Relations School (ILR) is accorded a great degree of autonomy. It controls its own hiring, establishes vacation and holiday schedules independently, and proposes its own programs and curricula tailored to the particular needs and demands of its New York City clientele. Its location further requires that certain employment practices be followed in conformance with area standards. For example, employees are frequently hired above the minimum wage to compete with the higher wage market in the city. The workweek is 35 hours, whereas at the main campus it is 38¾ hours. Holidays are in accord with those granted in the area.

However, there is testimony to the effect that the autonomy accorded to the ILR School's New York City office merely reflects Cornell's policy to grant relative independence to all its administrative departments. Thus, other department heads have considerable latitude in such matters as hiring and arranging work schedules and vacation leave. The three other ILR extension branches located in Ithaca, Albany, and Buffalo also gear their programs to meet specific local needs. Additionally, Cornell has other facilities in New York City which adapt employment practices to meet area standards.

Further, it does not appear that the functions of the nonprofessional employees at the New York City ILR office are distinct. Their job classifications and duties parallel similar titles and duties on the Ithaca campus.

Statewide Unit

There is considerable evidence that the operations of Cornell's facilities scattered throughout the State are integrated and centralized, and that a community of interests is shared by all of its nonprofessional employees. Thus, the director of personnel testified that the personnel department establishes employment practices and labor relations policies for the entire University. This department conducts recruitment, interviews applicants, and refers them to job vacancies, although actual hiring is done by the respective department heads. It also determines the benefits to which employees are entitled and slots employees into various levels of the wage scale. Job titles of Cornell employees are identical throughout the State. Meetings are held occasionally for new employees, and there is some secretarial training offered. Job vacancies are posted throughout the University, and there is campuswide bidding and transfers. Although recruitment and hiring for installations remote from Ithaca are decided at the particular site, classification of positions is still done by a central office at the main campus. Financial records are maintained and checks are issued from the Ithaca campus.

Additionally, Cornell has developed uniform guidelines covering such matters as attendance, leaves of absence, vacations, holidays, tardiness, discipline, overtime, and seniority applicable to all its employees. With few exceptions, all Cornell employees participate in many of the same fringe benefit programs such as workmen's compensation, disability, life insurance, retirement,[40] and a tuition scholarship plan for children.

In determining whether a particular group of employees constitutes an appropriate unit for bargaining where an employer operates a number of facilities, the Board considers such factors as prior bargaining history, centralization of management particularly in regard to labor relations, extent of employee interchange, degree of interdependence or autonomy of the plants, differences or similarities in skills and functions of the employees, and geographical location of the facilities in relation to each other.[41] We are mindful that we are entering into a hitherto uncharted area. Nevertheless, we regard the above principles as reliable guides to organization in the educational context as they have been in the industrial, and will apply them to the circumstances of the instant case.

Although ACE has acted informally in behalf of the library employees in the handling of grievances, it has never negotiated a collective-bargaining contract for them, nor has it been recognized as their bargaining representative. Apart from the fact that these employees have organized themselves separately, there is little which justifies establishing a separate bargaining unit for them. Their work and skills are similar to those of many other employees on the Ithaca campus, and they enjoy the same working conditions and benefits as other Cornell employees. In view of the foregoing, we do not find that the library employees possess a sufficiently separate community of interest which would warrant establishing the separate unit sought by ACE.

We reach the same conclusion as to the employees of the Industrial Relations School. In the industrial context, our practice is to find a single plant of a multiplant employer presumptively appropriate where that facility is geographically separated from the others, where the operations of the single plant are not integrated with those of other plants, where there is a degree of local man-

---

40. Employees of the four "contract" colleges at Cornell; i.e., those which are funded by the State of New York, participate in a separate State retirement program.
41. See, e.g., J. W. Mays, Inc., 147 NLRB 968; American Linen Supply Co., Inc., 129 NLRB 993.

agerial autonomy, and where no other union is seeking a larger unit.[42]

In the instant proceeding, a few of these factors are present. The ILR School New York City branch is located at a considerable distance from the main campus and it is relatively autonomous in its operations. Were there no countervailing considerations involved, we might find justification for the bargaining unit claimed by the UFCT.

There are, however, other criteria which must be taken into account here. We find it significant that the nonprofessional employees of the ILR School perform the same duties as many other Cornell employees in the same job classifications, and they are equally subject to the uniform and centralized employment practices of the University. Further, there is no prior collective-bargaining history for these employees. Finally, there is a union which is seeking a broad inclusive unit coextensive with the Employer's administrative and geographic boundaries.[43] In light of these circumstances, we find that a unit limited to the employees of the New York City ILR School is not appropriate. We find, instead, that the appropriate unit is one which is statewide in scope.

Accordingly, we shall dismiss the petitions in Cases 3-RC-4768, 3-RM-440, and 3-RM-441 and, in agreement with Cornell and CSEA, we find that the following employees constitute a unit appropriate for the purposes of collective bargaining within the meaning of Section 9(b) of the Act:

All nonsupervisory, nonprofessional employees of Cornell University within the State of New York, excluding employees of the medical college and nursing school in New York City, skilled trades employees on the Ithaca campus who are currently represented, guards, confidential employees, professional employees and supervisors as defined in the Act.

Direction of Election

An election by secret ballot shall be conducted among the employees in the unit found appropriate, as early as possible, but

---

42. See, e.g., Haag Drug Company, 169 NLRB No. 111; Sav-On-Drugs, Inc., 138 NLRB 1032.
43. See, e.g., Pacific Drive-In Theatres Corp., 167 NLRB 661; Adams Drug Co., Inc., 164 NLRB 594, enforcement · denied 414 F.2d 1194 (C.A.D.C.); State Farm Mutual Automobile Insurance Co., 158 NLRB 925.

not later than 30 days from the date below. The Regional Director for Region 3 shall direct and supervise the election, subject to National Labor Relations Board Rules and Regulations. Eligible to vote are those in the unit who were employed during the payroll period immediately preceding the date below, including employees who did not work during that period because they were ill, on vacation, or temporarily laid off. Also eligible are employees engaged in an economic strike which commenced less than 12 months before the election date and who retained their status as such during the eligibility period and their replacements. Those in the military services of the United States may vote if they appear in person at the polls. Ineligible to vote are employees who have quit or been discharged for cause since the designated payroll period and employees engaged in a strike who have been discharged for cause since the commencement thereof, and who have not been rehired or reinstated before the election date, and employees engaged in an economic strike which commenced more than 12 months before the election date and who have been permanently replaced.[44] Those eligible shall vote whether or not they desire to be represented for collective-bargaining purposes by Civil Service Employees Association.

Order

IT IS HEREBY ORDERED that the petitions filed in Cases 3-RM-433, 3-RC-4768, 3-RM-440, and 3-RM-441 be, and they hereby are, dismissed.

Dated, Washington, D. C.

John H. Fanning, Member
Frank W. McCulloch, Member
Gerald A. Brown, Member
Howard Jenkins, Jr., Member

NATIONAL LABOR RELATIONS BOARD

---

44. An election eligibility list, containing the names and addresses of all the eligible voters, must be filed by the Employer with the Regional Director for Region 3 within 7 days after the date of this Decision and Direction of Election. The Regional Director shall make the list available to all parties to the election. No extension of time to file this list shall be granted by the Regional Director except in extraordinary circumstances. Failure to comply with this requirement shall be grounds for setting aside the election whenever proper objections are filed. Excelsior Underwear Inc., 156 NLRB 1236.

APPENDIX E

The Million Dollar Rule
of the NLRB*

C.F.R. Title 29—Labor

Chapter I—National Labor Relations Board

Part 103—Other Rules

Subpart A—Jurisdictional Standards

Colleges and Universities

By virtue of the authority vested in it by the National Labor Relations Act, approved July 5, 1935,[1] the National Labor Relations Board hereby issues the following rule which it finds necessary to carry out the provisions of said Act.

The rule is issued following proceedings conforming to the requirements of 5 U.S.C. section 553 in which notice was given that any rule adopted would be immediately applicable. The National Labor Relations Board finds for good cause that this rule shall be effective upon publication in the *Federal Register* and shall apply to all proceedings affected thereby which are pending at the time of such publication or which may arise thereafter.

Jurisdictional standards applicable to private colleges and universities; notice of issuance of rule. On July 14, 1970, the Board having determined in Cornell University, 183 NLRB No. 41, to assert jurisdiction over private nonprofit colleges and universities as a class published in the *Federal Register*, (35 F.R. 11270) a

---

* Notice of Issuance of Rule and Text of Rule, 35 Fed. Reg. 18370 (Dec. 3, 1970).
1. 49 Stat. 449; 29 U.S.C. secs. 151-166, as amended by act of June 23, 1947 (61 Stat. 136; 29 U.S.C. secs. 151-167), act of Oct. 22, 1951 (65 Stat. 601; 29 U.S.C. secs. 158, 159, 163), and act of Sept. 14, 1959 (73 Stat. 519; 29 U.S.C. secs. 141-168).

notice of proposed rule making which invited interested parties to submit views, data, and recommendations to assist the Board in formulating a standard to be applied in determining whether to assert jurisdiction over specific institutions within the class. Thirty-three responses to the notice were received containing proposals and information. After giving careful consideration to all the responses, the Board has concluded that it will best effectuate the purposes of the Act to apply a $1 million annual gross revenue standard to private, nonprofit colleges and universities. A rule establishing that standard has been issued concurrently with the publication of this notice.

Although it is well settled that the National Labor Relations Act gives to the Board a jurisdictional authority coextensive with the full reach of the commerce clause,[2] it is equally well established that the Board in its discretion may set boundaries on the exercise of that authority.[3] In exercising that discretion, the Board has consistently taken the position "that it would better effectuate the purposes of the Act, and promote the prompt handling of major cases, not to exercise its jurisdiction to the fullest extent possible under the authority delegated to it by Congress, but to limit that exercise to enterprises whose operations have, or at which labor disputes would have, a pronounced impact upon the flow of interstate commerce."[4]

In determining where to draw such a dividing line, the Board here, as in the past, must balance its statutory obligations to extend the rights and protections of the Act to those employers and employees whose labor disputes are likely to have a substantial impact on commerce against the need to confine its caseload to manageable proportions. We are satisfied that the standard announced above accommodates these considerations.

In arriving at a $1 million gross revenue figure,[5] the Board con-

---

2. See N.L.R.B. v. Fainblatt, et al., 306 U.S. 601.
3. Office Employees International Union, Local No. 11 v. N.L.R.B., 353 U.S. 313; section 14(c)(1) of the Act.
4. Hollow Tree Lumber Company, 91 NLRB 635, 636. See also, e.g., Floridian Hotel of Tampa, Inc., 124 NLRB 261, 264; Butte Medical Properties, d/b/a Medical Center Properties, 168 NLRB 266, 268.
5. As reflected in the rule, this figure includes revenues from all sources, excepting only contributions which, because of limitations placed thereon by the grantor, are not available for operating expenses. These contributions encompassing, for example, contributions to an endowment fund or building fund, are excluded because of their generally nonrecurring nature (cf. Magic Mountain, Inc., 123 NLRB 1170). Income derived from

sidered the nature of the impact upon commerce made by private, nonprofit colleges and universities, as well as the number of employers and employees potentially affected. Thus, statistical projections based on data submitted by responding parties disclosed that adoption of such a standard would bring some 80 percent of all private colleges and universities and approximately 95 percent of all full- and part-time nonprofessional personnel within the reach of the Act. It has been argued that because the current annual gross revenue standards set for other types of enterprises are all lower than $1 million the Board is thereby precluded from adopting, or ought not to adopt, any gross revenue standard higher than the highest current standard which is $500,000 per annum. However, this argument overlooks the interplay between the various relevant considerations.

For example, available data revealed that the $250,000 gross revenue standard established for the hospital industry extended the Board's jurisdiction to approximately 76 percent of the institutions in that field.[6] In adopting a $500,000 annual gross revenue standard for the hotel industry, the Board observed that only 3.5 percent of the employers, but over 60 percent of the hotel employees, would be covered.[7] The same gross revenue standard applied to the retail industry encompassed 6.5 percent of the retail store employees.[8] Thus, although the standard set for private, nonprofit colleges or universities is higher on its face than gross revenue standards currently existing for other enterprises, its practical effect is to extend the protections of the Act to a greater proportion of the employers and employees in the affected class. Further, the industries to which the Board applies gross revenue standards of $500,000 or less conduct their business through large numbers of relatively small units, a substantial number of which must be embraced by the relevant jurisdictional standard if the Board effectively is to regulate the labor relations of the industry. Here, in contrast, effective regulation of the labor relations of the industry can be achieved, in our opinion, under the higher standard. Finally, the Board has rejected contentions that a standard higher than $1 million should be adopted because the Board is satisfied that colleges and universities with gross revenues of $1 million

---

investment of such funds will, however, be counted in determining whether the standard has been satisfied.

6. Butte Medical Properties, 168 NLRB 266.
7. Floridian Hotel of Tampa, Inc., 124 NLRB 261, 265.
8. Id. at 265-266, footnote 19.

have a substantial impact on commerce; and that the figure selected will not result in an unmanageable increase on the Board's caseload.

We recognize that there remains a small number of colleges and universities and their employees who will be excluded from the coverage of the Act. We are nevertheless satisfied that this standard will bring within the Board's jurisdiction those labor disputes in the industry which exert or tend to exert a pronounced impact on commerce. Moreover, adoption of a particular standard now in light of prevailing conditions does not foreclose future reevaluation and revision of that standard should subsequent circumstances make that appropriate.

There are, of course, criteria other than gross revenue by which to assess the impact of an institution on commerce. For example, responding parties suggested tests based on numbers of employees, numbers of students, or annual expenditures for commercial purposes. However, after considering all the various alternatives, the Board concludes that a gross revenue test is preferable, for it has the advantages of simplicity and ease of application. Board experience has demonstrated that such figures are readily available and relatively easy to produce, thereby reducing the amount of time, energy, and funds expended by the Board and staff as well as imposing less of a burden on the parties involved.

In light of the foregoing considerations, the Board is satisfied that the $1 million annual gross revenue standard announced today will bring uniform and effective regulation of labor relations to labor disputants at private, nonprofit colleges and universities, and at the same time enable the Board to function as a responsive forum for the resolution of those disputes.

103.1 Colleges and universities

The Board will assert its jurisdiction in any proceeding arising under sections 8, 9, and 10 of the Act involving any private nonprofit college or university which has a gross annual revenue from all sources (excluding only contributions which, because of limitation by the grantor, are not available for use for operating expenses) of not less than $1 million.

Dated, Washington, D.C., November 30, 1970.

By direction of the Board.

Ogden W. Fields,
Executive Secretary.

APPENDIX F

The Fordham Case

193 NLRB 23
United States of America
Before the National Labor Relations Board

Fordham University, Employer

and

American Association of University Professors,
Fordham University Chapter, Petitioner

⎫
⎬ Case 2-RC-15500
⎭

Fordham University, Employer

and

Law School Bargaining Committee, Petitioner

⎫
⎬ Case 2-RC-15507
⎭

Decision

Upon petitions duly filed under Section 9(c) of the National Labor Relations Act, as amended, a hearing was held before Hearing Officer Mary W. Taylor. Thereafter, pursuant to Section 102.67 of the National Labor Relations Board Rules and Regulations, Series 8, as amended, and by direction of the Regional Director for Region 2, these cases were transferred to the National Labor Relations Board for decision. The Employer[1] and the Petitioners filed briefs,[2] and the Association of American Law Schools filed a brief as *amicus curiae*. The Employer and the Petitioners also filed reply briefs.

Pursuant to the provisions of Section 3(b) of the National Labor

---

1. The requests for oral argument made by the Employer and Florida Southern College are hereby denied, as the record, including the briefs, adequately presents the issues and the positions of the parties.
2. United Federation of College Teachers, Local 1460, American Federation of Teachers, AFL-CIO, was permitted to intervene on the basis of a showing of interest, but has not filed a brief.

Relations Act, as amended, the National Labor Relations Board has delegated its powers in connection with these cases to a three-member panel.

The Board has reviewed the rulings of the Hearing Officer made at the hearing and finds that they are free from prejudicial error. They are hereby affirmed.

Upon the entire record in these cases,[3] the Board finds:

1. Fordham University is a New York corporation engaged in conducting a university for the education of young men and women. Its annual revenues from tuition fees and donations exceed $1 million, of which more than $50,000 are received from outside the State of New York. The parties stipulated that Fordham meets the jurisdictional standard for colleges and universities set forth in Section 103.1 of the Board's Rules and Regulations. Accordingly, we find that the Employer is engaged in commerce within the meaning of the Act and it will effectuate the policies of the Act to assert jurisdiction herein.

2. The labor organizations involved claim to represent certain employees of the Employer.[4]

3. Questions affecting commerce exist[5] concerning the representation of employees of the Employer within the meaning of Section 9(c)(1) and Section 2(6) and (7) of the Act.[6]

---

3. The Employer's motion to reopen the record for the introduction of two documents is hereby denied, as the matter therein cannot affect the outcome of these cases.

4. The Employer contends that the American Association of University Professors is not a labor organization. However, it is abundantly clear that AAUP meets the definition of "labor organization" set forth in Section 2(5) of the Act.

5. We reject the Employer's contention that the selection of any bargaining representative for the faculty members would result in having the faculty sit on both sides of the bargaining table because some faculty members serve on committees with policymaking functions. As we find below, such faculty members are not supervisors and serve on committees only as representatives of the faculty. Further, there is no reason to believe that the Employer would be represented in collective-bargaining negotiations by anyone other than members of the administration who are clearly supervisors and would be excluded from the bargaining unit for all purposes. We thus find no indication in this record of an actual or potential conflict of interest.

6. The Employer contends that the showing of interest of the Petitioner in Case 2-RC-15500 is fatally tainted by the participation of department chairmen and the law school librarian. Since we find *infra* that the department chairmen are not supervisors, and since the law school librarian is

4. AAUP, the Petitioner in Case 2-RC-15500, seeks a unit of all full-time and regular part-time teaching faculty, including department chairmen, professional librarians, and ancillary support professionals. It would exclude the law school faculty, but is willing to represent any unit found appropriate by the Board. The Intervenor is in substantial agreement with AAUP's contentions as to the appropriate bargaining unit. The Law School Bargaining Committee, Petitioner in Case 2-RC-15507, seeks a separate unit of full-time and regular part-time faculty of the law school.

The Employer contends that no bargaining unit can be appropriate, since all faculty members are supervisors, with the exception of the instructors, who constitute only a small part of the bargaining unit sought herein. In any event, it contends, all department or division chairmen and assistant chairmen and all faculty members who serve on policymaking committees are supervisors. If any unit is found appropriate, the Employer would exclude all professional librarians, ancillary support professionals, and part-time faculty. It contends that the law school faculty does not constitute a separate appropriate unit and should be included in a unit with the remainder of the faculty if any such unit is found appropriate.

Fordham University has two campuses, one at Rose Hill in the Bronx and the other at Lincoln Center in Manhattan. In addition, it has an interdisciplinary research center, the Calder Center for Ecological Studies, located in Westchester County. The Rose Hill campus includes the graduate school of arts and sciences, the undergraduate college of business, the school of graduate studies, the graduate institute of religious education, two undergraduate liberal arts colleges—Fordham College for men and Thomas More College for women—and an experimental undergraduate college, Bensalem College, as well as the school of pharmacy which is scheduled to be discontinued after 1 more year of operation. The Lincoln Center campus includes the schools of law, education, and social service; the Martino graduate school of business; and the liberal arts college, an undergraduate college.

The ultimate authority in the University is possessed by an in-

---

not a supervisor of any employees in the proposed bargaining unit, this contention is clearly without merit. The Employer's motion to dismiss the petition is therefore denied.

dependent and self-perpetuating board of trustees, which appoints the president, the chief executive officer. Faculty and student representatives sit on all committees of the board of trustees except the executive committee. The board of trustees appoints the executive vice president, the vice president for business and finance, and the vice president for academic affairs on the recommendation of the president. Each school has a dean, appointed by the president but responsible to the vice president for academic affairs, and a council consisting of students, faculty, and administration, with faculty members constituting a majority. In addition, there is a Faculty Senate, whose members are elected by the faculties of their respective schools; a Rose Hill Council, consisting of 16 students, 10 administrators, and 21 faculty representatives elected by the full-time faculty members of each department in the schools at the Rose Hill campus; and various universitywide committees composed of administrators, faculty members nominated by the Faculty Senate, and students. The chairmen of the departments offering graduate degrees at the Rose Hill campus constitute a graduate council. There is conflicting testimony as to whether these bodies play a significant role in policy formulation or merely have advisory authority.

There are approximately 501 full-time and 245 part-time faculty members employed by the University, of whom 21 full-time and 10 part-time faculty members teach at the school of law. Of the 480 full-time faculty members outside the school of law, approximately 244 are tenured and can be discharged only for gross incompetence or moral turpitude. The full-time faculty has a significant voice in determining curriculum, admissions standards, standards for granting degrees, and decisions on appointment, promotion, and tenure of other faculty members. Two grievance committees—the Ombudsman Committee for the Rose Hill campus and the Intown Committee for the Lincoln Center campus—handle grievances of faculty members. Both committees consist of faculty members appointed by the Faculty Senate.

There are more than 150 graduate assistants and teaching fellows whom all parties agreed to exclude from any bargaining unit. They assist the faculty members in instruction by grading papers, passing out syllabi of the courses, and preparing bibliographies for courses. Some of them work for several faculty members or for a department as a whole; almost every faculty member utilizes the services of a graduate assistant or teaching fellow at least part of the time. All graduate assistants and teaching fellows are full-time students seeking graduate degrees; an assistantship or fellowship is automatically terminated if a student fails in his academic work or receives his degree. Normally each department selects its most promising students as graduate assistants or teaching fellows; the assistant or fellowship is awarded for 1 year and may be renewed.

A number of faculty members administer research grants, mostly funded by the Federal Government, and employ persons to work on the grants. They may hire and fire such persons without the approval of the University, and salary questions are worked out in negotiations with the funding agency, although the school of education requires that appointments and salaries be approved by the dean.

Upon the foregoing facts, we reject the Employer's contention that the faculty members are supervisors.[7] It is clear that the faculty exercises its role in policy determination only as a group. Under our decision in C. W. Post Center of Long Island University, 189 NLRB No. 109, this is insufficient to make the faculty members supervisors. In our view, the presence of faculty members in the Faculty Senate and on a number of universitywide committees does not require a different result, even assuming that such bodies have power effectively to recommend major policy decisions. The faculty members serving on these committees are elected by other faculty members to represent the faculty as a whole, and no one faculty representative can make the policy decisions in question. The role played by these representatives in governing the University is thus one of participation in a group determination and does not make them individually supervisors. Similarly, the selection of graduate assistants and teaching fellows and the renewal of their assistantships or fellowships are determined collectively by each department. While many assistants work under particular faculty members, the faculty member in such cases is often the same person who is supervising the assistant's studies, and the assistant's work for him may consist of a research project which is part of the assistant's dissertation for his degree. In such cases, the

---

7. All parties agree that the president, the vice presidents, and the deans, associate deans, and assistant deans are supervisors. Accordingly, we exclude them from the units hereinafter found appropriate.

faculty member is simply exercising the same kind of supervision over the assistant that he would exercise over any graduate student working toward his degree. Furthermore, an individual may remain a graduate assistant or teaching fellow only as long as he remains a student. It seems clear, therefore, that the relationship between a faculty member and his graduate assistant is basically a teacher-student relationship which does not make the faculty member a supervisor.

Finally, individuals hired by faculty members directing research grants are not employees of the Employer. Therefore, even if such faculty members are supervisors with respect to these individuals, they are not supervisors in their relationship to the Employer.[8] For these reasons, we find that the faculty members are not supervisors, but are professional employees within the meaning of Section 2(12) of the Act, and are entitled to all the benefits of collective bargaining if they so desire.[9]

We have previously held a universitywide unit of professional employees to be appropriate,[10] and it is clear that such a unit may be appropriate here. The scope and composition of that unit must be considered, however, as the labor organizations involved agree that the law school faculty should be represented separately, while the Employer contends that it must be included in a universitywide unit if such unit is found appropriate. In addition, questions as to the supervisory status of certain categories of professionals must be resolved.

The law school is located in a separate building on the Lincoln Center campus. Activities of the law school are normally carried out only in this building; other schools never use the law school's classrooms and rarely use its other facilities. While some members of the law school faculty have participated in interdisciplinary programs such as environmental studies, they have not independently taught courses in any other schools, nor have faculty members from other schools independently taught courses at the school of law. All full-time faculty members at the law school are either full professors or associate professors; approximately 57 percent of them are full professors, while less than 20 percent of the full-time faculty members in the University as a whole hold this

8. Eureka Newspapers, Inc., 154 NLRB 1181, 1185, and cases cited therein.
9. C. W. Post Center of Long Island University, *supra*, third par. under Background and cases cited in fn. 5 therein.
10. C. W. Post Center of Long Island University, *supra*.

rank. Law school faculty members are eligible for tenure after 3 years, while faculty members in the remainder of the University must have at least 7 years of service, of which at least 4 must be at Fordham, before acquiring tenure. However, the law school, like other schools, must meet the requirements of the American Association of University Professors (AAUP) with respect to rank and tenure.

On the average, the salary of law school faculty members is higher than that of faculty members in the University as a whole, although at least one other professional school has salary levels comparable to those at the law school. In determining initial salaries for newly hired faculty members, the dean of the law school takes into account the prevailing rates paid by private law firms, as well as prevailing rates at Fordham and other law schools. All members of the law school faculty have law degrees.

The New York Court of Appeals regulates admission to the practice of law in New York and has issued rules and regulations concerning legal education in this connection. Law schools must be approved by the American Bar Association (ABA), and all major law schools, including Fordham, are members of the Association of American Law Schools (AALS), an organization dedicated to raising standards of law schools. Each of these bodies has detailed regulations, some of which affect the terms and conditions of employment of law school faculty members. Thus, the court of appeals regulates the hours during which classes are to be held and the length of class periods; the ABA requires that law schools have certain financial independence and a certain faculty-student ratio, and that each faculty member have his own office; and the AALS has fixed 8 hours per week as the maximum proper teaching load. Most faculty members in the remainder of the University teach 6 to 9 hours per week, but a few may teach as many as 12 hours.

Law school faculty members serve on the Faculty Senate and other University committees. The law school has its own faculty committees, which determine curriculum, course schedules, tenure, and other matters in the same manner as faculty committees in the remainder of the University. There are no departments; the dean of the law school prepares its budget and exercises all the functions of a department chairman as well as those exercised by deans in other schools. The law school, like every other school in the University, has its own calendar, and its opening and closing dates and vacation periods do not wholly coincide with those of other schools. There is no formal bargaining history for any of the faculty of the University, but in March 1970, the president and two vice presidents met with the law school faculty and student and alumni representatives and discussed a number of matters, including faculty salaries and promotions. Several members of the law school faculty are members of the Fordham chapter of the AAUP, which is the Petitioner in Case 2-RC-15500.

In *C. W. Post, supra,* we stated that we would apply the same principles in making unit determinations with respect to faculty members that we have applied in cases involving other types of employees. On consideration of these principles, we find that the law school faculty constitutes an identifiable group of employees whose separate community of interests is not irrevocably submerged in the broader community of interest which they share with other faculty members. Members of the law school faculty have specialized training, work in a separate building under their own supervisor (the dean of the law school), and, acting as a group, have a voice, separate from that of the faculty of the remainder of the University, in determining their working conditions. There is little or no interchange between them and other faculty members. As a result of its separate calendar, the law school is open for brief periods while other parts of the University are shut down, and vice versa. There is nothing in this record to indicate that these situations could not continue for longer periods in the event of a work stoppage. On this record, we cannot conclude that the operation of the law school is so highly integrated with that of the remainder of the University as to compel a finding that an overall unit alone is appropriate. Finally, we note that there is no bargaining history on a broader basis and that no labor organization seeks to include the law school faculty in a broader bargaining unit.

For all these reasons, we find that the law school faculty constitutes a separate appropriate unit.[11] Accordingly, we further find

---

11. Many of the factors set forth herein are equally applicable to the University's other professional schools. As an overall unit including the faculty of professional schools is appropriate, and as no party contends that the faculty of any professional school other than the law school should constitute a separate unit, we need not pass upon the appropriateness of any such separate unit.

that the faculty members in the remainder of the University constitute a unit appropriate for collective bargaining.

There remain questions as to the inclusion or exclusion of the following categories:[12]

Department chairmen are appointed by their respective deans for 3-year terms and may be reappointed once. In making these appointments, the deans have traditionally consulted with faculty members in the department. When the faculty members in a department agree that a particular person should be chairman, they recommend his selection to the dean. Recommendations based on a faculty consensus are usually followed.

The chairman, with the "advice and consent" of other members of his department,[13] makes recommendations to the dean concerning hiring of applicants.[14] The approval of the University administration is required before a new faculty member may be hired. When a faculty member seeks to be promoted to associate professor or full professor, a promotion committee is selected to consider his application. The department chairman is an *ex officio* member of the promotion committee; two of the other four members are nominated by the applicant for promotion, and two are nominated by the dean. Each member of the committee submits a recommendation to the dean; the committee does not act as a

---

12. The disputed categories relate only to the universitywide unit, except that the question as to part-time faculty applies to both units herein found appropriate.
13. The University handbook provides that department chairmen are to carry out their duties *"in accordance with policies of the School and the University* and the procedures, policies and rules of the Department." (Emphasis supplied.) The general policies and rules are set forth in the recommendation of the Committee on Chairmen of Departments, which the University administration has adopted, that "the most important duties of the chairmen be carried out with the advice and consent of members of the department...." The duties there enumerated include most of those listed by Member Kennedy in his partial dissent. For reasons more fully discussed in the text of this opinion, *infra*, this structure of collegiality, while recognizing the respect due to a department chairman, falls short of creating in him that kind of fully vested authority which we require for a finding of true supervisory status. The status of department chairmen varies in different university structures, and the fact that we found department chairmen to be supervisors in one case does not compel us to find that all department chairmen in all universities are supervisors.
14. In some departments, the recommendation is based on the decision of a recruitment committee headed by the department chairman.

group in making a recommendation. If the committee is divided on whether to recommend promotion, the chairman's recommendation may be given greater weight because it is more detailed, but is not always followed by the administration. Decisions with respect to the granting of tenure are recommended by a committee consisting of tenured faculty of the department in which the individual seeking tenure teaches. Again, the chairman's views may be given greater weight than those of other faculty members because of his greater knowledge of the applicant's qualifications, but they are not conclusive.

Each department chairman prepares his department's budget with the advice and consent of the other faculty members in the department. He presents the department's views to the dean, and indicates which items should receive highest priority. The budget, after being reviewed by the dean, is further reviewed by the academic vice president, and then goes to the board of trustees for final approval. Most of the budget is allocated to salaries. The department chairman is asked to evaluate the faculty members in his department to determine what merit increases should be given, but in larger departments a committee recommends the increases. This year the University gave an across-the-board increase to all faculty members; the merit increases recommended were in addition to this increase. Last year the administration failed to tell the department chairmen what salary increases the members of their departments were receiving; when the department chairmen protested, they were told that the failure to notify them was inadvertent. Grievances of individual faculty members concerning salaries can be discussed with the department chairman, but are ultimately resolved by the dean or academic vice president.

The department chairman, with the advice and consent of the faculty of the department, determines what courses will be offered by the department, when they will meet, and whether large classes should be split. If a large class is split into two or more sections, the faculty member in charge of the course may assign graduate assistants to some of the sections. A number of departments have curriculum committees which determine these matters. The administration interferes with the department's action only if it requires authorization for additional personnel.

The faculty member in charge of each course determines the content of the course, the manner of teaching it, and the content, number, and grading of examinations. The department chairman exercises no control over the day-to-day work of a faculty member, but will call the faculty member's attention to serious derelictions, such as a failure to meet his classes for a week. The chairman has no authority to dismiss a faculty member; if charges are filed against a faculty member, the president refers them to a faculty hearing committee. On one occasion, the administration attempted to terminate two language informants in the Russian department[15] without consulting the new chairman of the department or his predecessor, both of whom had recommended retention of the language informants. These individuals were retained only after the new chairman threatened not to assume the duties of the chairmanship.

The chairman's teaching load is reduced, and he receives a stipend of $500 to $1,250 in addition to his regular salary. This stipend amounts to less than 10 percent of his salary. Some department chairmen are associate professors; even with the stipend, they earn less money than full professors who are not department chairmen. The chairman may spend up to half of his time on administrative duties; the remainder is spent teaching.

Each department has a secretary. When a new secretary is to be hired, the department chairman interviews applicants referred by the personnel office and selects one. The secretary does routine secretarial work for the chairman and other members of the department. If the chairman finds a secretary unsatisfactory for the needs of his department, he can ask the personnel office to have her transferred. Once a secretary's probationary period has expired, she can be discharged only in accordance with the terms of the contract between the University and the labor organization representing the clerical employees; this contract is not part of the record herein. On at least one occasion, a pay raise was not given to a secretary whose department chairman recommended that she receive one.

A number of department chairmen serve on the Faculty Senate

---

15. The AAUP would include these individuals in the unit, while the Employer would exclude them. The record discloses that the language informants teach languages on a full-time basis and have the same duties and obligations as other faculty members. They differ from other faculty members only in teaching only language, whereas other faculty members may also teach courses in literature and other subjects. Accordingly, we shall include them in the unit.

and two faculty grievance committees. The University Budget Committee and a commission created to draft a constitution for a University Senate contain representatives of students, faculty, and administration; department chairmen were elected to these bodies as faculty representatives. One chairman testified that he frequently found himself having to defend the department against the dean. The catalogues published by the various schools in the University list department chairmen among members of the faculty rather than members of the administration.

In summary, it is apparent that decisions as to appointment, promotion, and tenure are in fact made not by the chairman alone, but by the faculty of the department, acting as a group. To the extent that the chairman's recommendations concerning these matters are given more weight than those of other faculty members, this fact appears to reflect the chairman's superior knowledge and experience, and does not indicate possession of the type of authority contemplated in the statutory definition of a supervisor.[16] The chairman does not direct the work of faculty members. While the chairman prepares the budget for his department, he does so only with the advice and consent of the faculty members. His recommendations as to salaries are subject to review at three levels of administrative authority, and his views are not always followed. We cannot, therefore, find that the chairman has power effectively to recommend salary increases. While the chairman exercises some direction over his secretary, and plays some part in the selection, it does not appear that he has statutory authority over that employee. The mere fact that professional employees may have secretaries does not necessarily constitute them supervisors.[17] Thus, the record does not indicate that a chairman makes the final selection for hiring, or has authority to discharge a secretary or effectively to recommend discharge, or that he can effectively recommend a pay raise. We therefore conclude that department chairmen do not exercise statutory supervisory authority over secretaries.[18]

---

16. *Cf.* United States Gypsum Company, 119 NLRB 1415, 1421; Central Mutual Telephone Company, 116 NLRB 1663, 1665; N.L.R.B. v. Magnesium Casting Company, 427 F.2d 114, 118 (C.A. 1), *affd.* 401 U.S. 137.
17. E.g., Air Line Pilots Association, International, 97 NLRB 929.
18. Even if the department chairmen were supervisors of secretaries, their alleged activities on behalf of the AAUP would not invalidate its showing of interest, since the secretaries are not in the bargaining unit sought herein.

In addition, it is significant that the department chairmen consider themselves, and are considered by faculty members, to be representatives of the faculty rather than of the administration. There is some indication that the University views them similarly. Thus, the catalogues of the various schools refer to chairmen as members of the faculty rather than as part of the administration. The letter of appointment used by the University indicates that a faculty member is responsible to the president or dean, rather than to his department chairman. A full-time faculty member who wishes to accept outside employment must obtain the approval of the academic vice president, rather than the department chairman.

Accordingly, we find that the department chairmen are not supervisors[19] and shall include them in the unit.[20]

A number of departments have *assistant chairmen*, who counsel students in selecting courses or research projects, in addition to assisting the chairmen in preparing the budget. As there is no evidence that assistant chairmen possess any supervisory authority, we shall include them in the unit.

Part-time faculty members are appointed for one or two semesters to teach one or two specific courses, and may be reappointed for 1 year at a time. They are paid on the basis of the number of credit hours taught. Most of them have full-time jobs outside the University; many are full-time faculty members at other institutions. Part-time faculty members are not eligible for tenure or

---

19. Unlike our dissenting colleague, we do not view our conclusion that the department chairmen herein are not supervisors as contrary to our recent decision in *C. W. Post Center of Long Island University, supra*, that the department chairmen there were supervisory. There is expert testimony in the instant case that department chairmen are part of the administration at some universities and representatives of the faculty at others. In *C. W. Post*, the statutes of Long Island University listed the department chairmen under the heading "Officers of the Centers"; before a faculty member could be granted tenure the recommendation of his department chairman was specifically required, the Faculty Tenure Committee having advisory authority only; the dean was to "act on the recommendation of the chairman of the appropriate department" in appointing new faculty members; and a faculty member who wished to accept outside teaching employment had to have the recommendation of his department chairman as well as the approval of the dean. It is thus clear that department chairmen at Fordham do not possess authority comparable to that of department chairmen at Long Island University.

20. As the *division chairmen* in the school of education appear to have substantially the same duties as the department chairmen, we shall also include them in the unit.

for fringe benefits enjoyed by the full-time faculty, and, unlike the full-time faculty members, do not participate in faculty policy decisions on department or school levels. We held in *University of New Haven, Inc.,* 190 NLRB No. 102, that regular part-time faculty members must be included in the same unit as the full-time faculty, absent agreement of the parties to exclude them. As the facts here are essentially the same as in the *New Haven* case, we shall include regular part-time faculty members in both units found appropriate herein. If the parties cannot reach agreement as to the regularity of employment of any individual part-time faculty members, such individuals may vote subject to challenge.[21]

Approximately 70 of the 500 full-time faculty members are *members of the Society of Jesus.* The AAUP would include them in the unit, while the Employer takes no position as to their placement. Most Jesuits live in a separate building, and their salaries are paid to the Jesuit community, an incorporated body, which houses and feeds them. The Jesuits may, with the permission of their religious superior, live away from this building and receive their own salaries; such permission has never been refused, but only 2 of the 70 Jesuits on the full-time faculty presently live away from the community. The Jesuits are hired in the same manner as other faculty members, and their salaries and other terms and conditions of employment are determined in the same manner. A Jesuit who leaves the Order may remain a faculty member and receive the same salary formerly paid to the community on his behalf. He may remain at Fordham and accept tenure despite the objection of the Order. There is no evidence that membership in the Order is in any way inconsistent with collective bargaining with respect to a Jesuit's salary or other terms and conditions of employment. Accordingly, we shall include the Jesuits in the unit.

The AAUP would include, and the Employer would exclude, all *professional librarians.* While the librarians do not have faculty status, it is clear that some of them are professional employees

---

21. The AAUP has moved to reopen the hearing to determine the issue of regularity if the parties do not reach a stipulation on this issue. This motion is hereby denied, as any disagreements concerning the unit placement of particular part-time faculty members are, in our view, best resolved through the challenged ballot procedure.

and should be included in the unit.[22] The record does not contain sufficient evidence to determine whether any of them are supervisors. Accordingly, any librarians whose status either as a professional employee or as a supervisor is in dispute may vote subject to challenge.

The AAUP would also include, while the Employer would exclude, *ancillary support professionals*. While the precise meaning of this term is unclear, it appears to encompass such employees as counselors, employees in the admissions office and placement office, and laboratory technicians. As we are unable to determine from the record which, if any, of these employees are professional employees, we shall permit them to vote subject to challenge.

For the reasons stated above, we find that the following units constitute units appropriate for the purposes of collective bargaining within the meaning of Section 9(b) of the Act:

1. All professional employees of Fordham University, including full-time and regular part-time members of the teaching and research faculty, department chairmen and assistant chairmen, division chairmen, members of the Faculty Senate, faculty members serving on University committees as faculty representatives, faculty members directing research grants, members of the Society of Jesus, nonsupervisory professional librarians, and language informants; but excluding the president, vice presidents, deans, associate deans, assistant deans, members of the faculty of the school of law, graduate assistants, teaching fellows, guards and supervisors as defined in the Act, and all other employees.

2. All full-time and regular part-time members of the faculty of the school of law, including members of the Faculty Senate and University committees; but excluding the dean of the school of law, the law librarian,[23] guards and supervisors as defined in the Act, and all other employees.

5. At Fordham, as at most universities, the various schools are in session from September until June. While the University has a

22. C. W. Post Center of Long Island University, *supra*.
23. The parties agreed that the law librarian is a supervisor. As the record does not indicate whether other librarians at the law school are professional employees, we shall permit them to vote subject to challenge.

summer session, it is clear that many faculty members do not teach during the summer. Accordingly, we shall not direct that elections be held at this time, but shall direct that they be held after the commencement of classes for the fall term at all schools of the University, on a date to be determined by the Regional Director, among the employees in the appropriate units who are employed during the payroll period immediately preceding the date of issuance of the Notice of Election.[24]

Direction of Elections

Elections by secret ballot shall be conducted among the employees in the units found appropriate as early as possible, at a date to be determined by the Regional Director for Region 2. The Regional Director shall direct and supervise the elections, subject to the National Labor Relations Board Rules and Regulations. Eligible to vote are those in the units who were employed during the payroll period immediately preceding the date of issuance of each Notice of Election by the Regional Director, including employees who did not work during that period because they were ill, on vacation, or temporarily laid off. Also eligible are employees engaged in an economic strike which commenced less than 12 months before the election date and who retained their status as such during the eligibility period and their replacements. Those in the military services of the United States may vote if they appear in person at the polls. Ineligible to vote are employees who have quit or been discharged for cause since the designated payroll period and employees engaged in a strike who have been discharged for cause since the commencement thereof, and who have not been rehired or reinstated before the election date, and employees engaged in an economic strike which commenced more than 12 months before the election date and who have been permanently replaced.[25]

---

24. This postponement of the elections is in accordance with our customary practice in seasonal industries. E.g., Garin Company, 148 NLRB 1499, 1502.
25. In order to assure that all eligible voters may have the opportunity to be informed of the issues in the exercise of their statutory right to vote, all parties to the elections should have access to a list of voters in their respective units, and their addresses, which may be used to communicate with them. Excelsior Underwear Inc., 156 NLRB 1236; N.L.R.B. v. Wyman-Gordon Co., 394 U.S. 759. Accordingly, it is hereby directed that election eligibility lists, containing the names and addresses of all the

Those eligible in unit 1 shall vote whether they desire to be represented for collective-bargaining purposes by American Association of University Professors, Fordham University Chapter; by United Federation of College Teachers, Local 1460, American Federation of Teachers, AFL-CIO; or by neither. Those eligible in unit 2 shall vote whether or not they desire to be represented for collective-bargaining purposes by the Law School Bargaining Committee.
Dated, Washington, D.C.

Edward B. Miller, Chairman
Howard Jenkins, Jr., Member
NATIONAL LABOR RELATIONS BOARD

MEMBER KENNEDY, dissenting in part:
I cannot agree with my colleagues' conclusion that the University department chairmen are not supervisors within the meaning of Section 2(11) of the Act.

Under circumstances substantially similar to those revealed by the record in the instant case, the Board found department chairmen to be supervisors in *C. W. Post Center of Long Island University,* 189 NLRB No. 109. There the department chairmen interviewed prospective candidates for faculty positions, discussed the selected candidate's appointment with the dean, hired department clerical employees, recommended faculty members' change of status to the dean and board of trustees, and were assigned a reduced teaching load in order to carry out these duties.

According to the Fordham University Handbook, the department chairmen's duties include, *inter alia,* promulgating department policies and procedures; calling and presiding at department meetings; appointing department committees; preparing the department budget and supervising expenditures; recommending faculty appointments, reappointments, tenure, and promotions; and establishing course offerings and schedules and assigning schedules to

eligible voters, must be filed by the Employer with the Regional Director for Region 2 within 7 days after the date of issuance of each Notice of Election by the Regional Director. The Regional Director shall make the lists available to all parties to the elections. No extension of time to file these lists shall be granted by the Regional Director except in extraordinary circumstances. Failure to comply with this requirement shall be grounds for setting aside the elections whenever proper objections are filed.

each department member after consultation. A special stipend of between $500 and $1,250 is awarded the department chairmen as well as a reduced teaching load.

Chairmen at Fordham handle initial negotiations for appointments to the faculty and submit recommendations to the dean. The faculty and students are involved in this procedure too. The tenured faculty votes by secret ballot to grant a colleague tenure but the chairmen make a separate report to the dean explaining in full the reasons for the decision. Each faculty member also informs the dean of the reason for his vote. The dean is annually told by the chairmen which faculty members should be considered for promotion. A faculty committee chaired by the chairman votes on promotions, and this decision is transmitted to the dean by the respective chairman. Before recommending individual faculty member's salaries, the dean consults the chairman; the vice president for academic affairs makes the ultimate decision. Finally, chairmen select the department clerical employees from among the candidates referred to them by the University personnel office.

I find that the department chairmen's situation at Fordham is substantially akin to that at C. W. Post. Accordingly, as the Board did in *C. W. Post*, I would find the department chairmen at Fordham to be supervisors within the meaning of the Act.[26]

Dated, Washington, D.C.

Ralph E. Kennedy, Member

NATIONAL LABOR RELATIONS BOARD

---

26. In view of my conclusion that department chairmen are supervisors, I would reach the issue raised in Case 2-RC-15500 whether the showing of interest was tainted by supervisory participation in the solicitation of signatures for authorization cards.

Association of
American Law Schools
Position Statement and Brief

In February, 1971, the Executive Committee of the Association of American Law Schools (AALS) authorized appointment of an Emergency Committee on Law Faculties in Collective Bargaining Units. Its charge was to prepare recommendations to the Executive Committee concerning the position the AALS should take regarding inclusion of a law school faculty in a universitywide bargaining unit. That committee prepared a memorandum, dated March 11, 1971, on the basis of which the Executive Committee subsequently issued the following statement:

The Executive Committee of the Association of American Law Schools has considered the problem presented by demands for collective bargaining for the academic staffs of universities. The Committee takes no position on whether collective bargaining is appropriate for university faculties generally. It believes, however, that in most situations it would be unfortunate to include the law faculty in any university-wide bargaining unit. It therefore recommends that, in proceedings before administrative and judicial tribunals and in any voting on the establishment of representational units, law faculties oppose their inclusion in university-wide bargaining units.*

The Emergency Committee's memorandum of March 11, 1971, is given here, followed by a summary of the *amicus curiae* brief.

---

* *AALS Newsletter* 71, no. 2 (May 3, 1971), p. 3. The memorandum is used by permission of the AALS and is quoted in full as presented by Robert A. Gorman, Walter E. Oberer, and Michael I. Sovern. Of some 165 law schools in the United States, 124 are accredited by the AALS.

Memorandum

The representation proceeding presently pending before the National Labor Relations Board concerning the faculty of Fordham University has brought to the fore the question whether the faculty of a university law school is properly to be included within a university-wide unit for purposes of collective bargaining or, instead, itself constitutes an "appropriate bargaining unit." This Committee was designated to outline the position which the Association should take on this question. The Committee's conclusions are as follows: (1) The typical law school faculty should seek exclusion from a university-wide professional or faculty bargaining unit, in order autonomously to secure protection of its own special economic and professional interests. (2) The Association should endorse publicly this principle of autonomy of the law faculty, setting forth the reasons therefor. (3) The Association should be prepared to defend this principle in the context of particular legal proceedings, whether of a legislative or judicial character.

A representation proceeding before a state or federal labor relations board invites a determination regarding the group of employees among whom an election is to be held and on whose behalf collective bargaining may be conducted. Typically, the agency administering the collective bargaining law is given little guidance in determining the appropriate bargaining unit other than the statutory injunction to effectuate the purpose of the law or to group the employees in accordance with their community of interests. Groups of employees whose interests are in conflict, or who have interests which are so special as to caution against submergence in a larger and more homogeneous group, will typically be accorded autonomous status for purposes of deciding whether and through whom to engage in collective bargaining.

A number of overlapping bargaining-unit questions may thus be presented within the university setting. First, there may be a question whether university faculty are within the jurisdiction of the agency at all, or whether that jurisdiction is limited to employees whose activities are "commercial" within the conventional understanding. Second, there may be a question whether university faculty (or the tenured members thereof), who will often make effective decisions regarding calendar, curriculum and workload, and appointments, promotion and tenure, should properly be treated as managerial or supervisory employees who either are not covered at all by collective bargaining legislation or, if covered, are required to deal separately from other professionals (or from the non-tenured members of the faculty). Third, there may be a question whether department heads or deans fall within or without an appropriate faculty bargaining unit. Fourth, there may be a question whether faculty members employed within certain divisions, departments or schools within the university have a community of interest sufficiently distinct from other university faculty as to warrant exclusion therefrom and autonomy in choosing a collective bargaining representative (or none at all). It is to this last question that the attention of the AALS and this Committee has been addressed.

This Committee urges the Association to support the exclusion of law school faculty from a university-wide bargaining unit. The Committee also believes, however, that in the event that autonomy is achieved, the question whether law faculty at a particular institution should choose to settle terms and conditions of employment by collective bargaining rather than in the manner which currently obtains is a question which should be left for that faculty to decide in light of local traditions and imperatives; at least at this early stage of development, the Association should not purport to give uniform advice regarding whether to adopt the principle of collective bargaining, the mode in which such bargaining is to be carried on or the organization properly to be selected as faculty spokesman.

While institutional patterns vary, it is fair to state that the law school faculty is in most pertinent respects independent of centralized university control. The law school faculty will typically, for example, set its own standards for the nature and quality of the educational experience offered there: the size of the student body, the qualifications for admission, the qualifications for continued membership in the student body and for award of the degree, the course requirements, the curriculum, the number of classroom hours, the teaching materials, the teaching methods, the examination procedures, the calendar. In all of these respects—which have implications not only for the student but for the "terms and conditions of employment" of the faculty—the law school typically regulates its affairs independently of the university. Indeed, in structuring such matters, the law school will commonly pay greater heed to such extra-university professional and accrediting agencies as the American Bar Association and the Association of American Law Schools than to the university authorities themselves. The same is true to regarding matters which bear yet more directly upon personnel administration, which is of perhaps central importance in determining "community of interest" among employee groups. Thus, the law faculty will—usually in consonance with only the most minimum guidelines set by the central university administration—establish the criteria for appointments, promotion and tenure, make specific decisions regarding specific persons at those various stages, determine the number of faculty teaching hours and teaching weeks, assign specific courses, determine the extent to which resources will be allocated between teaching and research, establish educational programs (often in cooperation with the professional bar) of a special nature involving work during vacations and beyond the academic year, safeguard principles of academic freedom within the law school, and select the chief administrative officer of the school. It perhaps goes without saying that the determination of financial compensation for law faculty is made by standards typically quite distinct from those which obtain within the university generally, again reflecting the intimate relationship among all "law professionals" whether in teaching, in government or in private practice. Moreover, the teaching credentials of the law school teacher—normally the LL.B. or J.D. degree awarded without an eye toward special preparation for a career of teaching and scholarship, followed by a period of practical experience serving public or private clients—are vastly different from those of the typical university teacher, and further contribute to the felt community of interest within the law school faculty.

In the judgment of this Committee, this separate identity of the law school faculty is worthy of preservation, but such may be jeopardized if that faculty were to be engrossed within a university-wide unit for purposes of collective bargaining. A bargaining representative is obviously inclined to be responsive to a majority of its constituents when framing its bargaining position. To the extent that the law faculty, typically a small proportion of the university faculty, is absorbed into a larger unit, there is a likelihood that its interests will at best be ignored and at worst actually sacrified to the interests of the majority (e.g., by reducing the salary differential between law faculty and other faculty, or by bringing the hourly teaching load of the law faculty more in line with the generally more onerous burden obtaining elsewhere within the university). This likelihood is heightened when the university-wide unit includes not only non-law faculty but also non-teaching professionals, such as vocational and guidance counselors, librarians and laboratory and clinical assistants.

It may well be, however, that the hazards to the law faculty of absorption in a university-wide bargaining unit are overstated. If the traditions of present-day university governance carry over into the era of collective bargaining, it is not unlikely that representatives of the law faculty will continue to speak with an authority on matters of university policy which far outweighs their numerical proportion within the body corporate. Similarly, to the extent there is the common tendency on the part of the bargaining representative to negotiate a percentage increase for all faculty within the unit—rather than to redress felt inequalities among various faculty groups—the economic status of the law faculty would not be jeopardized by absorption within a university-wide unit. Moreover, although it is unlikely that the typical law faculty will resort to a work stoppage or other job action as a means of reinforcing its position on a matter of economic or professional concern, should that day ever come a law faculty which is a part of a larger professional unit will find solace in the unified support of their brethren in other divisions of the university. (This would, however, bring the correlative obligation on the part of the law faculty to support job action by professionals outside of the law school, a prospect perhaps less attractive if only because likely to come to pass with greater frequency.)

On balance, this Committee would urge the Association publicly to support the principle of exclusion of law faculty from university-wide bargaining units. The Association is perhaps uniquely equipped—and therefore obliged—to speak forth on the issue. No other organization can better articulate the traditions and aspirations of the law faculty as a unique branch both of the teaching profession and of the legal profession. Those traditions and aspirations must be communicated to the decision-making agency in order to make more realistic the possibility of continued autonomy in the determination of terms and conditions of employment. We reiterate that the decision by any particular law faculty regarding the manner in which that autonomy is to be exercised—through a continuation of non-collective bargaining, or a movement toward collective bargaining (or some hybrid) for law school faculty alone, or perhaps even for cooperative efforts with the university faculty outside of the law school—is properly to be made by the particular law school faculty in light of local traditions and imperatives. The Association should not, however, be reluctant to point out to law school faculties that any movement toward formalized collective bargaining (whether conducted autonomously or on a university-wide basis) under the aegis of an existing administrative agency brings with it the risk that that agency will invoke bargaining models, developed in private industry or in public employment, which may be wholly inapt to the employment setting in higher education; e.g., the far narrower range of subjects outside of academe in which the "employees" have unilateral or shared control.

It remains for this Committee briefly to suggest how the Association's support for the principle of law-faculty autonomy might be manifested, some possible legal theories which can be marshalled in our tentative prognosis for success.

This Committee recommends that the Association take the affirmative steps of:

(a) preparing a statement of policy embodying the Association's position along with supporting arguments; this statement would be published in appropriate Association communications and made available to law schools and to other interested parties;

(b) securing counsel for the purpose of preparing a brief with more detailed legal argumentation and citation of relevant authorities; the Association should take steps to file such a brief *amicus curiae* in pending representation proceedings;

(c) taking further steps to bring this statement and brief to the attention of any appropriate legislative or quasi-legislative body about to embark upon the regulation of employment relations in higher education; the Association might in fact urge the National Labor Relations Board to establish, through its rarely invoked "rule-making" procedures, general guidelines for unit determinations in the setting of a legislative-style hearing rather than in ad hoc adjudicatory proceedings. The major cost to the Association in such a program of publicity would be the preparation of the brief, a cost which we believe worth bearing in light of the potentially frequent use of the document and in light of the emerging significance of this issue for law faculties throughout the country. (In any event, the Association should stand willing to lend its name to any brief, independently prepared on behalf of a law school faculty, which espouses the principles recommended in this report.)

Any legal arguments supporting law faculty autonomy will have to rest upon the notions of "community of interest" and the "professional employee." A number of factors have already been set forth above which indicate a community of interest among law school faculty which is separate and distinct from other faculty members—and yet more clearly from non-teaching professionals—within the university. To the extent that the locus of decisionmaking on matters of educational and personnel policy at the law school is decentralized and independent of effective control by university administration, support may be found in precedents outside of academe dealing with claims for separate representation in single plants in a multi-plant business operation, as well as in single-store and single-office units. The National Labor Relations Board appears over the past decade to have become rather more hospitable to such "fragmented" units. To the extent that the professional skills and training, teaching methods and ties to the practicing bar mark the law faculty as professionals who have interests distinct from other teachers, reference can be made to decisions outside of academe dealing with claims for separate representation by professional employees apart from a unit of nonprofessionals. This principle of separate representation is frequently expressly written into legislation; the federal Labor Management Relations Act provides that professional employees are not to be included in a unit with nonprofessional employees unless the former first approve such inclusion by majority vote. While it is true that all university faculty (and some non-faculty university employees) may be deemed "professional employees" such that this provision strictly applied would not speak to the question of autonomy for "law faculty professionals," it is possible to argue that the same principle of elective autonomy should apply when a group of teaching professionals have a distinct community of interest from all other teaching professionals. The alternative is to enshrine in every case a university-wide unit, typically comprised of hundreds and occasionally thousands of professionals (faculty and non-faculty), as the only appropriate unit in higher education.

Despite the vigor with which this Committee unanimously embraces the above views, we are equally unanimous in putting forth a most guarded prognosis of success. The obstacles to prevailing on an argument for autonomy of law faculty are substantial indeed. The counter-arguments are at least of two kinds. First, despite some measure of educational and administrative independence from the rest of the university, the law school faculty in considerable measure shares a community of interest with all faculty within the "university family." There is typically a substantial degree of fiscal dependence upon central university administration, which, through ultimate control over the pursestrings, can exercise considerable influence over faculty size and composition, faculty salaries and fringe benefits, student composition, curriculum development, research activities, physical plant and the like at the law school. The law school faculty commonly demonstrates its felt community of interest with other university faculty by actively participating in university governance through representative bodies and policymaking committees. The catalogue need not be extended indefinitely. The second major obstacle to autonomy, even assuming that the law faculty can make a case for a separate community of interest, is that there are other divisions or schools within the university which can perhaps lay equal claim to exclusion from a university-wide unit. A university medical school—and other professional schools training in the medical arts—is perhaps the most obvious example. Schools of business, engineering and other applied sciences, and faculty groups working on special projects perhaps with the aid of government funds, can all raise plausible arguments for separate representation not unlike those asserted herein on behalf of the law schools. The proliferation and fragmentation that might characterize collective bargaining in higher education could make a labor relations agency most reluctant to grant autonomy to the law school, thereby opening the door to similar claims by other faculty groups. (It may well be, however, that as a practical matter this proliferation would not come to pass, with only the law and medical schools seeking and being granted autonomy in light of their educational goal of training practicing professionals.) With many labor relations agencies already engrossing within the unit all university professionals, those who do not teach, as well as those who do, it may well be a considerable victory to secure separate bargaining status for all full-time teaching faculty as distinct from other university professionals. Separate representation for faculty of the professional schools will not likely come easily.

In conclusion, this Committee interposes the further caveat that the above report has been based on some generalized model of the "typical" law school. (The three schools from which we come provide the archetype for us; but many would dispute our treating them as "typical.") The extent of educational and administrative autonomy of specific law schools will no doubt vary, and our conclusions and recommendations may well have to be adjusted accordingly in particular instances. Indeed, there may be cases in which the law school faculty would wish affirmatively to seek incorporation within a larger university-wide unit; surely in such cases the Association, after rendering any requested advice on the matter, should take no formal position inimical to the desires of the specific faculty in question.

Amicus Curiae Brief

In May, 1971, the AALS *amicus curiae* brief in the *Fordham* case was submitted to the National Labor Relations Board (NLRB). The brief, chiefly prepared by Alvin L. Goldman, together with Walter E. Oberer and Robert A. Gorman, supported the AALS position that law faculty should be in a representational unit separate from the rest of the university in NLRB-directed elections. The National Labor Relations Act (NLRA) and its subsequent interpretations since 1947, which display an awareness of the need for certain professional groups to have separate representation, were cited as the basis of the AALS position.

Four Criteria for a Separate Unit

The brief presented four criteria for separating the law faculty from a larger group of professionals. (1) It notes a lack of functional integration:

The Board [NLRB] tends to establish separate units where there is little or no integration in the functional responsibilities of the several groups of employees.[1] Functional integration of an operation provides a basis for projecting the extent to which there will be job related interpersonal contact and a sense of mutual identity between the members of the various proposed units. Perhaps even more importantly, the extent of functional integration indicates the potential viability of a voting unit for bargaining purposes—that is, whether a particular unit can muster meaningful bargaining leverage—and the degree to which the bargaining behavior of a separate unit will disrupt the work activities of members of a larger or other separate unit.

The law schools lack functional integration with the rest of the universities to which they belong. Some prominent universities such as Princeton, Brown, and Dartmouth have no law faculty; others like the Detroit College of Law have no university affiliation; several are physically distant from the main university campus. Functionally, universities and law schools do not depend on each other. They usually have different academic calendars. Because the bulk of the students will enter the legal profession, distinctive demands are placed on law faculty. For example, law schools must coordinate their efforts with professional organizations, especially in view of bar examinations, bar association and legal institute programs, and continuing legal education needs; convey legal ethics; provide supervised practice; and grade comprehensive examination papers.

(2) The brief further argues that law schools have a separate sense of identity:

A realistic opportunity to collectively organize and establish meaningful collective bargaining goals is fostered by a sense of mutual identity amongst the unit members. For this reason, a separate bargaining unit is preferred where a group has a separate and distinctive sense of identity. The Board [NLRB] seeks to ascertain the mutuality or separateness of employee identity in making its voting unit determinations by examining a number of factors. Included is the nature of the differences or similarities in job skills and functions.[2] The lack of perma-

---

1. E.I. DuPont de Nemours, 162 NLRB 49.
2. Cornell University, 183 NLRB 41; Ladish Co., 178 NLRB 5; Arnold Constable Corp., 150 NLRB 80; Standard Oil Co., 107 NLRB 311.

nent interchange or temporary job transfers are additional factors frequently used by the Board in weighing the quality of mutual identity.[3] Differences in benefits policies amongst professional, departmental or plan groups suggest that there will be an accompanying lack of mutual identity.[4] Dissimilarities in employee background and training will also reduce the likelihood of a mutual sense of identity.[5] The same is true with respect to differences in employee licensing requirements.[6] Differences in job progression criteria and patterns provide yet another indicator that there may be an absence of a sense of mutuality of identity.[7] And, still another indicator used by the Board is the extent to which work schedules vary between the two groups of employees in question.[8]

In their separate physical and professional environment, law faculties have a characteristically different type of academic background, work experience, promotional criteria, and salary schedule. Most were professionally employed outside the university before becoming faculty members. Their higher salaries are influenced by the larger marketplace of the profession. Almost all are admitted to legal practice. Part-time teachers are normally full-time practicing lawyers or judges. Very few law faculty members hold research doctorates. On the average, promotion to full professor occurs in the sixth year of their appointment and tenure is obtained earlier than is true for other faculty groups. Transfers from other academic units into law are extremely rare. Law faculties are a tightly knit community, with a unique form of curriculum and a high degree of professional autonomy. They select their own deans, conduct separate fund drives, determine their own teaching loads and curriculum, and at times pay greater heed to their own special public than to the university itself. Their students tend to reflect a similar sense of identity, even in the way

3. Empire State Sugar Co., 166 NLRB 22, aff'd, 401 F.2d 559 (2d Cir. 1968); Douglas Aircraft Co., 157 NLRB 68; Georgia-Pacific Corp., 156 NLRB 92.
4. Parke Davis & Co., 173 NLRB 53; Empire State Sugar Co., supra.
5. Ladish Co., 178 NLRB 5; Standard Oil Co., 107 NLRB 311.
6. Parke Davis & Co., 173 NLRB 53.
7. Georgia-Pacific Corp., 156 NLRB 92; Parke Davis & Co., 173 NLRB 53; Douglas Aircraft, 157 NLRB 68.
8. Parke Davis & Co., 173 NLRB 53.

they spend their extracurricular time. An expression of this is seen in the absorption of the American Law Student Association, established in the late 1940s, into the newly created Law Student Division of the American Bar Association. Student groups have had a major role in the transition of the first law degree from the LL.B. to the J.D. and in the increase of legal service programs at law schools.

(3) Among the four interlocking criteria for exclusion, the brief also indicates physical proximity of the work situs.

> Physical separation of the work situs, too, contributes to the Board's [NLRB] evaluation that a separate professional, departmental, or plant type unit is preferable.[9] Physical separation is a relevant criterion for much the same reason as is lack of a sense of mutuality of identity. In addition, lack of physical proximity poses serious problems to the organizational opportunities for different groups of employees. The specification of the "plant unit" as one of the enumerated unit categories in section 9(b) of the Act [NLRA] demonstrates that Congress viewed the characteristic of the physical separateness of the work situs as particularly significant.

Law schools usually have distinctive facilities in a separate physical plant. The law faculty typically has its own classrooms and maintains its own library, at a much higher number of volumes per student than in university libraries. With few exceptions, all full-time teachers and the law librarians have separate offices.

(4) Finally, the brief points out the degree of unit autonomy.

> Decisionmaking autonomy increases the likelihood that a unit will have distinctive terms and conditions to collectively negotiate and independent bargaining interests to be served by a bargaining agent. Further, the degree of autonomy will influence the extent to which one group of employees must depend on another group for bargaining effectiveness. It will also influence the prospect that the bargaining conduct of one group will or will not have direct consequences for the other; that is, for an autonomous employee group, a separate unit provides the most meaningful opportunity to negotiate effectively on a

---

9. Parke Davis & Co., 173 NLRB 53; Douglas Aircraft Co., 157 NLRB 68.

collective basis. Therefore, the presence of autonomy strongly indicates that a separate unit will be preferred.[10]

A number of factors which the Board [NLRB] traditionally examines, in determining whether a separate professional, departmental or plant unit will be preferred, provide insight into the extent to which the unit is autonomous. These factors include whether there is independent control over recruitment and hiring in the unit;[11] whether the group is separately supervised;[12] whether the group has a different work schedule.[13] Bargaining history provides still another item in the Board's evaluation.[14] And, factors such as job progression patterns and comparative compensation benefits are relevant to evaluating the extent of autonomy as well as in weighing the mutuality of identity.

Law faculties have traditionally had a very high degree of autonomy which far exceeds that found to warrant a separate unit in past decisions.[15] In a consent agreement reached at St. John's University, the law school was therefore appropriately excluded from the universitywide unit.[16] Law school self-governance is both a tradition and a standard for AALS accreditation. Individual faculty members normally determine, without review or supervision, how and what they will teach in courses assigned them and how the grading will be done. The AALS encourages the practice of raising funds from outside the university sources.

Dangers of Inclusion

The concluding arguments of the brief emphasize dangers inherent in immersing the law faculty within a larger faculty unit:

The foregoing discussion should make it evident that all of the usual considerations in voting unit determination cases compel the result that a separate unit be preferred by the Board [NLRB] for the law faculty. But were the usual con-

---

10. Metropolitan Life Ins. Co., 156 NLRB 113.
11. Ladish Co., 178 NLRB 5; Douglas Aircraft Co., 157 NLRB 68.
12. Georgia-Pacific Corp., 156 NLRB 92; Parke Davis & Co., 173 NLRB 53.
13. Parke Davis & Co., 173 NLRB 53.
14. Georgia-Pacific Corp., 156 NLRB 92.
15. Douglas Aircraft Co., 157 NLRB 68; Arnold Constable Co., 150 NLRB 80; Lumbermen's Mutual Casualty Co., 75 NLRB 129.
16. St. John's University, N.Y.S. Lab. Rel. Bd., Doc. No. 12630, April 22, 1970.

siderations the only ones involved in the present issue, the AALS might not have deemed it necessary to make this amicus appearance. Rather, there are at least two additional concerns respecting the instant issue which elevate the question to one of great urgency for an association dedicated to the purpose of improving the legal profession through legal education.

Professor Donald Wollett is probably the nation's most experienced academic observer of unionizational activities in higher education. In a recent article he pointed out that to attract and retain quality faculty in a professional area such as law, "universities often find it necessary to prescribe lighter work loads and larger salaries than those of other faculty groups. . . ." Reflecting on the impact of a university-wide unit determination, he goes on to state: "Collective bargaining agents tend to favor policies that treat all employees alike. . . . If collective negotiations result in a reduction in the favorable differentials enjoyed by professional school faculties, the ability of those schools to attract and retain quality faculty and to function at present performance levels will probably be diminished."[17] The AALS concurs in Professor Wollett's prediction that negotiation on a university-wide unit basis will adversely affect the quality of legal education. There is no good reason for risking that result in as much as the intent of Congress in promulgating 9(b) of the Act [NLRA] is more accurately served by preferring a separate unit for law faculty.

Secondly, legal education (as, perhaps, all of higher education) is in a phase of considerable reappraisal and transition. The law faculties, the bench, and the bar are all actively engaged in this reevaluation.[18] Encompassed in the current review of legal education are such questions as the optimum duration of formal professional education in law; course and curriculum content; teaching methodology; expansion, protraction or revision of clinical programs; the direction, tools and content of scholarly efforts in law; financial resources for legal education; budgetary priorities; and the relationship of law

---

17. Donald Wollett, "The Status and Trends of Collective Negotiations for Faculty in Higher Education," 1971 *Wis. L. Rev.* 2, 18.
18. Statement of the AALS to Senate Subcommittee on Education, reported in the Association of American Law Schools, *Proceedings, 1971 Annual Meeting,* Part One (Washington, D.C.: AALS, 1971), p. 49.

teaching and legal scholarship to other academic disciplines.[19] Presently the locus of decisionmaking on matters of educational and personnel policy in legal education is decentralized and independent of effective control by university administration. There are those (usually persons in university administration) who argue that the law schools should surrender a significant part of that autonomy and become more comprehensively integrated into the university system.[20] Law faculties, on the other hand, as the academic representatives of the legal profession, see many reasons to be cautious against submergence of their special and distinctive role into a larger and more homogeneous group.

A decision by the National Labor Relations Board to immerse the law faculty into the larger faculty unit could well have the effect of a *fait accompli* respecting the role of the law school in a modern university. As we have seen, that decision could be quite detrimental to the quality of legal education. In any event, surely, if change in that relationship is to come, it should result from a decision made by those entrusted with the responsibility for guiding legal education.

A decision to immerse the law school within the larger university-wide faculty unit might well foreclose any further reappraisal of, or adjustment in, the law school's role within the university and its relation to the profession. Rather, such a determination would tend to move that relationship in the specific direction of total submergence within the university faculty. On the other hand, recognizing that the law faculty is a preferred voting unit apart from the larger university faculty would permit continued reappraisal and adjustment in the law school-university relationship.

---

19. *Ibid*, at pp. 50-52, 55-72.
20. *See, e.g.,* various commentaries in Haber & Cohen, *The Law School of Tomorrow* (New Brunswick, N.J.: Rutgers University Press, 1968), pp. 5-80.

NLRB Denial of the American Association of University Professors Petition

United States of America
Before the National Labor Relations Board

*Petition for Proceedings for Rule-making
in Representation Cases Involving Faculty
Members in Colleges and Universities*

American Association of University Professors, Petitioner

Order Denying Petition

Pursuant to Section 6 of the National Labor Relations Act, as amended, and Section 4 of the Administrative Procedure Act, and in accordance with Section 120.124 of the National Labor Relations Board Rules and Regulations, Series 8, as amended, the American Association of University Professors, hereinafter called the AAUP, filed the above Petition with the National Labor Relations Board in Washington, D.C. The AAUP requested that the Board institute proceedings for the purpose of determining what, if any, rules may be promulgated to guide the determination of issues in representation cases involving faculty members in colleges and universities, and submitted a statement in support of its Petition. Subsequently, The Association of American Universities advised that it wishes to be associated with the AAUP in the Petition, and various other organizations and individuals wrote in support of the Petition.

The Board, pursuant to Section 102.125 of the Board's Rules and Regulations, has considered the Petition. The Board considers that the Petition properly points out that the Board's unit determinations in this area should take into account certain practices and organizational structures which do not parallel the traditional practices and organizational structures in private industry. The Board's information to date, however, suggests that there is also a great variety in this regard within the academic community, and also that the practices and structures in universities and colleges are undergoing a period of change and experimentation. The Board believes that to adopt inflexible rules for units of teaching employees at this time might well introduce too great an element of rigidity and prevent the Board from adapting its approach to a highly pluralistic and fluid set of conditions. Accordingly, the Board shall deny the Petition.

The Board would welcome the fruits of any research which has been done or can be done in this subject area, to supplement its own efforts to compile source data. Surveys of existing structures and practices in universities and colleges, for example, could provide the Board with a set of empirical data which could be most helpful to it as reference material. The Board invites all interested persons or organizations, including the Petitioner, to submit to the Board in Washington, D.C., any such materials which they believe could be of assistance to the Board in this connection. Information of this nature should be sent to Mr. Standau Weinbrecht, Chief, Legal Research and Special Projects Branch, National Labor Relations Board, 1717 Pennsylvania Avenue, N.W., Washington, D.C. 20570. Mr. Weinbrecht will have the responsibility of compiling such materials into a useful research tool for the Members of the Board and their professional staffs.

IT IS HEREBY ORDERED that the AAUP's Petition requesting the Board to engage in rule-making for the purpose of developing guidelines for the establishment of units of teaching employees of universities and colleges be, and it hereby is, denied.

Dated, Washington, D.C., July 16, 1971

By direction of the Board:

John C. Truesdale

Acting Executive Secretary

Bargaining Agents at
163 Colleges and Universities

The following 163 colleges and universities are those where faculty are known to have named agents to represent them in collective bargaining, as of January, 1972. About 55,000 academic personnel are involved, over 30,000 of these in New York. In a few cases legal status has not yet been accorded by the states. Note that all campuses of the City University of New York are included as one, as are those of the State University of New York, the Maine Vocational-Technical Institutes, and the state college systems of Nebraska, New Jersey, and Pennsylvania. These bring the actual number of campus units to 233. In two cases—Dutchess Community College and St. John's University, both in New York—there is joint affiliation. At City University of New York, lecturers and part-time academic staff are separately represented.

Of the total 233 units listed, 80 are in New York, 30 in Michigan, 22 in Pennsylvania, 19 in New Jersey, 18 in Minnesota, 15 in Wisconsin, 13 in Illinois, and 10 in Massachusetts—a total of 207 in these eight states and only 26 in the remaining nine states.[1] Membership of the larger units is noted here, as are the 1971 additions by AFT. The 1971 dates were not available from NEA, though its list is up-to-date. At present NEA represents about 35,000 academic personnel in 169 units and AFT about 13,000 in 67 units (the 19 CUNY units overlap). A latecomer, AAUP represents about 2,500 in eight units.

Colorado

Arapahoe Community College   NEA

---

1. The help of NEA's Charles Belknap and AAUP's Wilfred Kaplan in forming this list is gratefully acknowledged; also, that of the AAUP, AFT, and NEA national offices.

District of Columbia

Washington Technical Institute (1971)	AFT

Guam

*University of Guam	AFT

Illinois

Belleville Area College	AAUP

Chicago City College (also a clerical unit)	AFT
Highland Community College	AFT
Illinois Valley Community College	AFT
Joliet Junior College	AFT
Lincoln-Land Community College (1971)	AFT
Morton Junior College	AFT
Prairie State College (Cook Co.)	AFT
Thornton Community College (Cook Co., 1971)	AFT
Waubonsee Community College	AFT

College of Lake County	NEA
Lakeland College	NEA
Sauk Valley College	NEA

Kansas

Butler County Community Junior College	NEA
Cloud County Community Junior College	NEA
Colby Community Junior College	NEA
Garden City Community Junior College	NEA
Hutchinson Community Junior College	NEA
Independence Community Junior College	NEA
Kansas City Kansas Community Junior College	NEA
Labette Community Junior College	NEA

Maine

Vocational-Technical Institutes (5 institutes)	NEA

Maryland

Baltimore Community College	AFT

---

* Denotes four-year institutions.

Massachusetts

*Boston State College	AFT
Bristol Community College (1971)	AFT
*Lowell State University (1971)	AFT
*Massachusetts College of Art	AFT
*Southeastern Massachusetts University	AFT
*Westfield State University (1971)	AFT
*Worcester State College (1971)	AFT
*Fitchburg State College	NEA
Massasoit Community College	NEA
*Salem State College	NEA

Michigan

*Oakland University	AAUP
Henry Ford Community College	AFT
Highland Park College	AFT
Lake Michigan College	AFT
Wayne County Community College	AFT
Alpena Community College	NEA
*Central Michigan University (ca 570 members)	NEA
*Detroit College of Business	NEA
Genesee Community Junior College	NEA
Glen Oaks Community College	NEA
Gogebic Community College	NEA
Jackson Community College	NEA
Kalamazoo Valley Community College	NEA
Kellogg Community College	NEA
Lansing Community College	NEA
Mid-Michigan Community College	NEA
Monroe County Community College	NEA
Montcalm Community College	NEA
Muskegon Community College	NEA
Oakland Community College	NEA
*Saginaw Valley State College (Jan. 1972)	NEA
St. Clair County Community College	NEA
Schoolcraft College	NEA
Southwestern Michigan College	NEA
Washtenaw Community College	NEA

Bay De Noc Community College	INDEP.
Grand Rapids Junior College	INDEP.
Kirtland Community College	INDEP.
Macomb County Community College	INDEP.
West Shore Community College	INDEP.

Minnesota

Anoka Ramsey State Junior College	NEA
Austin State Junior College	NEA
Brainerd State Junior College	NEA
Fergus Falls State Junior College	NEA
Hibbing State Junior College	NEA
Itasca State Junior College	NEA
Lakewood State Junior College	NEA
Mesabi State Junior College	NEA
Metropolitan State Junior College	NEA
Normandale State Junior College	NEA
North Hennepin State Junior College	NEA
Northland State Junior College	NEA
Rainy River State Junior College	NEA
Rochester State Junior College	NEA
St. Mary's Junior College	NEA
Vermilion State Junior College	NEA
Willmar State Junior College	NEA
Worthington State Junior College	NEA

Nebraska

*Nebraska State Colleges (4 colleges: Chadron, Kearney, Peru, Wayne; ca 475 members)	NEA

New Jersey

*Rutgers University (ca 750 members)	AAUP
Middlesex County College	AFT
Atlantic Community College	NEA
Bergen Community College	NEA
Burlington Community College	NEA
Camden County College	NEA
Cumberland County College	NEA

Essex County College	NEA
Gloucester County College	NEA
Mercer County College	NEA
*Monmouth College	NEA
*New Jersey State Colleges (6 colleges: Glassboro, Jersey City, Montclair, Newark, Paterson, Trenton; ca 2,000 members)	NEA
Ocean County College	NEA
Somerset County College	NEA

New York

*Brooklyn Polytechnic Institute	AAUP
*Dowling College (formerly Adelphi)	AAUP
*New York Institute of Technology	AAUP
*St. John's University (with independent association, ca 500 members)	AAUP
*City University of New York (19 units; lecturers, part-time and support personnel; ca 6,200 members)	AFT
Dutchess Community College (with NEA)	AFT
Fashion Institute of Technology	AFT
*Long Island University (C. W. Post Center and Brooklyn Campus, 1971; ca 750 members)	AFT
Nassau Community College (1971)	AFT
Onondaga Community College	AFT
*Pratt Institute (1971)	AFT
Rockland Community College	AFT
*Taylor Business Institute	AFT
*U.S. Merchant Marine Academy	AFT
Westchester Community College	AFT
Adirondack Community College	NEA
Auburn Community College	NEA
Broome Technical Community College	NEA
*City University of New York (19 units; full-time academic staff; ca 6,000 members)	NEA
Clinton County Community College	NEA
Dutchess Community College (with AFT)	NEA
Erie Community College	NEA
Fulton-Montgomery Community College	NEA

Genesee Community College   NEA
Hudson Valley Community College   NEA
Jamestown Community College   NEA
Jefferson Community College   NEA
Monroe Community College   NEA
Mohawk Valley Community College   NEA
North Country Community College   NEA
Orange County Community College   NEA
Schenectady Community College   NEA
*State University of New York (26 units; ca 15,000 members)   NEA
Suffolk County Community College   NEA
Tompkins-Cortland Community College   NEA
Ulster County Community College   NEA

Niagara Community College   INDEP.

Pennsylvania

Allegheny County Community College (1971)   AFT
Bucks County Community College (1971)   AFT
Community College of Philadelphia   AFT
Moore College of Art (1971)   AFT

Beaver County Community College   NEA
Lehigh Community College   NEA
Luzerne Community College   NEA
*Pennsylvania State College and University System (14
    units, 1971; ca 4,000 members)   NEA
Williamsport Area Community College   NEA

Rhode Island

*University of Rhode Island (Dec. 1971)   AAUP

*Bryant College of Business Administration   AFT

Washington

Olympia Vocational-Technical Institute (1971)   AFT
Seattle Community College   AFT

Yakima Valley College   NEA

Wisconsin

Eau Claire Area Technical Institute	AFT
Green Bay Area Technical Institute	AFT
Madison Area Technical College	AFT
Milwaukee Area Technical College	AFT
Racine Area Technical Institute	AFT
Superior Area Technical Institute	AFT
Fond du Lac Area Technical Institute	NEA
Fox Valley Area Technical Institute	NEA
Kenosha Area Technical Institute	NEA
Lake Shore Area Technical Institute	NEA
Mid State Area Technical Institute	NEA
North Central Area Technical Institute	NEA
Waukesha Area Technical Institute	NEA
*University of Wisconsin (teaching assistants)	INDEP.
Western Wisconsin Area Technical Institute	INDEP.

APPENDIX J

Contracts

The few faculty contracts thus far achieved through collective bargaining yield valuable information for those who need to know the specifics of negotiating a contract and for those who are exploring alternatives to collective bargaining. The following analysis uses contracts from eight representative institutions to illustrate some of the more noteworthy features. All eight are included in the Institute of Continuing Legal Education *Course Materials* cited in the Preface and are referred to by their abbreviations. The bargaining agents follow the college name.

Belleville Area College, Illinois (AAUP, 1970)	BAC
Central Michigan University (NEA, 1971, second contract)	CMU
City University of New York (Legislative Conference	
NEA, 1969)	CUNY
Nassau Community College, New York	
(Faculty Senate, 1969)	NCC
New Jersey State Colleges (NEA, 1971)	NJSC
St. John's University, New York (AAUP, 1970)	St. John's
Southeastern Massachusetts University (AFT, 1970)	SEMU
Washtenaw Community College (NEA, 1971)	WCC

Among the more recent contracts, that from Michigan's Oakland University is outlined at the close of this discussion.

The aim here is not to explain the order in which a contract should be written but to consider what can be included. The outline represents an order of philosophical reflection, starting with basic principles. A few items discussed are not taken from the eight contracts but have been under consideration in other institutions.

Basic Principles

A key issue to be faced in negotiating any contract is the best method of dealing with institutional rights. There are at least three possible solutions: (1) Assume that such rights are implicit within traditional relationships. *Pro:* This solution avoids having to go by the book, reinforces an atmosphere of mutual trust, and allows a more appropriate sense of rights to develop with experience. *Con:* It fails to deal with the changed relationships to be brought about by collective bargaining, leaving rights open to subsequent bargaining and the risk of serious misunderstandings later on. (2) Recognize institutional rights in general terms, e.g., by reference to the American Association of University Professors (AAUP) statements on rights. *Pro:* This solution allows specifics to be developed with further experience. *Con:* It is too vague to be useful for some purposes, such as determining the nature of faculty participation in governance, and it tends to entrench the status quo. (3) Specify institutional rights in concrete terms. *Pro:* This solution meets the objections to the first two solutions. *Con:* It presupposes a capacity for agreement that may not be achievable at the time; it may develop out of hasty, ad hoc consideration; and the results may be difficult to alter later on.

Whatever solution or combination of solutions is adopted, it should allow for mechanisms to permit change. Otherwise, both the contract and the bargaining process could become restrictive factors at a time when rapid institutional change is required. Sufficient flexibility for change can be assured by arranging for joint advisory or decisionmaking committees, outside the bargaining structure, to speak to such matters as academic affairs, long-range planning, program evaluation, budgeting and allocation, relation to the state, research, tenure review, and student affairs. Community members other than senior faculty and administrators can be profitably involved in some of these areas.

Other areas where basic principles are regularly involved include:

1. Recognition of Bargaining Agent and Composition of Unit
2. Continuation of Established Patterns
3. Relationship of Faculty, Administration, and Governing Board
4. Academic Freedom
5. Management Rights
6. Codetermination in Governance
7. Mechanisms for Institutional Change
8. Nondiscrimination

9. Access to Information
10. Strikes and Lockouts
11. Impasse Resolution
12. Participation of Other Community Members

1. Recognition of Bargaining Agent and Composition of Unit

Although these matters are largely determined before negotiations leading to the first contract, the immense importance of the issues involved should be anticipated. Any marked changes in the bargaining unit would have to be cleared with the labor relations board having jurisdiction. The WCC contract includes paragraphs defining community of interest and indicates how title changes on these and related matters can be made. CMU notes categories of employees excluded from the bargaining unit. CUNY adds an article on unit stability (3.1): "Any group of employees in the present collective negotiation unit whose group classification is changed during the life of this Agreement will remain in this unit for the duration of this Agreement." CUNY further provides (2.2): "The parties agree to extend the period of unchallenged representation status for the maximum period authorized by law." St. John's (1.2) includes an agreement to carry over the unit in case of institutional merger or consolidation. Unless rights are the subject of a separate article, it is appropriate to state in the contract that nothing prevents officials from meeting with any party on matters not specifically included as subjects of collective bargaining (CUNY 2.3).

2. Continuation of Established Patterns

The items discussed under this and the following five headings could be covered in a single article or series of articles. Unfortunately, in most of the contracts studied they are scattered or missing altogether. St. John's (Premable, 2, 3, and 4:3) is far more explicit on many of these items than any of the other contracts. More often than not, established patterns of governance and decisionmaking are retained in practice simply by not mentioning them at all in the contract.

3. Relationship of Faculty, Administration, and Governing Board

WCC (2,3) states governing board rights in general terms, but the faculty association rights and responsibilities are specifically listed in sixteen items, many of which are usually put in separate articles in other contracts. CUNY's first article on relationships between the board and the faculty Legislative Conference deals specifically with board bylaws, agendas, and the right to be heard by the board, if proper notice is given. St. John's (2.4) adheres to the AAUP's 1966 "Statement on Government of Colleges and Universities." SEMU includes federation-trustees relations in a single article. The eleven sections of this article include such items as nondiscrimination, dues check-offs, continuing consultation, use of bulletin boards, and provision of an agency office. Similar features are included in NJSC in articles entitled administration of agreement, policy statements, and association rights and privileges.

4. Academic Freedom

St. John's (4.3) accepts the AAUP's 1940 "Statement of Principles on Academic Freedom and Tenure." In preambles, SEMU vaguely refers to "the democratic ideal" and NJSC to "the traditional principles of academic freedom and professional ethics." SEMU, however, adds an article establishing an academic review committee to work on such matters and defines academic freedom in some detail (e.g., determination of course content and texts, teaching assignments, publication and speaking, and discussion of controversial issues). NCC includes a lengthy definition of academic freedom which emphasizes specific limits: "The teacher is entitled to freedom in the classroom in discussing his subject, but he should be careful not to introduce into his teaching controversial matter which has no relation to his subject." This definition is also included in the SEMU contract.

A very different mood, more restricted in scope, is displayed in WCC: "The instructor shall have the freedom to report the truth as he sees it both in the classroom and in reports of research activities. There shall be no restraints which would impair the instructor's ability to present his subject matter in this context." The chief difficulty in defining academic freedom is the risk of saying too much or too little. In traditional parlance, academic freedom includes a broad range of rights and privileges and widely divergent interpretations. The 1940 AAUP statement, as refined in subsequent AAUP reports,[1] probably comes closest to meeting the

---

1. See *AAUP Bulletin,* Fall, 1970.

difficulty. In most AAUP reports, principles of academic freedom often appear to be too closely allied to the definition of tenure practices to fit the current scene.

5. Management Rights

Employee and management representatives regularly disagree on management rights. The two sides of the issue: Will statements of such rights preempt bargaining? Or, will management give away rights, difficult or impossible to bargain back, by failing to include their recognition in the initial contract? Recognition of some management rights will inevitably emerge through bargaining; others are already established by law. Bargainers should avoid the presumption that all previous rights on one side may be reserved unless otherwise specified, while those on the other side may be won only through bargaining. This can be done by stating the respective rights and responsibilities in general or specific terms in the contract, by recognizing the institutional means by which such areas are customarily singled out (e.g., cooperation between administration and organs of faculty governance), or by inserting a general statement that the agreement is not to be construed as either affirming or denying customary administrative rights and responsibilities not explicitly covered in the agreement.

WCC includes a reserve clause: "All rights and authority of the Board prescribed by law or stated in this Contract are retained. This Contract covers all subjects of bargaining and there shall be no duty on either party to bargain collectively regarding those matters covered in this Contract unless otherwise specified for the duration of this Contract." St. John's (3) retains "past practices" of the administration "not in conflict" with the provisions of the agreement. The management rights provision (12) in NJSC states:

A. The STATE, the Board, the Department and the Boards of Trustees retain and reserve unto themselves all rights, powers, duties, authority and responsibilities conferred upon and vested in them by the laws and constitutions of the State of New Jersey and the United States of America.

B. All such rights, powers, authority and prerogatives of management possessed by the STATE, the Department and the Boards of Trustees are retained and may be exercised without restrictions or prior notice, subject to limitations imposed by law, except as they are specifically abridged or modified by this Agreement.

C. The STATE, the Board and the Boards of Trustees retain their responsibility to promulgate and enforce rules and regulations, subject to limitations imposed by law, governing the conduct and activities of employees not inconsistent with the express provisions of this Agreement.

The provisions above maintain the administrative autonomy provided by law for a system of state colleges.

6. Codetermination in Governance

A separation of powers is emphasized in NCC (2,4), where the faculty senate is the bargaining agent. That contract states:

The Board and President should [not shall], on matters where the faculty has the primary responsibility, concur with the faculty judgment except in rare instances and for compelling reasons which should be stated, in detail, and an opportunity for further consideration and transmittal of views to both the President and the Board of Trustees shall be provided.

Apparently none of the eight institutions, at the time their contracts were made, had organs for codetermination which were sufficiently influential to be recognized or protected in their contracts; but such recognition will surely be a major issue in future contracts. Stated formally, the issue is: Can the development of collective bargaining prove compatible with, and supportive of, a concurrent development of organs for codetermination of basic policy and procedure between faculty and administration? Viewed in terms of basic academic values, the issue is: To what extent is collective bargaining justifiable within a given institution if such collegial relations are not promoted through the bargaining process?

7. Mechanisms for Institutional Change

Apart from arrangements for bargaining and decisionmaking on items like tenure, mechanisms for institutional change have been mentioned in these contracts only in the broadest terms. The development of such mechanisms largely depends on achievements in joint governance—stronger faculty participation and administrative capacity to build structures to promote needed change.

8. Nondiscrimination

In CUNY (7) nondiscrimination simply refers to a joint agreement to give equal treatment to nonagency and agency members of the bargaining unit. CUNY explicitly permits all unit members to become agency members, which is prohibited in some contracts. St. John's (11) provides only that:

Nothing contained in this Agreement shall prevent any faculty member from bringing before any governmental administrative agency any complaint regarding discrimination with regard to race, creed, color, national origin, age, sex or marital status.

The provision omits reference to agency or nonagency faculty members. NJSC (3.D) is more inclusive:

The BOARD and the ASSOCIATION agree that there shall be no discrimination in the hiring, training, assignment, promotion, transfer, or discipline of faculty or in the application or administration of this Agreement on the basis of race, creed, color, religion, national origin, sex, marital status, or Association membership.

9. Access to Information

Although agency access to economic and personnel information is becoming increasingly important, only WCC among these eight contracts includes a comprehensive provision. NJSC (13) simply arranges for an exchange of current lists of association and administrative officers. CUNY (1.5) has the board furnish agendas and minutes of its meetings; WCC (3) adds "all normal attachments" to the agenda. At CUNY (8.1):

The Board shall make available to the Conference, upon its reasonable request and within a reasonable time thereafter, such statistics and financial information related to the collective negotiation unit and in possession of the Board as are necessary for negotiation and implementation of this Agreement. It is understood that this shall not be construed to require the Board to compile information and statistics in the form requested not already compiled in that form unless mutually agreeable.

SEMU (2.H) restricts the requirement to "public information," as does NJSC. WCC includes the CUNY statement almost verbatim but adds another paragraph:

> The Board agrees to furnish the Association information available to it concerning the professional staffing projections and financial resources of the college and such other information as will assist the Association in contract negotiation or in the processing of any grievance or in support of any member against whom a complaint is pending involving a demand for dismissal.

Several contracts have provisions carefully defining access to personnel files.

10. Strikes and Lockouts

No-strike provisions occur in most of the contracts and are sometimes accompanied by a prohibition against lockouts. The St. John's faculty association (12) agrees not to "instigate, engage in, support, encourage or condone any strike, work stoppage, or other concerted refusal to perform work," while the administration agrees not to lock out any or all faculty members. In case of violation, each party not only has recourse to the courts but may also opt for binding arbitration provided by the American Arbitration Association, which is available within a few days. WCC, one of the most recent Michigan contracts, omits any reference to strikes or lockouts.

11. Impasse Resolution

Especially where state law provides no special services, it would seem advisable to set up some procedure for resolving impasses (such as the St. John's provision just referred to). NJSC (17) explicitly adopts the procedure provided in the 1968 New Jersey law.

12. Participation of Other Community Members

The contracts have been virtually silent on the issue of what other community members might participate in the bargaining process. Experts generally agree that representation in negotiations should be restricted to faculty and administrators. Should other community members—e.g., students, academic support staff, and faculty outside the bargaining unit—have some input? If so, at what points and in what capacities? To preserve confidentiality in the negotiations themselves, some of these interests could be served through open or closed hearings, communiques, or even adjunct negotiations.

Major Contract Provisions

Differing institutional needs and partisan perspectives chiefly determine what contract provisions are thought essential. The following items are usually included in some form.

1. Meeting and Consultative Procedures
2. Collection of Dues
3. Provisions for the Agency and Its Representatives
4. Salary Increments and Schedules
5. Merit Increases
6. Fringe Benefits
7. Grievance Procedures
8. Disciplinary Action (Removal or Suspension)
9. Reduction and Elimination of Programs
10. Work Load
11. Tenure, Appointments, Evaluation, Promotion, Notice of Non-reappointment
12. Retirement
13. Participation in Selection of Deans and Other Administrative Officers
14. Priority in Relation to Other Contracts
15. Duration of Contract

1-3. The Bargaining Process

Arrangements closely related to the bargaining process deserve a separate place in a contract. They need not be elaborate to be sufficient, and they chiefly relate to (1) meeting and consultative procedures, (2) collection of dues, and (3) provisions for the agency and its representatives.

4-5. Salaries and Merit Increases

CUNY provides a standard salary schedule with automatic annual increments up to a maximum for each rank or category. In special circumstances, a deserving faculty member's position on the scale presumably can be accelerated. No separate merit provisions are made. St. John's (6) grants all full-time faculty an equal percentage increase for the contract period, a lesser percentage increase for all adjunct faculty, an adjustment fund to assure at least a stated amount of increase at each rank, and specific promotional increments. SEMU (5) adds merit increases to its salary schedule and sets up a joint committee "to develop policies for distributing future merit monies as provided by the Acts of the State legislature." BAC puts degrees earned and longevity factors into the salary schedule. WCC uses a point system to determine at what step in the schedule each member is to be placed, with additions to be earned through work experience or educational attainment.

6. Fringe Benefits

St. John's (7) lists the following fringe benefits in a single article: pension and annuity plan, medical, group life, disability, and travel insurance, and tuition waiver for faculty families. Some of these are provided by the university but paid for by the insured. CUNY (24.1) provides a per capita contribution by the university to the City University Faculty Welfare Fund. NJSC does not mention fringe benefits, while SEMU (5.F) simply continues "all fringe benefits as provided by law." BAC includes "legal service in defense of litigations that arise out of and in the course of performance of official duties"; NCC has a dental plan; WCC grants the privilege of buying at cost in the bookstore. As a rule of thumb it would be useful to divide faculty benefits other than salary into two categories: (1) fringe benefits in a special sense, i.e., compensated items that are provided on a mandatory or optional basis to all members (these are usually not subject to taxation and are, therefore, an especially important consideration in bargaining about compensation levels, and (2) service benefits in a special sense, i.e., those for which compensation is offered indirectly through administered programs or according to special qualifications (such as tuition waivers for children of faculty). Most existing contracts present these items in a random, fragmented way.

7. Grievance Procedure

Several matters regarding grievance procedures are of extreme importance. These include (a) acceptable subjects for grievance, (b) informal procedures for handling complaints, (c) steps and time limits within the formal process, (d) the nature of faculty participation, and (e) who pays the bills. There is much open ground here, especially where faculty members feel they have been inequitably treated outside the contract provisions, or possibly by virtue of its provisions, and such matters are not covered by the formal grievance procedures.

8. Disciplinary Action

Disciplinary actions against faculty members are customarily provided in the institutional bylaws. CUNY (19) puts them into the contract. St. John's has a lengthy section on "retention of employment" to cover emergency situations and bona fide need to reduce or eliminate programs. WCC has instituted its Professional Practices Committee to handle proposals to dismiss faculty members holding a probationary contract, with binding arbitration as a final recourse in case of conflict with the board of trustees' eventual decision.

9. Reduction and Elimination of Programs

A valuable addition to a few contracts specifies in what way review of programs is to be conducted, particularly when proposals involve reduction or elimination of programs. St. John's (4.17) specifies:

> The Administration may abolish programs and reduce the size of the faculty in a particular program, provided that (a) it consults with the faculty in accordance with the [AAUP] 1966 "Statement on Government of Colleges and Universities" and (b) it follows the provisions of Section 4.18 hereof [on retention of employment].

10. Work Load

Work load has not yet become a major item in most contracts, although an article broadly defining work load is normally included. BAC devotes all but a small portion of the contract to the matters of service and work load standards and of leave provisions. BAC sets maximum class sizes differentially for the various fields and provides formulas for establishing the equivalents of a regular faculty load in each field.

11-13. Personnel Decisions

The contracts are not consistent in specifying exactly who controls the complex personnel procedures and how it is to be done. Matters of tenure, appointments, evaluation, promotion, and notice of nonreappointment should be covered in any contract. Evaluation of tenured faculty has not yet become a major issue in bargaining, but in a tight budget situation it can be expected to arise. Such evaluation will be critical as the need for new programs increases, the average age of faculty climbs, and traditional tenure procedures come under attack. In some contracts provision is made for participation of faculty in selection of deans and other administrative officers.

14. Priority Clauses

Several contracts include a priority clause, which indicates the priority of contract provisions over any previous rules, policies, or practices and over any previous contracts between individual faculty members and the administration. St. John's (2:2) specifies that all provisions of the university statutes, or any amendments to them, remain in force, except that the terms of the bargained agreement shall be "controlling" where conflict arises between the two. CUNY (1.2-3) states:

> Nothing contained in this Agreement shall be construed to diminish the rights granted under the Bylaws of the Board to the entities and bodies within the internal structure of CUNY so long as such rights are not in conflict with this Agreement. If provisions of this Agreement require changes in the Bylaws of the Board, such changes will be effected. . . .

> If there is any inconsistency or conflict between the Bylaws of the Board and this Agreement, the provisions of this Agreement shall apply.

NJSC (3.B) and SEMU (II.B) refer their "controlling" clause only to individual contracts; both also have management rights clauses not present in the other two agreements.

15. Duration of Contract

The final article is usually a duration of contract clause. Sometimes provisions for automatic renewal, resumption of new contract negotiations, or completeness of contract are associated with it. NJSC (18) alone has an elaborate complete contract statement:

A. This Agreement, including the Appendix, incorporates the entire understanding of the parties on all matters which were or could have been the subject of negotiations. During the term of this Agreement neither party shall be required to negotiate with respect to any such matter whether or not covered by this Agreement and whether or not within the knowledge or contemplation of either or both of the parties at the time they negotiated or executed this Agreement.

B. By mutual agreement negotiations may be undertaken for the purpose of amending this Agreement. Amendments shall be in writing, be signed by the parties to this Agreement, appended thereto in order to become effective and published by the Board for the members of the unit and other parties concerned.

Secondary Provisions

The following subjects, which are included in some contracts, require little comment.

1. Seniority and Review of Tenured Faculty
2. Distinguished Professorships
3. Additional Teaching
4. Outside Employment
5. Travel Funds
6. Research Support
7. Office hours
8. Facilities
9. Housing
10. Other Academic Staff
11. Transfers Within the System

12. Sabbaticals and Other Leaves
13. Tuition Waivers
14. Transfer of Ownership
15. Legislative Action and Savings Provisions

There is one special issue, however. What consideration should be given to academic staff who are not members of the bargaining unit, how should this be done, and how can the results be reflected in the contract? CUNY has a separate bargaining unit for almost all these people.

Regarding transfer of ownership, St. John's (14-15) includes two clauses in view of a possible consolidation with Notre Dame College of Staten Island. One clause makes the agreement (especially noting retention of employment and reduction or elimination of programs) binding on "the successors, assigns, transferees, etc., of the University." It also provides for any reopening of negotiations in case consolidation occurs.

CUNY deals with legislative action and savings provisions in Article 32:

> It is agreed by and between the parties that any provision of this agreement requiring legislative action to permit its implementation by amendment of law or by providing the additional funds therefor, shall not become effective until the appropriate legislative body has given approval.

SEMU (16) and NJSC (16) have a savings provision:

> If any provision of this Agreement or any application of this Agreement to any employee or group of employees shall be found [NJSC is "held"] contrary to law, then such provision or application shall not be deemed valid and subsisting, except to the extent permitted by law, but all other provisions or applications will continue in full force and effect.

NJSC also has a legislative action clause like CUNY's and further adds: "Whenever legislation is necessary to implement this Agreement, the STATE and/or Department [i.e., state administration] shall assume responsibility for seeking the introduction of such legislation."

Oakland University

Among the more recent contracts is the Oakland University (Rochester, Michigan) and American Association of University Professors (AAUP) *Faculty Agreement 1971-1972,* dated November 12, 1971. This contract contains an unusually large number of bargained items, on the whole stated in clear, uncluttered language. Some of its features are as follows:

(1) Visiting lecturers, honorary professors, executive and supervisory employees, and postdoctoral fellows or research assistants whose wages are not determined by Oakland University are all excluded from the bargaining unit. Special instructors, as full-time employees who lack academic qualifications for a regular appointment, are included and are entitled to job security after seven years as long as the position is part of the university's program. They also receive all other faculty perquisites except sabbatical leaves. Department chairmen and certain other program directors are also included in the unit.

(2) Rigorous restrictions are placed on who may teach credit courses and on the use of visiting lecturers, who can be part-time only. Further (III.5): "In any semester, the number of extra-departmental and extraschool part-time employees shall not exceed three percent, figured on a full-time faculty equivalent basis, of the total number of faculty members in the bargaining unit."

(3) Time limits are set on the association's notification of the university regarding dues to be deducted and on handling any remittance to faculty members who choose not to have membership in the association. Nondiscriminatory policy toward these persons is required.

(4) Discipline and discharge procedures are set according to the national AAUP standards.

(5) There is a broad agreement that faculty members shall not be asked to spend "an excessive or unfair amount of time" on matters other than teaching (which includes academic counseling, professional library service, and research).

(6) The compensation program includes salary minimums for four levels of instructor, six of assistant professor, eight of associate professor, and eleven of professor, with differing nongrievable departmental and school factors for computing each individ-

ual's salary. For example, 1.000 is the factor for the library and 1.180 for the School of Economics and Management. In most cases (Appendix B of the contract): "Excepting assistant instructors, each full-time faculty member's regular salary shall be the product of the university salary minimum for his level multiplied by his assigned department-school factor, multiplied by his merit factor." The exception is that any member receiving the maximum merit factor available to him (ranging from 1.000 to specified figures at each level—1.030 at the lowest level and 1.226 at the highest) will receive base compensation equal to his 1970-1971 salary multiplied by 1.037 times the standard base compensation increment factor of 1.0419 if the amount yielded is greater than that afforded by his field. For example, the amount yielded will not be greater than that afforded in chemistry, which has a factor of 1.037, but it will be higher in mathematics with a factor of 1.111.

(7) Other compensation items: hospitalization, major medical, group travel, professional liability, long-term disability and life insurance programs, retirement, and faculty travel. Elaborate provisions are made for leaves with pay for both sabbaticals and research purposes, and for unpaid leaves.

(8) Further, strikes, work stoppages or interruptions, and lockouts are prohibited. A four-step grievance procedure is spelled out, with strict time limits (except by mutual consent), which ends in arbitration by the American Arbitration Association. Management rights and past practices by faculty and administration are retained. A nondiscrimination clause is inserted. Procedure regarding meetings, exchange of information, offices, keys, parking, assignment of assistants, physical examinations, and amendments are all indicated, as are means for offering terms and conditions of employment above the scale provided in the agreement. Dismissal procedures are given in great detail. Special letters of agreement are appended which deal with supplies and support services, research funds, the university calendar, duration of salary structure, student-faculty ratio, and librarians' work schedule.

APPENDIX K

Bargainable Issues

J. David Kerr and Kenneth M. Smythe

In Michigan, there is a vast range of bargainable issues supported by some authority, although not necessarily final authority. The issues listed below were ruled to be bargainable by the Michigan Employment Relations Commission (MERC) in the *North Dearborn Heights School District*[1] case. There may be a question as to whether the discussion of any of these issues interferes with the constitutional power of university boards of trustees to govern the university, but this has not been tested in the courts.

1. Right of the union to appear on the board agenda
2. Right of teachers to appeal discharges or demotion
3. Right of teachers to evaluate curriculum
4. Right of teachers to evaluate class schedules
5. Size of classes
6. Selection of supplies
7. Selection of textbooks
8. Planning of facilities
9. Special education
10. Establishment of in-service training for teachers
11. Procedures for the rating of effectiveness of teachers
12. Establishment of self-sustaining summer school programs
13. Compensated release time
14. Right of union to have a regular staff member of the collective bargaining agent visit to investigate teacher conditions or teacher problems

---

1. 1966 MERC Lab. Op. 434.

The following six Michigan decisions on the issues named are similar to some in other states.

15. Vacations—*Reese Public School District and Reese Teacher's Education Association,* 1967 MERC Lab. Op. 489.
16. Holidays—*Reese Public School District and Reese Teacher's Education Association,* 1967 MERC Lab. Op. 489.
17. University calendar—*Reese Public School District and Reese Teacher's Education Association,* 1967 MERC Lab. 489, and *W.K. Kellogg Community College and Kellogg Community Chapter, Michigan Association for Higher Education,* 1968 MERC Lab. Op. 407.
18. The weight to be given clinical or laboratory hours in relation to teaching hours in connection with evaluating the teaching load of particular instructors—*W.K. Kellogg Community College and Kellogg Community Chapter, Michigan Association for Higher Education,* 1968 MERC Lab. Op. 407.
19. Standards for employee promotions—*City of Detroit Board of Fire Commissioners,* 1968 MERC Lab. Op. 492.
20. Wage increases—*Mount Morency Road Commission,* 1967 MERC Lab. Op. 176.

Decisions under the National Labor Relations Act (NLRA) will guide future Michigan decisions because MERC tends to follow the NLRA industrial pattern. In 1967, Robert Howlett, MERC chairman, underscored this point in a speech before the Association of Labor Mediation Agencies: "Michigan's Public Employment Relations Act applies the industrial procedures of representation, unfair labor practices and collective bargaining to the public sector."[2]

The following thirteen cases, taken from the federal experience under the NLRA represent areas in which employers were prevented from making unilateral decisions without consulting the collective bargaining agent. Therefore, these are also bargainable areas:

21. Discharge of employees—*National Licorice Co.,* 7 NLRB 537 (1938).
22. Seniority policy—*Inland Steel v. NLRB,* 170 F.2d 247 (7th Cir. 1948).

---

2. *Labor Relations Yearbook 1967,* Bureau of National Affairs, Inc.

23. Working schedules—*NLRB v. Hallam and Boggs Truck and Implement Co.*, 198 F.2d 751 (10th Cir. 1952).
24. Vacations—*Phelps Dodge Corp.*, 98 NLRB 726 (1952), supplemented by 30 LRRM 1030 and 30 LRRM 1125 (1952).
25. Individual merit increases—*NLRB v. J. H. Allison & Co.*, 165 F.2d 766 (6th Cir. 1948), *cert. denied*, 335 U.S. 814 (1948), *reh. denied*, 335 U.S. 905 (1949).
26. Pensions—*Inland Steel v. NLRB*, 170 F.2d 247 (7th Cir. 1948).
27. Insurance—*Cross & Coe, Inc. v. NLRB*, 174 F.2d 875 (1st Cir. 1949).
28. Christmas bonuses—*Niles-Bement-Pond Co.*, 97 NLRB 30 (1951).
29. Subcontracting—*Town & Country Mfg. Co.*, 136 NLRB 111 (1962).
30. Adoption of technological improvements—*Renton News Record*, 136 NLRB 55 (1962). Note the new type teaching machines which have an impact with respect to technological improvements.
31. In *Westinghouse Electric Corp.*, 156 NLRB 96 (1966), the duty to bargain was held to require the employer to advise the union of a proposed five-cent change in food prices and a one-cent increase for coffee in the employer's cafeterias and to bargain with the union concerning the same.
32. Fringe benefits have been held to be bargainable by a Michigan circuit judge—*Rayburn v. Mt. Morris Board of Education*, 71 LRRM 2177, opinion by Judge Elliott.
33. Agency shop is a question presently before the Michigan Supreme Court in an appeal of the case of *Smigel v. Southgate Community School District*, 24 Mich. App. 179 (1970), *leave to appeal granted*, Oct. 26, 1970. Briefs have been submitted in this matter and it awaits oral argument.

APPENDIX L

Bylaws:
Legislative Conference of the
City University of New York

Article I   Name, Purposes, Relationship to Collective Negotiating Agreement, Eligibility for Membership

Section 1. This organization shall be known as "The Legislative Conference of the City University of New York" (hereinafter referred to as "the Conference").

Section 2.   The purposes of the Conference shall be:

    a) To act as collective negotiating agent for employees of the City University of New York and other educational institutions of higher learning.

    b) To represent employees of CUNY for whom it is the collective negotiating agent, its members, and the Conference in:

        (1) the processing of grievances, arbitrations, and all other matters related to the implementation of collective bargaining agreements with the Board of Higher Education of the City of New York and other educational institutions of higher learning;

        (2) their interest in proceedings before appropriate governmental agencies.

    c) To serve as public spokesman for those it represents.

    d) To assist in all other ways in the protection and advancement of its membership and the principles of higher education everywhere.

    e) To maintain and protect the academic freedom of its members and to advance their professional interests.

319

Article II Membership, Dues, and Assessments

Section 1. Membership shall be open to employees of the City University of New York and other educational institutions of higher learning.

Section 2. The specific dues to be paid by members shall be determined by a two-thirds (2/3) majority of the members of the Governing Board voting at a special meeting convened for the purpose of voting thereon after fourteen (14) days advance notice thereof to the members of the Governing Board.

Section 3. Dues for each year shall be payable by checkoff or in advance of an annual or semi-annual basis.

Section 4. Any member who is six (6) months in arrears in the payment of dues, shall be automatically suspended from membership.

Section 5. No assessment shall be levied except by vote of the membership at a general meeting or by mail referendum, and in either case, after twenty (20) days' notice to the membership that voting will take place on such proposed assessment. Non-payment for thirty (30) days of any assessment levied shall carry automatic loss of good standing.

Article III Organization

Section 1. The organizational structure of the Conference shall be
    a) A Governing Board
    b) An Executive Committee
    c) Elected Officers
    d) Standing Committees and their Chairmen
    e) Appointed Committees and their Chairmen
    f) Campus Units
    g) Cross Campus Units

Article IV The Governing Board

Section 1. The Governing Board shall consist of delegates elected by the Campus and Cross Campus Units as hereafter prescribed.

Section 2. The Governing Board shall have the following powers and duties:

a) To formulate and supervise the execution of the policies of the Conference.

b) To issue specific directives to appropriate executive and administrative bodies and personnel of the Conference to implement policies adopted.

c) To adopt an annual budget.

d) To approve and establish new cross campus units.

e) To engage counsel and other specialized professional assistance.

f) To establish dues and levy assessments, pursuant to Article II.

g) To do all things necessary and proper to further the purposes and well being of the Conference and its members.

Section 3. Each Campus and Cross Campus Unit shall be entitled to one delegate to the Governing Board, plus one (1) additional delegate for each one hundred (100) Conference members of the unit or major fraction thereof.

Section 4. The Delegates to the Governing Board shall be elected in May of 1970. One-third of the delegates elected shall serve for a term of one year, one-third for a term of two years, and the 3rd third for a term of three years. The determination of the respective thirds shall be by lot except that in establishing such terms of office, all the delegates of any unit shall serve for the same term. All terms of office shall commence at the end of the first meeting of the Governing Board following the election. After 1970 all delegates shall be elected for a term of three years.

Section 5. Delegates shall be elected in their respective units during the month of May, 1970 and every appropriate May thereafter, on a specific date or dates to be established by the Governing Board. Delegates shall be elected from nominees by mail ballot which shall be mailed to the members of the unit at least seven (7) days before the return date on which such ballots are due.

Section 6. Nomination for Delegate to the Governing Board shall be by nominating petition. To qualify as a candidate, nominating petitions must be signed by twenty-five (25) members or ten percent (10%) of the unit's Conference membership, whichever is less, and endorsed by the candidate indicating his willingness to run and serve if elected.

Section 7. The electorate shall vote for one more candidate than the number of delegates to which the unit is entitled.

Section 8. Those delegates, to the number of delegates to which the unit is entitled, who receive the highest number of votes shall be declared elected. The delegate receiving the next highest number of votes shall be declared to be an alternate delgate.

Section 9. The alternate delegate may serve as delegate at any meeting of the Governing Board where a regular delegate of his unit is absent.

In case of the death, disqualification, or resignation of a delegate, the alternate shall take his place. A special election shall be held to replace an alternate or other absence among delegates for any unexpired term of more than one (1) year.

Article V   The Executive Committee

Section 1. The Executive Committee shall consist of the Chairman, First Vice-Chairman, Secretary, Treasurer, Vice-Chairman for Senior Colleges, Vice-Chairman for Community Colleges, Vice-Chairman for Cross Campus Units, and three (3) members at large elected from the Governing Board.

Section 2. The Executive Committee shall have the following powers and duties:

a) To implement and execute the policies established by the Governing Board.
b) To authorize the expenditure of funds of the Conference in accordance with the budget adopted by the the Governing Board.
c) To hire and supervise members of the Staff and agents hired for special purposes and set the compensation therefor.
d) To establish and supervise an official publication of the Conference.
e) To review, supervise, and be responsible for the work of the several committees in accordance with

the various responsibilities with which such committees are charged.

f) To prepare the Annual Budget for submission to the
Governing Board.

g) To act in the name of the Conference in any emergency between meetings of the Governing Board.

h) To appoint a Legislative Representative or Representatives to represent the Conference before legislative bodies.

Article VI Officers

Section 1. The following officers shall be elected by the members
of the Governing Board from among the members of the Governing Board:

> Chairman
> First Vice-Chairman
> Secretary
> Treasurer

Section 2. The term of office of the officers specified in Section 1
shall be one year. In case of a vacancy in any of these offices,
the unexpired term shall be filled by appointment by the Executive Committee.

Section 3. The election and installation of the offices of Chairman,
First Vice-Chairman, Secretary, and Treasurer shall be held at
the first regular meeting of the Governing Board, held each year
following the election of the Governing Board.

Section 4. In addition to the officers specified in Section 1 hereof:

a) The delegates elected by the Senior Colleges shall
elect from among themselves a Vice-Chairman for
Senior Colleges.

b) The delegates elected by the Community Colleges
shall elect from among themselves a Vice-Chairman
for Community Colleges.

c) The delegates elected by the Cross Campus Units
shall elect from among themselves a Vice-Chairman
for Cross Campus Units.

d) Elections for these Vice-Chairmen and installations

shall take place at the first regular meeting of the Governing Board held each year following the election of the Governing Board. The term of office shall be one year. In case of a vacancy in any of these offices, a replacement for the unexpired term shall be made from among the qualified delegates by appointment by the Executive Committee.

Section 5. Powers and Duties

a) Chairman. The Chairman shall be the Chief Executive Officer of the Conference. He shall preside at meetings of the Governing Board and the Executive Committee. He shall, with the advice and consent of the Executive Committee, make all appointments to all committees other than standing committees. He shall be the official spokesman for the Conference. He shall have all powers and duties usually attendant upon the position of a chief executive officer.

b) First Vice-Chairman. The powers and duties of the First Vice-Chairman shall be: To assist the Chairman in the performance of his duties; to substitute for the Chairman in his absence; direct organizational efforts and activities; supervise the official publication of the Conference.

c) The duties and powers of Vice Chairman for 1) Senior Colleges, 2) Community Colleges, and 3) Cross Campus Units shall be: To coordinate the activities of the Conference in their respective areas; to arrange for, conduct, and chair meetings with the Campus Chairmen within their respective areas for exchange of knowledge and information of particular interest or importance to such areas; to develop programs of interest to the members of such areas and recommend the same to the Governing Board.

d) Secretary. The Secretary shall keep minutes of meetings of the Governing Board and the Executive Committee. He shall send out notices of meetings and conduct the correspondence of the Conference.

e) Treasurer. The Treasurer shall have custody of the funds of the Conference; he shall pay bills as authorized by the Executive Committee; he shall keep an accurate account of all receipts and expenditures and all financial transactions. His accounts shall be audited annually by a CPA. He shall render a financial statement annually and at such other times as directed by the Governing Board. He shall be bonded at the expense of the Conference in an amount to be set by the Executive Committee. He shall be an ex officio member of the Finance Committee.

Article VII Units

Section 1. The following shall constitute the Campus Units:
Each College of the City University of New York, and Hunter High School and Elementary School as one unit, and additional units as may be determined by the Governing Board.

Section 2. The following shall constitute a Cross Campus Unit:
Any special interest group with membership in two or more Campuses, as may be determined by the Governing Board.

Section 3. a) Conference members in Cross Campus Units shall vote in such units only for the election of delegates to the Governing Board and shall not be counted in any Campus Unit in the determination of the number of delegates to the Governing Board to which the Campus Unit is entitled.

b) Any dispute concerning the placement of any member or group of members in either a Campus or Cross Campus Unit shall be resolved by the Executive Committee.

Section 4. The Governing Board may create new Campus or Cross Campus Units or, in the interest of promoting greater effectiveness, merge existing Units.

Section 5. Each Unit, whether Campus or Cross Campus, shall elect from among its members a Unit Chairman, a Unit Vice-Chairman, and a Chairman of the Unit Grievance Committee. The Unit Chairman or Unit Vice-Chairman may also serve as Chairman of the Grievance Committee and may, but need not be, a delegate to the Governing Board. The term of office shall be one

(1) year. Vacancies for the balance of any term shall be filled by appointment by the Executive Committee.

Section 6. Election for Unit Chairman, Unit Vice-Chairman, and Chairman of the Unit Grievance Committee shall take place at the first meeting of the Unit in each academic year. Such meeting shall be held in the month of September or October.

Section 7. It shall be the function of the Unit Chairman to coordinate the affairs of the Unit, represent the Unit as its spokesman, and promote the interest of the Conference within the Unit.

Article VIII Committees

Section 1. The Standing Committees shall be:
   a) The Executive Committee
   b) Legislative Committee
   c) University Grievance Committee
   d) Finance & Budget Committee
   e) Committee on Pensions and Fringe Benefits
   f) Membership Committee
   g) Committee on Liaison With Other Organizations
   h) Elections Committee
   i) Public Relations Committee
   j) Committee on Schools of General Studies
   k) Committee on Educational Planning and Policy

Section 2. The Chairman of the Conference shall, with the advice and consent of the Executive Committee, appoint the Chairman and members of the Legislative Committee, the Finance & Budget Committee, the Committee on Pensions & Fringe Benefits, the Membership Committee, the Committee on Liaison With Other Organizations, the Elections Committee, the Public Relations Committee, the Committee on Schools of General Studies, and the Committee on Educational Planning and Policy.

Section 3. University Grievance Committee
   a) The University Grievance Committee shall consist of a Chairman appointed by the Chairman of the Conference with the approval of the Executive Committee, and the Unit Grievance Chairmen of the several Units.
   b) It shall have jurisdiction over and be responsible for all collective bargaining grievances which reach the

University level. It shall act as a resource, on request, to the Unit Grievance Committees.

Section 4. Membership Committee

The Membership Committee shall be charged with the responsibility of conducting membership enrollment efforts.

Section 5. Negotiating Committee

a) The Negotiating Committee shall consist of one member elected by the Governing Board from each Unit together with the Chairman of the Conference and the Chairman of the University Grievance Committee who shall be members of this committee ex officio.

b) The Committee shall elect its Chairman and Vice-Chairman from among its members.

c) The Committee shall have the power to add additional personnel to its membership and may form sub-committees to facilitate its work, provided however, that in any discussion or negotiation involving issues peculiar to any particular Unit, a representative of such Unit shall have been consulted.

d) The election of the members of the Negotiating Committee shall take place at a time selected by the Executive Committee, approximately six (6) months before negotiations for each new agreement.

e) Following the conclusion of each negotiation, the Negotiating Committee shall submit to the membership the text of the proposed agreement, together with its recommendation. Such submission shall be presented to the membership not less than seven (7) days prior to a general meeting of the membership. The membership shall vote whether to accept or reject the proposed agreement. No agreement shall be signed or agreed to without the prior consent of the membership.

Section 6. Elections Committee

The Elections Committee shall have the authority to make arrangements for and conduct all elections except those conducted within a particular Unit.

Section 7. Public Relations Committee

The Public Relations Committee shall be responsible for publicity on behalf of the Conference, including publications of the Conference, and for liaison with the news media.

Section 8. Unit Grievance Committee

Each Unit shall be responsible for handling the grievances and complaints of its members at preliminary steps. This shall be done under the leadership of the elected Chairman of the Unit Grievance Committee for his Unit.

Section 9. The Chairman and/or the Executive Committee may establish ad hoc committees for specific purposes and appoint the members thereof.

Article IX Meetings

Section 1. At least one (1) General Membership meeting shall be held each academic year at a date to be established by the Executive Committee.

Section 2. The Chairman shall report at such meetings on the state of the Conference and a financial statement shall be rendered to the membership.

Section 3. Special meetings of the General Membership shall be held by direction of a majority of the Governing Board or upon petition of twenty percent (20%) of the membership.

Section 4. a) The Governing Board shall meet regularly on the last Thursday of each month during the academic year.

b) Special meetings of the Governing Board shall be held on request of the Executive Committee or on petition of twenty percent (20%) of the Governing Board.

Section 5. a) The Executive Committee shall meet at least once each month during the academic year.

b) The time and place for such meetings shall be established by the Chairman.

c) Special meetings shall be held on request of the Chairman or any three (3) members of the Executive Committee.

Section 6. No matter shall be brought before any specially convoked meeting of the membership, or the Governing Board, unless notice thereof shall have been given to the members entitled to vote at such special meeting at least five (5) days in advance of the date of such meeting.

Section 7. All meetings shall be conducted pursuant to Roberts Rules of Order, except where these Bylaws may be inconsistent, in which case these Bylaws shall prevail.

Section 8. a) The Chairman of each Campus and Cross Campus Unit shall convoke at least one (1) meeting of his Unit each semester at a time and place selected by him.

b) Special meetings of such Units shall be held on petition of ten percent (10%) of the membership of the Unit.

c) Each unit shall constitute a separate chapter which shall be headed by the Chairman of the Unit. It shall establish its own operating structure to represent its members' interest, which shall not be inconsistent with these Bylaws.

Article X Discipline

Any member who shall violate the provisions of these Bylaws or who shall be found guilty of conduct designed to cause irreparable harm to the Conference or its membership, shall be subject to expulsion from the Conference, provided that the accepted canons of academic freedom and academic due process be observed.

Article XI Miscellaneous

Section 1. These Bylaws shall be presented to the Governing Board of the Legislative Conference as presently constituted, and if approved by them or if approved as modified, shall then be presented to the membership for approval.

Section 2. Amendments. Amendments to these Bylaws may be proposed in writing by any ten (10) members of the Governing Board or any one hundred (100) members of the Conference. Amendments must be approved by a two-thirds (2/3) majority of the Governing Board. The membership shall be notified of each proposed amendment at least ten (10) days prior to any meeting at which the amendment is to be voted on.

Bibliography

This bibliography covers most of the published literature on collective bargaining in higher education that has appeared since 1965, including a selection of books and articles that provide background information. It also presents a modest selection of published literature on college and university governance. Recent unpublished papers, dissertations, and reports (e.g., from Harvard, Minnesota, Michigan State University, and scores of other institutions where such matters have recently been under study) are not included.

Very few studies on junior colleges done before 1965 are relevant to the current situation. Within the major literature, faculty were seldom thought to have much right to exercise power at that level of higher education. Almost all the empirical studies on governance and bargaining in junior colleges have been done within the past four years and are as yet unpublished.[1]

As of January, 1972, over 150 college and university faculties had elected bargaining agents (see Appendix I for a separate list of these). Several dozen contracts had been negotiated. The three principal bargaining agents have sample contracts for distribution. NEA distributes contracts from CUNY and other four-year institutions (or for CUNY's one can write City University of New York, 535 East 80th St., New York, New York 10021). NEA also has a prototype master agreement for use by two-year colleges and copies of contracts made thus far, through its National Faculty Association of Community and Junior Colleges (1201 16th St., N.W., Washington, D.C. 20036). AFT also has sample contracts for all levels, available through its College and University Division (1012 14th St., N.W., Washington, D.C. 20005). AAUP will send copies of

---

1. See J.E. Roueche and J.R. Boggs, *Junior College Institutional Research: The State of the Art* (Washington: American Association of Junior Colleges, 1968), viii, 66 p.

contracts negotiated at St. John's University, Oakland University (published in January, 1972), and elsewhere (AAUP, One Dupont Circle, N.W., Washington, D.C. 20036).

This bibliography has been classified to aid the user in locating articles covering various aspects of faculty collective bargaining. The basic classification is by subject, and then alphabetically by author. To aid in following the development of issues, the works listed in section I, Collective Bargaining on Campuses, are grouped chronologically before being grouped alphabetically by author. The basic scheme of the bibliography is as follows:

I. *Collective Bargaining on Campuses*
   A. *Books*
   B. *Articles*
      1. *Related Labor Law and Practice*
      2. *Collective Bargaining in Higher Education*
      3. *Faculty and Professional Bargaining*

II. *College and University Governance*
   A. *Books*
   B. *Articles*

I. COLLECTIVE BARGAINING ON CAMPUSES

A. Books

1965 Fleming, Robben W. *The Labor Arbitration Process.* Champaign: University of Illinois Press, 1965. 233 p.

Marceau, Le Roy. *Drafting a Union Contract.* Boston: Little, Brown, 1965. 321 p.

Detailed advice on every aspect of drafting, with special attention to step by step procedures and to meanings of terms.

1966 Lieberman, Myron, and Michael Moskow. *Collective Negotiations for Teachers.* Chicago: Rand McNally, 1966. 768 p.

1967 Hanslowe, Kurt L. *The Emerging Law of Labor Relations in Public Employment.* Ithaca: New York School of Industrial and Labor Relations, Cornell University, 1967. vi, 117 p.

A general survey, already made somewhat out-of-date for New York State by passage of the Taylor Law.

Warner, Kenneth O., ed. *Collective Bargaining in the Public Service: Theory and Practice.* Chicago: Public Personnel Association, 1967. viii, 200 p.

Warner, Kenneth O., and Mary L. Hennessy. *Public Management at the Bargaining Table*. Chicago: Public Personnel Association, 1967. 490 p.
Includes an example, a how-to-do-it outline, discussion of the future of collective bargaining, and bibliography.

1968 Anderson, Howard J., ed. *Public Employee Organization and Bargaining: A Report on the Joint Conference of the Association of Labor Mediation Agencies and the National Association of State Labor Relations Agencies, August 19 to August 24, 1968*. Washington: Bureau of National Affairs, 1968. ii, 117 p.

Rubin, Richard S. *A Summary of State Collective Bargaining Law in Public Employment*. Public Employee Relations Reports, no. 3. Ithaca: New York State School of Industrial and Labor Relations, Cornell University, 1968.

Smith, Russell A., Leroy S. Merrifield, and Theodore J. St. Antoine. *Labor Relations Law: Cases and Materials*. 4th ed. Indianapolis: Bobbs-Merrill, 1968. xlvii, 1196 p.

1969 Elam, Stanley, and Michael H. Moskow, eds. *Employment Relations in Higher Education*. Bloomington, Indiana: Phi Delta Kappa, 1969. 215 p.
Proceedings of a symposium at Temple University Nov. 1968; not comprehensive; contrasting views of faculty representation by Myron Lieberman and Walter Oberer.

Marx, Herbert L., Jr., ed. *Collective Bargaining for Public Employees*. New York: Wilson, 1969. 215 p.
Background, plus discussions of particular types of union (e.g., AFGE, AFSCME, policemen, and firefighters) and teacher negotiations; sections on strikes, the federal and state laws, public unionism abroad, and "what's ahead."

Nigro, Felix A. *Management-Employee Relations in the Public Service*. Chicago: Public Personnel Association, 1969. 433 p.

1970 Bureau of National Affairs. *Collective Bargaining Today, Proceedings of the Collective Bargaining Forum—1969*. Washington: Bureau of National Affairs, 1970. xvii, 503 p.
A basic collection of papers on numerous current topics in the field; no material on colleges and universities.

Haehn, James O. *A Survey of Faculty and Administrator Attitudes on Collective Bargaining, A Report to the Aca-*

demic Senate, California State Colleges. Chico, Calif.: Chico State College, 1970.

Smith, Russell A., Leroy S. Merrifield, and Donald P. Rothschild. *Collective Bargaining and Labor Arbitration: Materials on the Negotiation, Enforcement and Content of the Labor Agreements.* Indianapolis: Bobbs-Merrill, 1970. xxiv, 919 p.
A volume containing materials reflecting the expanding boundaries of collective bargaining is to follow.

Wollett, Donald H., and Robert H. Chanin. *The Law and Practice of Teacher Negotiations.* Washington: Bureau of National Affairs, 1970. 1567 p. (looseleaf).

B. Articles

1. Related Labor Law and Practice

1967   Clary, Jack R. "Pitfalls of Collective Bargaining in Public Employment." *Labor Law Journal* 18, no. 7 (July 1967), 406-411.
An early article, written after the Feb. 15, 1967, report of Michigan Governor Romney's blue-ribbon Advisory Committee on Public Employee Relations.

March, William E. "The Rights of a Public Employee in Nebraska." *Nebraska Law Review* 46, no. 4 (July 1967), 884-901.

1968   Aksen, Gerald, et al. "Public Employees and Collective Bargaining." Symposium in *Conference on Labor, New York University, Proceedings, 21st* (1968), 447-575.
Includes discussions on comparison of state and local experience, unit determination, arbitration, factfinding, and how to prevent strikes.

Morris, Charles J. "Public Policy and the Law Relating to Collective Bargaining in the Public Service." *Southwestern Law Journal* 22, no. 4 (October 1968), 585-609.
A careful statement on principles in the context of recent developments; includes a statutory proposal.

Schoenthal, Val L. "Collective Bargaining in the Public Sector: A Survey of Major Options." *Drake Law Review* 18, no. 1 (December 1968), 26-46.
A general essay, with brief appendix on major sources of information.

Spindel, Frederic T. "Union Authorization Cards: A Reliable Basis for an NLRB Order to Bargain?" *Texas Law Review* 47, no. 1 (December 1968), 87-107.

1969   Anderson, Arvid. "Public Employee Bargaining." *Urban Lawyer* 1, no. 3 (Fall 1969), 312-319.
Essay on several critical questions by the chairman, Office of Collective Bargaining, New York City.

Comment, "Collective Bargaining for Public Employees and the Prevention of Strikes in the Public Sector." *Michigan Law Review* 68, no. 2 (December 1969), 260-302.
Special reference to Michigan.

Crowley, Joseph R. "The Resolution of Representation Status Disputes under the Taylor Law." *Fordham Law Review* 37, no. 4 (May 1969), 517-534.
Discussion by a member of the New York State Public Employment Relations Board.

Dole, Richard F., Jr. "State and Local Public Employee Collective Bargaining in the Absence of Explicit Legislative Authorization." *Iowa Law Review* 54, no. 4 (February 1969), 539-559.
A thoroughgoing study of the problems, amply footnoted—with special reference to Iowa, which lacks a comprehensive collective bargaining statute.

Hartley, Roger. "Pennsylvania's Proposed Public Employees Relations Act: A Landmark of Sound Progress or an Invitation to a Quagmire?" *University of Pittsburgh Law Review* 30, no. 4 (Summer 1969), 693-714.

Oberer, Walter E. "The Future of Collective Bargaining in Public Employment." *Labor Law Journal* 20, no. 12 (December 1969), 777-786.
Address to NEA's Fourth Annual National Seminar on Professional Negotiations in Public Employment by Cornell professor of law and industrial and labor relations.

Smith, Russell A. "State and Local Advisory Reports on Public Employment Labor Legislation: A Comparative Analysis." *Michigan Law Review* 67, no. 5 (March 1969), 891-918.
Part of a symposium on "Labor Relations in the Public Sector," 891-1082; the article by Ralph S. Brown, cited in section 3 (Faculty and Professional Bargaining) below, is also especially relevant to higher education; the other articles are: Charles M. Reh-

mus, "Constraints on Local Governments in Public Employment Bargaining," 919-930; Theodore H. Kheel, "Strikes and Public Employment," 931-942; Arvid Anderson, "Strikes and Impasse Resolution in Public Employment," 943-970; H.W. Arthurs, "Collective Bargaining in the Public Service of Canada: Bold Experiment or Act of Folly?", 971-1000; Eli Hook, "The Appropriate Unit Question in the Public Service: The Problem of Proliferation," 1001-1016; Donald H. Wollett, "The Coming Revolution in Public School Management," 1017-1032; Ida Klaus, "The Evolution of a Collective Bargaining Relationship in Public Education: New York City's Changing Seven-Year History," 1033-1066; Ralph S. Brown, Jr., "Collective Bargaining in Higher Education," 1067-1082.

Wellington, Harry H., and Ralph K. Winter. "The Limits of Collective Bargaining in Public Employment." *Yale Law Journal* 78, no. 7 (June 1969), 1107-1127.

Werne, Benjamin. "Collective Bargaining in the Public Sector." *Vanderbilt Law Review* 22, no. 4 (May 1969), 833-874.

Includes sections on details of the bargaining process and administration of the agreement; the principal reference is to cities by Mr. Werne, who is Management Labor Counsel to the National League of Cities and National Association of County Organizations.

Zwerdling, A.L. "Collective Bargaining in Public Employment." *Michigan State Bar Journal* 48, no. 5 (May 1969), 18-23.

Arguments in favor, with special reference to the situation in Michigan; discussion of recent federal cases.

1970 Corbett, William L. "The Right of Wyoming State and Municipal Employees to Organize, Receive Exclusive Recognition, and Bargain Collectively." *Land and Water Law Review* 5 (1970), 605-619.

"Current Perspectives in Labor Law: A Symposium." In *Georgia Law Review* 4, no. 4 (Summer 1970), 643-829.

Especially Elihu Platt, "The Supreme Court Looks at Bargaining Orders Based on Authorization Cards," 779-801.

Evers, I.C. "First Year of Public Collective Bargaining in New Jersey." *Urban Lawyer* 2, no. 4 (Winter 1970), 78 ff.

McEvilly, James Patrick, Jr. "Retirees' Status as 'Employees' under the National Labor Relations Act for the Purpose of Collective Bargaining." *Temple Law Quarterly* 43, no. 4 (Summer 1970), 373-380.

On the Pittsburgh Plate Glass case, 1969.

Marshall, Schuyler B. "Public Employee Bargaining Rights —A Proposal for Texas." *Texas Law Review* 48, no. 3 (February 1970), 625-645.
Includes a suggested bill.

Monk, Richard C. "Exclusive Representation and the Right of Employees to Engage in Concerted Activity—Conflicting Policies of the NLRA." *University of San Francisco Law Review* 4, no. 2 (April 1970), 354-372.
History, cases, analyses, policy considerations, and proposals.

Rains, Harry H. "Dispute Settlement in the Public Sector." *Buffalo Law Review* 19, no. 2 (Winter 1970), 279-287.

Shinn, John C., et al. "Collective Bargaining in the Public Sector." Symposium in *Conference on Labor, New York University, Proceedings, 23rd* (1970), 359-426.
Includes discussion of Executive Order No. 11491, bargaining units, grievance arbitration, and ability to pay.

Steinbach, Sheldon E. "Public Employee Unionization—A Constitutionally Protected Right?" *South Dakota Law Review* 15, no. 2 (Spring 1970), 258-272.
Especially discusses recent federal developments.

Sullivan, William B. "New Developments in Union Authorization Cards and the NLRB Order to Bargain." *Suffolk University Law Review* 5, no. 1 (Fall 1970), 99-138.

Waks, Jay W. "Impact of the Agency Shop on Labor Relations in the Public Sector." *Cornell Law Review* 55, no. 4 (April 1970), 547-593.
Thorough coverage; comparison of the various state laws; offers a Model Agency Shop Statute, with extensive comment.

Waks, Jay W. "Privilege of Exclusive Recognition and Minority Union Rights in Public Employment." *Cornell Law Review* 55, no. 6 (July 1970), 1004-1032.
Cites the relevant state laws.

Wellington, Harry H., and Ralph K. Winter. "Structuring Collective Bargaining in Public Employment." *Yale Law Journal* 79 (April 1970), 805-870.
"Structuring" means "limiting."

Zach, Arnold M. "Ability to Pay in Public Sector Bargaining." In *Conference on Labor, New York University, Proceedings, 23rd* (1970), 403-426.

1971   Abodeely, John E. "The Effect of Reorganization, Merger or Acquisition on the Appropriate Bargaining Unit." *George Washington Law Review* 39, no. 3 (March 1971), 488-531.

Anderson, Arvid. "Public Employee Collective Bargaining: The Changing of the Establishment." *Wake Forest Law Review* 7, no. 2 (March 1971), 175-188.

Gumbinger, Frank E. "Collective Bargaining—Is It Working?" *Loyola University Law Review* 4, no. 2 (April 1971), 361-381.
Includes a thumbnail legislative history, examination of some current problems notable between government and the unions, and proposed approaches toward solution.

Kelly, J.P. "Labor Law—NLRB's Remedial Powers." *Duquesne Law Review* 9, no. 3 (Spring 1971), 514-521.

Note, "Title VII, the NLRB, and Arbitration: Conflicts in National Labor Policy." *Georgia Law Review* 5, no. 2 (Winter 1971), 313-348.

Seidman, Joel. "State Legislation on Collective Bargaining by Public Employees." *Labor Law Journal* 22, no. 1 (January 1971), 13-22.

2. Collective Bargaining in Higher Education

1966   Blackwell, Thomas E. "How NLRB Views College Unionism." *College and University Business* 40, no. 5 (May 1966), p. 78.
By the author of *College Law: A Guide for Administrators and College and University Administration,* 1966.

1967   "The Impact of Labor Legislation on Colleges and Universities." *College Counsel* 2, no. 3 (1967).
Articles: (1) Earl F. Halvorson, "The Application of the Fair Labor Standards Act to Colleges and Universities," 146-158; (2) William P. Lemmer, "Federal Labor Legislation and Jurisdiction," 159-184; (3) Louis J. Sparvero, "State Labor Legislation and Jurisdiction," 185-194.

1968   Belcher, A. Lee. "Labor-Management Relations in Higher Education." *NACUBO Professional File* (March 1970).
The original of this slightly revised speech was published in *Proceedings of the Central Association of College and University Business Officers,* 1968, 127-137.

Ferguson, Tracy H. "Collective Bargaining in Universities and Colleges." *Labor Law Journal* 19, no. 12 (December 1968), 778-804.
Also published in *College Counsel* 3, no. 2 (1968), 95-152, and in *Journal of the College and University Personnel Association* (November 1968); comprehensive comparison of federal and state laws.

Lemmer, William P. "The Impact of the NLRB on Colleges and Universities—Jurisdiction and Other Aspects." *Journal of the College and University Personnel Association* 19, no. 2 (February 1968), 9-22.
The author is The University of Michigan attorney.

1969 Bilyea, C.G. "Unions on the Campus." *Journal of the College and University Personnel Association* 20, no. 3 (May 1969), 7-22.

Koslowe, Neil H., James H. Breay, and Howard A. Kenley. "A Model Public Employees Collective Bargaining Act." *Harvard Journal on Legislation* 6, no. 4 (May 1969), 548-562.
With comment.

1970 Begin, James P. "Employee Organization among Members of the College and University Personnel Association." *Journal of the College and University Personnel Association* 22, no. 1 (December 1970), 12-26.
The author is an assistant research professor, Institute of Management and Labor Relations, Rutgers University.

Belcher, A. Lee. "The NLRB Ruling: How It Affects Campus Administration." *College and University Business* 49, no. 2 (August 1970), 42-45.

Bucklew, Neil S. "Employment Relations of Staff Employees in Institutions of Higher Learning." *Journal of the College and University Personnel Association* 22, no. 1 (December 1970), 74-107.
The author is Vice Provost, Central Michigan University.

Gianopulos, John. "Collective Bargaining: What Part Should College Presidents Play?" *College and University Business* 49, no. 3 (September 1970), 71-72, 102.

Ten Boer, Martin H. "A Study of the Extent and Impact of Organized Labor in Colleges and Universities." *Jour-*

nal of the College and University Personnel Association 22, no. 1 (December 1970), 27-73.
Largely concerns staff services employees.

1971   Begin, James P. "Collective Bargaining Agreements in Colleges and Universities: Union Security Provisions." *Journal of the College and University Personnel Association* 22, no. 2 (March 1971), 33-43.

Begin, James P., and Jack Chernick. "Collective Bargaining Agreements in Colleges and Universities: Grievance and Job Allocation Provisions." *Journal of the College and University Personnel Association* 22, no. 3 (May 1971), 52-63.

Bucklew, Neil S. "Employment Relations of Staff Employees in Institutions of Higher Learning." *Journal of the College and University Personnel Association* 22, no. 2 (March 1971), 44-78.
Case studies of Wisconsin and Michigan, continued in his article in the next section.

3. Faculty and Professional Bargaining

The following periodicals are especially useful for information about what the major bargaining agents are doing. These and other related periodicals are indexed by subject, author, and title in Education Index *(N.Y.: Wilson), issued monthly with periodical and annual cumulations.*

AAUP Bulletin. Issued four times a year by the American Association of University Professors; address: One Dupont Circle, N.W., Washington, D.C. 20005.

American Federation of Teachers. *The American Teacher.* A periodical newsletter reporting the activities of AFT at all levels; address: 1012 14th St., N.W., Washington, D.C. 20005.

American Federation of Teachers. *On Campus.* A periodical newsletter from the AFT's colleges and universities department; address: 1012 14th St., N.W., Washington, D.C. 20005.

The Chronicle of Higher Education. Published weekly through most of the year; address: 1717 Massachusetts Ave., N.W., Washington, D.C. 20036.

Junior College Journal. A quarterly; issued by the American Association of Junior Colleges; address: One Dupont Circle, N.W., Washington, D.C. 20036.

National Education Association. *Higher Education Forum.* A periodical newsletter published by the NEA for the three higher education groups formed within the NHEA after the American Association for Higher Education withdrew: National Faculty Association for Community and Junior Colleges, National Society of Professors, and National Association of College and University Administrators; the first was established in June, 1967, the latter two in April, 1969; address: 1201 16th St., N.W., Washington, D.C. 20036.

National Education Association, Research Division. *Negotiations Research Digest.* Appears ten times each year, covering all levels; address: 1201 16th St., N.W., Washington, D.C. 20036.

1966 Howe, Ray A. "Faculty-Administrative Relationships in Extremis." *Junior College Journal* 37, no. 3 (November 1966), 14-15.
Written in aftermath of the first junior college strike at Henry Ford Community College, Michigan, by its Executive Dean.

1967 Day, James F., and William H. Fisher. "The Professor and Collective Negotiations." *School and Society* 95, no. 2291 (April 1, 1967), 226-229.

Livingston, John C. "Collective Bargaining and Professionalism in Higher Education." *Educational Record* 48, no. 1 (Winter 1967), 79-88.

1968 Buchalter, Sol S., and Harold H. Haak. "The California State Colleges: Systemwide Adoption of a Grievance Procedure." *AAUP Bulletin* 54, no. 3 (Autumn 1968), 365-370.

Davis, Bertram H. "Unions and Higher Education: Another View." *Educational Record* 49, no. 2 (Spring 1968), 139-144.
See articles by Kugler and Marmion.

Frankie, Richard J., and Ray A. Howe. "Faculty P~
the Community College." *Theory Into Pr~
(April 1968), 83-88.

Kadish, Sanford. "The Strike and the Professoriate." *AAUP Bulletin* 54, no. 2 (Summer 1968), 160-168.
This article is an abridged edition of his lecture *Dimensions of Academic Freedom*, Urbana: University of Illinois Press, 1968.

Kugler, Israel. "The Union Speaks for Itself." *Educational Record* 49, no. 4 (Fall 1968), 414-418.

Kutner, Luis. "Habeas Scholastica: An Ombudsman for Academic Due Process—A Proposal." *University of Miami Law Review* 23, no. 1 (Fall 1968), 107-159.

Livingston, John C. "Faculty and Administrative Roles in Decision-Making." In *Stress and Campus Response,* edited by G. Kerry Smith, 187-195. San Francisco: Jossey-Bass, 1968.

McConnell, John W. "How to Negotiate with a Professors' Union." *Association of Governing Boards Reports* 10, no. 6 (March 1968), 3-15.

Marmion, Harry A. "Unions and Higher Education." *Educational Record* 49, no. 1 (Winter 1968), 41-48.

Rehmus, Charles M. "Collective Bargaining and the Market for Academic Personnel." *Quarterly Review of Economics and Business* (Autumn 1968), 7-13.

1969   Brown, Ralph S., Jr. "Collective Bargaining in Higher Education." *Michigan Law Review* 67, no. 5 (March 1969), 1067-1082.

Hechinger, Fred M. "Toward One Voice for Teachers," *New York Times,* October 19, 1969, Section 4, p. 11.
The author sees AFT and NEA growing toward possible mergers at the national level. Trial balloons on this subject are going up here and there across the country but with scant notice in print.

Hixon, Richard, Robert W. Miner, Bertram Davis, and G. Kerry Smith. "Four Associations Look to the Junior College." *Junior College Journal* 39, no. 4 (December-January 1968-1969), 10-17.
The four associations are AAUP, AFT, NEA, and AAHE.

Livingston, John C. "Academic Senate Under Fire." In *Agony and Promise,* edited by G. Kerry Smith, 161-172. San Francisco: Jossey-Bass, 1969.
A paper delivered at the 1969 AAUP meeting.

McHugh, William F. "Collective Negotiations in Public Higher Education." *College and University Business* 47, no. 6 (December 1969), 41-44, 61-62.

Note, "Collective Bargaining and the Professional Employee." *Columbia Law Review* 69, no. 2 (February 1969), 277-298.
Early in the debate, but gives relevant background and discussion on some basic issues.

1970   Brown, Martha A. "Collective Bargaining on the Campus: Professors, Associations and Unions." *Labor Law Journal* 21, no. 3 (March 1970), 167-181.
Compares approaches of the major bargaining agents; discusses California State Colleges case.

Brown, Ralph S., and Israel Kugler. "Collective Bargaining for the Faculty." *Liberal Education* 56, no. 1 (March 1970), 75-85.

Brown, Ronald C. "Professors and Unions: The Faculty Senate: An Effective Alternative to Collective Bargaining in Higher Education?" *William and Mary Law Review* 12, no. 2 (Winter 1970), 252-332.
Now Assistant Professor of Law at William and Mary, Mr. Brown did most of the work for this article in preparing his L.L.M. thesis at the University of Michigan. Much of his material relates to Michigan colleges and universities and to Michigan law.

Buys, Larry M. "Collective Bargaining in Michigan Community Colleges." *Journal of the College and University Personnel Association* 21, no. 3 (May 1970), 33-49.

Gianopulos, John W. "The College Administrator and Collective Negotiations." *Junior College Journal* 41, no. 1 (August-September 1970), 26-29.

Gillis, John W. "Academic Collective Bargaining: Comment and an Annotated Bibliography." *Liberal Education* 56, no. 4 (December 1970), 594-604.

Logan, Albert A., Jr. "Ph.D. Surplus Seen Benefiting Faculty Unions." *Chronicle of Higher Education* 4, no. 38 (August 31, 1970), p. 3.

McHugh, William F. "National Labor Relations Board Goes to College." *College and University Business* 49, no. 1 (July 1970), p. 44.

McHugh, William F. "Recent Developments in Collective Bargaining in Higher Education." *College Counsel* 5, no. 1 (1970), 159-208.

Polishook, Sheila Stern. "Collective Bargaining and the City University of New York." *Journal of Higher Education* 61, no. 5 (May 1970), 377-386.

Young, Edwin. "Management and Collective Bargaining on the Campus." *Association of Governing Boards Reports* 13, no. 3 (November 1970), 17-23.
Also see remarks in same issue by Walter G. Barlow, a Cornell trustee, under the same title, pp. 8-16. Young was then Chancellor at Wisconsin.

1971   Bucklew, Neil S. "Administering a Faculty Agreement." *Journal of the College and University Personnel Association* 22, no. 3 (May 1971), 46-51.

Garbarino, Joseph W. "Precarious Professors: New Patterns of Representation." *Industrial Relations* 10, no. 1 (February 1971), 1-20.
See also in *Industrial Relations* 10, 231-233, Trevor Bain, "Comment," and Garbarino, "Reply."

Hanley, Dexter L., S.J. "Issues and Models for Collective Bargaining in Higher Education." *Liberal Education* 57, no. 1 (March 1971), 5-14.

Jacobson, Robert L. "Cost of Living Outpaces Rise in Faculty Pay." *Chronicle of Higher Education* 5, no. 28 (April 19, 1971), 1, 5.
Accompanied by charts from the AAUP study on faculty compensation, pp. 1, 4-5.

Kerr, J. David. "Faculty Bargaining in Higher Education— New Twists to the University." *Journal of the College and University Personnel Association* 22, no. 3 (May 1971), 37-45.
Some solid advice to personnel directors from a negotiator for Central Michigan University.

Lieberman, Myron. "Professors, Unite!" *Harper's Magazine* 243, no. 1457 (October 1971), 61-70.

McHugh, William F. "Collective Bargaining and the College Student." *Journal of Higher Education* 62, no. 3 (March 1971), 175-185.

Pfefferkorn, William G. "Professional Negotiations in North Carolina: An Alternative to Formal Collective Bargaining for Public Employees." *Wake Forest Law Review* 7, no. 2 (March 1971), 189-210.

Scully, Malcolm G. "Attacks on Tenure Mount: Limitations Are Proposed in 5 States." *Chronicle of Higher Education* 5, no. 24 (March 22, 1971), pp. 1, 4.

Scully, Malcolm G., and William A. Sievert. "Collective Bargaining Gains Converts Among Teachers; 3 National Organizations Vie to Represent Faculties." *Chronicle of Higher Education* 5, no. 31 (May 10, 1971), pp. 1, 6.

"Unions Woo the College Faculties." *Business Week*, no. 2174 (May 1, 1971).

"The Unionization of Attorneys." *Columbia Law Review* 71, no. 1 (January 1971), 100-117.

Wisconsin Law Review 1971, no. 1, 1-295: "Collective Negotiations in Higher Education: A Symposium."
Myron Lieberman, "Preface," 1; Donald H. Wollett, "The Status and Trends of Collective Negotiations for Faculty in Higher Education," 2-32; Michael H. Moskow, "The Scope of Collective Bargaining in Higher Education," 33-54; William F. McHugh, "Collective Bargaining with Professionals in Higher Education," 55-90; Frederick R. Livingston and Andrea S. Christensen, "State and Federal Regulation of Collective Negotiations in Higher Education," 91-111; Bernard Mintz, "The CUNY Experience," 112-124; Matthew W. Finkin, "Collective Bargaining and University Government," 125-149 [reprinted, in slightly revised and expanded form, in *AAUP Bulletin* 57, no. 2 (Summer 1971), 149-162]; C. Dallas Sands, "The Role of Collective Bargaining in Higher Education," 150-176; Pierre-Paul Proulx, "Collective Negotiations in Higher Education—Canada," 177-186; Frederick E. Sherman and David Loeffler, "Universities, Unions, and the Rule of Law: The Teaching Assistants at Wisconsin," 187-209; Arlen Christenson, "Collective Bargaining in a University: The University of Wisconsin and the Teaching Assistants Association," 210-228; Nathan P. Feinsinger and Eleanore J. Roe, "The University of Wisconsin, Madison Campus—TAA Dispute of 1969-70: A Case Study," 229-274; Thomas R. Wildman, "The Legislation Necessary to Effectively Govern Collective Bargaining in Public Higher Education," 275-295.

II. COLLEGE AND UNIVERSITY GOVERNANCE

A. Books

American Association for Higher Education. *Faculty Par-*

ticipation in Academic Governance. Washington, D.C.: American Association for Higher Education, 1967. 67 p.
Report of the AAHE task force on faculty representation and academic negotiations, Campus Governance Program.

Assembly on University Goals and Governance. *A First Report.* Cambridge, Mass.: American Academy of Arts and Sciences, 1971.
See also first item under II (B) in this bibliography.

Corson, John J. *Governance of Colleges and Universities.* New York: McGraw-Hill, 1960. vii, 209 p.

Daniels, Arlene K., Rachel Kahn-Hut, et al. *Academics on the Line: The Faculty Strike at San Francisco State.* San Francisco: Jossey-Bass, 1970. xvi, 269 p.
Faculty analyses of the strike of 1968-69; all the contributors are members of the AFT.

Demerath, Nicholas J., Richard W. Stephens, and R. Robb Taylor. *Power, Presidents, and Professors.* New York: Basic Books, 1967. viii, 275 p.

Dill, David. *Case Studies in University Governance.* Washington, D.C.: National Association of State Universities and Land-Grant Colleges, 1971. xii, 192 p.
The case studies are of Florida A. & M., Minnesota, Columbia. and New Hampshire.

Dressel, Paul L., and Sally B. Pratt. *The World of Higher Education: An Annotated Guide to the Major Literature.* San Francisco: Jossey-Bass, 1971. 175 p.

Dykes, Archie R. *Faculty Participation in Academic Decision Making: Report of a Study.* Washington, D.C.: American Council on Education, 1968. vii, 44 p.

Foote, Caleb, Henry Mayer, et al. *The Culture of the University: Governance and Education.* San Francisco: Jossey-Bass, 1968. xviii, 288 p.
Report of an official University of California, Berkeley, faculty-student commission.

Garrison, Roger H. *Junior College Faculty: Issues and Problems—A Preliminary National Appraisal.* Washington, D.C.: American Association of Junior Colleges, 1967. vi, 90 p.

Hodgkinson, Harold L., and L. Richard Meeth, eds. *Power*

and Authority: Transformation of Campus Governance. San Francisco: Jossey-Bass, 1971. xviii, 215 p.

Joughin, Louis, ed. *Academic Freedom and Tenure: A Handbook of the American Association of University Professors.* Madison: University of Wisconsin Press, 1967. xiv, 343 p.

Keeton, Morris. *Shared Authority on Campus.* Washington, D.C.: American Association for Higher Education, 1971. vii, 168 p.
Studies and recommendations from the AAHE's Campus Governance Program.

Kruytbosch, Carlos E., and Sheldon L. Messinger, eds. *The State of the University: Authority and Change.* Beverly Hills, Calif.: Sage Publications, 1970. 384 p.

McConnell, T.R. *The Redistribution of Power in Higher Education: Changing Patterns of Internal Governance.* Berkeley: University of California, Center for Research and Development in Higher Education, 1971. 67 p.

Mortimer, Kenneth P. *Academic Government at Berkeley: The Academic Senate.* Berkeley: University of California, Center for Research and Development in Higher Education, 1970. vii, 194 p.

Smith, G. Kerry, ed. *Agony and Promise: Current Issues in Higher Education, 1969.* San Francisco: Jossey-Bass, 1969. xvii, 282 p.
Papers of AAHE 24th National Conference; especially Section V—Governance: Lewis B. Mayhew, "Faculty in Campus Governance," 145-160, and John C. Livingston, "Academic Senate Under Fire," 161-172.

Thackrey, Russell I. *The Future of the State University.* Urbana: University of Illinois Press, 1971. 144 p.

B. Articles

American Academy of Arts and Sciences. "Governance of Universities: A Conference Report, The American Academy of Arts and Sciences," Part I, *Association of Governing Boards Reports* 13, no. 5 (February 1970), 2-61; Part II, no. 8 (May-June 1970), 3-44.

American Association of University Professors, American

Council on Education, and Association of Governing Boards of Universities and Colleges. "Statement on Government of Colleges and Universities." *AAUP Bulletin* 52, no. 4 (Winter 1966), 374-379.

Also published in *Academic Freedom and Tenure: A Handbook of the American Association of University Professors,* edited by Louis Joughin. Madison: University of Wisconsin Press, 1967, pp. 90-101.

American Association of University Professors. "Faculty Participation in Strikes." *AAUP Bulletin* 54, no. 2 (Summer 1968), 155-159.

In practice this position appears to have shifted somewhat since 1968.

American Association of University Professors. "Policy on Representation of Economic and Professional Interests." *AAUP Bulletin* 55, no. 4 (Winter 1969), 489-491.

American Association of University Professors, Survey Subcommittee of Committee T on Faculty Participation in College and University Government. "Report." *AAUP Bulletin* 55, no. 2 (Summer 1969), 180-185; 57, no. 1 (Spring 1971), 68-124.

Also see reports of Committee T on the role of Faculty in Budgetary and Salary Matters and of Committee N on Representation of Economic and Professional Interests—for 1970-71 in *AAUP Bulletin* 57, no. 2 (Summer 1971): Committee T, pp. 187-191; Committee N, by the chairman Ralph S. Brown, Jr., pp. 211-214.

Blackburn, Robert T. *The Professor's Role in a Changing Society.* Report no. 10. Washington, D.C.: ERIC Clearinghouse on Higher Education, 1971. 22 p.

Bowen, Howard R. "University Governance: Workable Participation, Administrative Authority and the Public Interest." *Labor Law Journal* 20, no. 8 (August 1969), 517-528.

Bundy, McGeorge. "Faculty Power." *Atlantic Monthly* 222, no. 3 (September 1968), 41-47.

Carnegie Commission on Higher Education. "A Model Bill of Rights and Responsibilities for Members of an Institution of Higher Education: Faculty, Students, Administration, Staff, and Trustees." *Chronicle of Higher Education* 5, no. 23 (March 15, 1971), p. 1.

Duryea, E.D. "Reform in University Government." *Journal of Higher Education* 42, no. 5 (May 1971), 339-352.

Hickman, C. Addison. "The Faculty Voice in Institutional Policy." *Association of Governing Boards Reports* 10, no. 4 (January 1968), 17-26.
From the AAHE study.

Hickman, C. Addison. "Faculty Role in Governance." In *Handbook of College and University Administration: Academia,* edited by Asa S. Knowles, sec. 6, pp. 85-103. New York: McGraw-Hill, 1970.

Ikenberry, Stanley O., et al. "The Invitational Seminar on Restructuring College and University Organization and Governance." *Journal of Higher Education* 42, no. 6 (June 1971), 421-542.

Levi, Julian H. "Legal Aspects of University Governance." *Educational Record* 50, no. 4 (Fall 1969), 405-410.

Lieberman, Myron. "Faculty Senates: Institutionalized Irresponsibility." *Phi Delta Kappa* 51 (September 1969), 16-20.

Livingston, John C. "Collective Negotiations." In *Handbook of College and University Administration: Academia,* edited by Asa S. Knowles, sec. 6, pp. 104-119. New York: McGraw-Hill, 1970.

Mayhew, Lewis B. "Faculty Demands and Faculty Militance." *Journal of Higher Education* 40, no. 5 (May 1969), 337-350.

Scully, Malcolm G. "Faculty Members: Liberal on Politics, Found Conservative on Academic Issues." *Chronicle of Higher Education* 4, no. 26 (April 6, 1970), p. 3.

Sturner, William F. "University Governance through the Bicameral Legislature." *Journal of Higher Education* 42, no. 3 (March 1971), 219-228.

Wilson, Logan. "Changing University Governance." *Educational Record* 50, no. 4 (Fall 1969), 388-404.
The articles by Wilson and Levi are part of a symposium on "University Governance," 388-448.

Table of Cases

Court Decisions

NLRB Decisions

State Labor Board Decisions

Index

Although cases are listed in the Table of Cases, a few landmark cases (e.g., Cornell, Fordham) are also listed under place names here. Federal and state statutes are included in the index either under popular name or by state. Only material directly pertinent to the rest of the volume is included from the appendixes.

Howlett, Robert G.,   23-36, 143, 146, 147, 316

Idaho,   30, 166
Illinois,   12, 60, 69, 72-73, 78, 143, 155, 291, 292
  See also Chicago City College; Rock Valley College; Wheaton College
  Cook County,   68, 78
  Federation of Independent Illinois Colleges,   232
  Rockford,   70
  state colleges,   60
Impasse resolution. *See* Dispute resolution
Indiana,   35, 155, 167
Interns and residents,   26, 64, 81-86
Iowa,   155

Jacobs, Karl J.,   67-74, 75, 78-79
Jencks, C.,   125
Jenkins, Howard,   63, 249
Junior colleges. *See* Community colleges

Kansas,   30, 167-168, 292
Kennedy, John F.,   10, 143, 223
Kennedy, Ralph E.,   63, 263, 267, 271-272
Kentucky,   155
Kerr, Clark,   121
Kerr, J. David,   49-54, 148-150
Kugler, Israel,   42

Labor-Management Relations Act,   279
Labor relations boards. *See* Laws; Michigan; National Labor Relations
  Board; *and individual states*
Landrum-Griffin Act (1959),   237
Laws (statutes),
  See also Advisory Commission on Intergovernmental Relations; Legisla-
    tures; Michigan Employment Relations Act; National Labor Relations
    Act; New York Public Employment Relations Act; Taft-Hartley Act;
    and individual laws by popular name
  common law,   9, 12
  comprehensive labor law,   10, 12, 155-156
  conflict between laws,   17-19, 31-34, 227-228
  constitutional law,   9, 12
  model laws,   191-221
  municipal law,   9, 12, 17-18, 23, 155-189
  state laws,   9-22, 45, 117-118, 132, 143, 155-189, 242
Law schools,   2-3, 38-39, 56, 62-63, 151, 257, 258, 260-263, 269, 273-287
  See also Association of American Law Schools; Michigan, University of,
    Law School
Legislatures (state),   52, 114, 120, 126, 129, 130, 132, 133-134, 142, 149, 166,
  170, 171, 178, 312, 326
  See also Politics